Understanding Users

Grounded in the user-centered design movement, this book offers a broad consideration of how our civilization has evolved its technical infrastructure for human purpose to help us make sense of our contemporary information infrastructure and online existence. The author incorporates historical, cultural, and aesthetic approaches to situating information and its underlying technologies across time in the collective, lived experiences of humanity.

In today's digital environment, user experience is vital to the success of any product or service. Yet as the user population expands to include us all, designing for people who vary in skills, abilities, preferences, and backgrounds is challenging. This book provides an integrated understanding of users, and the methods that have evolved to identify usability challenges, that can facilitate cohesive and earlier solutions. The book treats information creation and use as a core human behavior based on acts of representation and recording that humans have always practiced. It suggests that the traditional ways of studying information use, with their origins in the distinct layers of social science theories and models is limiting our understanding of what it means to be an information user and hampers our efforts at being truly user-centric in design. Instead, the book offers a way of integrating the knowledge base to support a richer view of use and users in design education and evaluation.

Understanding Users is aimed at those studying or practicing user-centered design and anyone interested in learning how people might be better integrated in the design of new technologies to augment human capabilities and experiences.

Andrew Dillon is the V.M. Daniel Professor of Information at the University of Texas at Austin, USA, where he served as dean of the School of Information from 2002 to 2017. Prior to this he was a founding member of the School of Informatics at Indiana University, where he directed the master's program in HCI. He earned a PhD in psychology at Loughborough University and a BA and MA (first class) at University College Cork, Ireland.

Understanding Users

Designing Experience through Layers of Meaning

ANDREW DILLON

NEW YORK AND LONDON

Designed cover image: © Getty Images

First published 2023
by Routledge
605 Third Avenue, New York, NY 10158

and by Routledge
4 Park Square, Milton Park, Abingdon, Oxon, OX14 4RN

Routledge is an imprint of the Taylor & Francis Group, an informa business

ISBN: 978-0-367-45927-7 (hbk)
ISBN: 978-0-367-45925-3 (pbk)
ISBN: 978-1-003-02611-2 (ebk)

DOI: 10.4324/9781003026112

Typeset in Avenir and Dante
by MPS Limited, Dehradun

Contents

Preface *vi*

1 Information as a Human Process 1

2 The Emergence of User-Centeredness 22

3 Designing Our Information World: Craft or Science? 48

4 Humans and the Vertical Slice 75

5 The Physio-Tech Layer 98

6 The Cogito-Tech Layer 114

7 The Socio-Tech Layer 135

8 The Culturo-Tech Layer 158

9 Usability as a Design Value 175

10 Acceptability as a Design Value 198

11 Augmentation as the REAL Value 220

Index *247*

Preface

One of the marvels of academic life is that time seems to pass in ways that make little objective sense. Certainly, we measure out semesters and the courses taught, academic years and the research published, programs of study and the graduates hooded, years in rank and the promotions obtained, all endlessly documented in repetitive annual reports of dubious worth. But for all these markers, it still surprises me occasionally to find a decade or two has passed while I obsessed over some problem or other, pursuing answers to questions that few people ask, only to find that the chase invokes deeper questions. In that spirit, this book amounts to a minor obsession of mine that has now stretched almost 40 years.

It was as a newly minted psychology graduate in 1984 that I joined the Human Factors Research Group at University College Cork in Ireland and began learning about an emerging concern for more user-centered design of computers. I was fascinated by the idea that here was an area of application where psychology might make a meaningful difference, where theories met the real world and effects could be measured in observable outcomes. What I imagined would be a focus of graduate studies became a career, first at Loughborough in the UK where I joined the Human Sciences & Advanced Technology Institute (HUSAT), then later in a post-doc at Indiana University in the US, where I ended up staying for 8 years, helping to launch the Informatics school and a new master's degree in Human-Computer Interaction. For the past two decades I've been at the School of Information at the University of Texas at Austin where we offer multiple degrees with a strong graduate program in user experience design. My roles and locations have changed but throughout it all I've always asked myself and my students to consider what makes any design work well for people and why?

I have never quite been satisfied with what we call user-centered design. First, it can be difficult to define, which seems odd, but the term gets bandied about by many people who share little common understanding of methods or values. Second, user-centeredness must involve more than asking users what they think. That's certainly a good start but what about situations where users do not yet recognize what they might need? What about the shift in views that can occur between first and later uses? We are still struggling to answer these questions and yet we continue to hear people push a simple "just ask them" mantra as the key to user-centered design. Third, why is our application of theoretical knowledge so piecemeal that it often feels tacked on at the end to give a veneer of science to design findings or claims? How can we educate the next generation of user experience designers to better apply what we know? Finally, why are we so committed to the rather limited values of usability and acceptability as primary goals without considering the broader implications of building a global information infrastructure that serves more than instrumental purposes?

I wrote this book in the spirit of these questions, less to provide direct answers than to share and hopefully prod others into considering them seriously. I believe we have too narrowly understood what it means to be user-centric and have too slavishly adopted the framing of social science, with its temporal boundaries on disciplines which has led to either weak application by those with the background or downright dismissal of science by those without. Consequently, even though I am delighted by the recognition user-centered design education now receives around the world, I am still concerned that we are not doing enough. It's nearly 60 years since Herb Simon advanced the idea of design as a core discipline that every university should teach but we are far from this ideal. Instead, we have a range of offerings that tend to stick closely to tradition, some in engineering, some in psychology, some in fine arts, and yes, some in information schools. The latter, I believe, are the only truly interdisciplinary academic homes that exist on many campuses and yet even some of those are merely rebranded traditional programs with little focus on design as a cohesive and fundamental act of problem solving. Meanwhile, user-centeredness has become a label that businesses use to market their product, less a description of a method or set of values for products or services than a claim or advertising line that ticks some boxes. The world needs something better.

One issue I do wish to speak directly to here is the readership. I believe user-centered design is a concern for everybody on the planet. We are reshaping the world we experience through a rapidly evolving set of technologies that are being embraced and contorted for use faster than we can control. In this realm where everything moves it is easy to lose perspective, captivated by the new and the changing, but the real drivers are not technical, or at least not entirely technical. Humans are the core of this world, and we all need to engage actively in shaping what is coming for ourselves, our loved ones, our world.

I have taught generations of students with a variety of backgrounds, many technical, with degrees in computer science and engineering, but many also from the arts and humanities. The former often come because they recognize that their technical education left them ill-prepared to design for real people where the seeming variability of humans and the lack of precision we have in predicting responses are worrisome. The latter often come because they want to get involved professionally but fear their lack of technical understanding will be an obstacle to them ever shaping a design. Each in their own way is a product of an educational system that divides us early and too often permanently. I take delight in seeing how high some of these students have risen in their subsquent careers and I hope they continue to push the message. In my user-centered design course, I try to create a space where disciplines are not important and where we piece together from existing sources what we might need to know to create better user experiences. There is science in this, that is what makes design knowledge replicable and useful, but there is art and narrative too, which is what helps us imagine and interpret opportunities to create.

We can't leave design to any one or even a few existing disciplines or we will create a world that works for some but never all. If you can read this book and start to question why the technology you use is the way it is and suggest some ways in which it could be improved to make your life better, then you are a participant in the user-centered design movement. If the book gives you the language to speak up about design decisions that impact your world, then you can get involved and make a difference. User-centered design needs more, not less input from real users. Some say we get the world we deserve but I believe we get the world we imagine then enable. Let's imagine and enable some more.

Andrew Dillon
Austin, Texas
August 2022

1 Information as a Human Process

Representation through the Ages

In 1879, Marcelino de Sautola, a lawyer by profession but an amateur archaeologist by choice, visited Altamira Cave in Spain with his nine-year old daughter, Maria. He had visited the cave on previous trips and returned this year to deepen his study of ancient fossil remains that had been found inside by a local hunter who stumbled onto the previously sealed off cave. By popular account, while the archaeology-loving Marcelino was digging around in the dirt, Maria gazed up and remarked "look Papa, a bison." What she pointed out is the now famous colored image of a beast on the roof of Altamira Cave (see Figure 1.1) a site that turned out to be so rich in images that it has since come to be commonly spoken of as the Sistine Chapel of Prehistory.

Altamira's was not the first cave art to have been discovered, other paintings had been found centuries before in various other sites in Europe, but once de Sautola had accurate renderings of this art produced and published a book in 1880, his discovery came to be considered the birthdate of serious scholarly consideration of cave paintings and their evidentiary value to studies of human cultural development (Clarke and Madariaga de la Campa, 2001). And much like other discussions of evolution and the nature of humans, or of revolutionary technologies and social development, his book triggered more than few controversies and competing interpretations.

Once the wonder of the images had sunk in, explanations of their origin and meaning became hotly contested. de Sautola's claim that such dramatic and colorful art must have been the product of our ancient ancestors was greeted with scepticism by some and even dismissed as impossible, on the

DOI: 10.4324/9781003026112-1

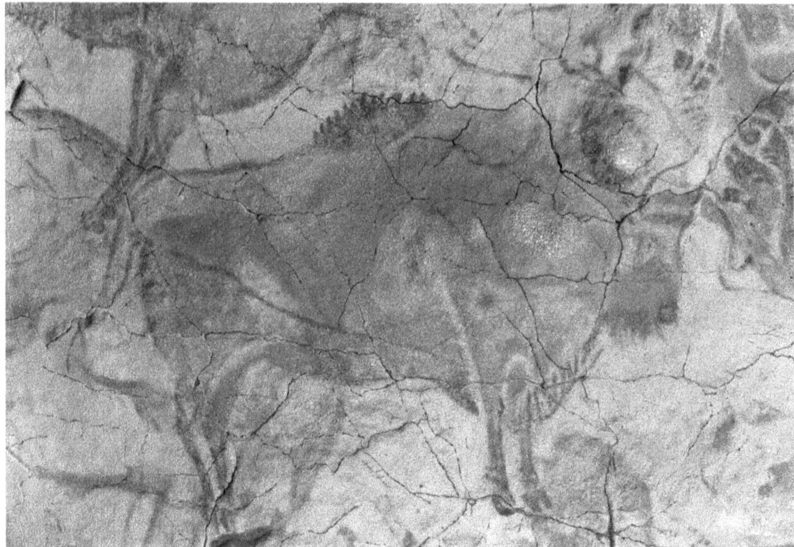

Figure 1.1 Image of a bison from the cave art at Altamira

assumption rather than evidence that our forebears could not possibly have possessed the necessary capacity to think so abstractly, a curiously persistent belief in the uniqueness of contemporary humans. Established scholars of the time were often the strongest in their dismissal, leading to suggestions that the art was probably a fraud, in so doing impugning de Sautola. The apparent absence of soot deposits in the surrounding area, a material which would necessarily have been present on the walls and floors if ancient people had ever tried to illuminate the dark cave with their torches and fires led many to conclude the artwork could not be what de Sautola claimed.

It was only with the continual discovery and documenting of similar works in other sites, and the development of better dating techniques and chemical analyses that cave art came to be treated as a reliable and serious window into the lives of ancient humans. By the time the tide of expert opinion shifted at the start of the 20th Century, including an apology from one of his harshest critics, Emile Cartailhac in 1902, it was too late for de Sautola. He died in 1888 unable to convince his peers of what we now consider to be the truth about these works.

Today, not only do we have a rich catalog of genuine cave art to examine, but continual technical advances in our measurement of the age of materials have revealed that the origins of such work are in fact much older than we previously imagined. Up to 20 years ago, the oldest works were deemed to have been created some 25,000–35,000 years ago. Since then, research has pushed that date back millennia, to 45,000 years, but even this now seems an under-estimate the history of our records. In 2018, the discovery of colored art in Africa led to extensive dating tests using Uranium-thorium mass spectrometry, which suggest our ancestors were painting cave walls 70,000 years ago (Hoffman et al, 2018). This estimate, more than a century after de Sautola's original estimates, push the origins of information representation back as far as Neanderthals, a claim that has some contemporary critics suggesting what we consider to be art and the representation of information is as old as, or maybe even older than, our species.

The lessons of de Sautola's discovery and its reception by others are still pertinent today in at least two ways. First, fashionable interpretations and superficial analyses of limited data points are still too common in our discussions of information technology. We are easily swayed by fantastic numbers that seem to suggest we now produce more information in two days than we did in the previous 2000 years up to this century, or that the amount of data captured and stored by industry is doubling every year (see e.g., the numbers reported by industry data analysts Cloudnine, n.d.) Media reports sensationalize many aspects of the new information world, from the naïve claims of the internet spreading either democracy or terror, to the fear that a generation weaned on digital documents will never be able to read like their parents, or, alternatively, will develop a new form of literacy that leaves the rest of us behind, there is no shortage of supposed experts and talking heads who want to tell us how it is and what it all means for humanity. But the arguments for the social impact of information technologies are frequently speculative, superficial, and trendy, as reactive to current events as de Sautola's early critics, who responded based on a world view that was not yet able to recognize the reality of our human history. Rather than follow the trends or seek to awe readers with impressive data quantities, in this book I will focus more on the longstanding and slow-changing consistencies of our human existence, not the continual changes in our inventions and tools, as a lens for considering the nature and the role of information in our lives.

What cave art and its analysis reveals is I believe, of considerable importance, and shapes the central tenets of this book. From the earliest times, humans have represented and recorded data to serve as accounts, reminders, and signs to others. From cave paintings to stone counters, through papyrus and the block printing press, to the biro and the iPad, humans have continually refined the technologies of information to enhance speed, reach, and usability of data. This is true but not really what is so important, technological progress on its own is a limited story. However, the technology does reflect our humanity, and the history of civilization can surely be viewed as a series of information ages characterized by different tools, mechanisms and media, continually building on a desire to create, manage, and share information across time and distance. What we experience today is different but not disconnected from the information tools and technologies of all people's since the first paintings.

A second lesson from de Sautola's story would also seem important to learn. Our reckoning of our own information progress is always inevitably partial, limited as it must be to our own understanding of our history and our lived experience. We are always at the mercy of an incomplete historical record while subject to the pressures to make sense of our rapidly moving present time. This means we yield to a narrow and time-bound view of what is happening, and we attempt, naturally, to make sense of this as best we can. But we can learn to recognize that shortcomings in our reactions and analyses are likely and therefore, perhaps show willingness to be open to new explanations that challenge our cherished views of how humans and the world must be, allowing for new perspectives as more findings are made. What will historians in the year 2200 make of our love of mobile phones, the battle for ownership of Twitter, or the rapid move to virtual meetings forced on us by a global pandemic? Do we really imagine our sense of these processes will be those historians deem an accurate, cohesive, and unbiased account?

Finally, we must acknowledge that we engage in our understanding of our information world with a cognitive architecture to perceive, process, and output information that is likely little changed from the mind and processing capabilities of those same artists who drew in caves. The world has changed rapidly in terms of technological infrastructure, and it is tempting to believe that the minds of contemporary humans have changed at this pace too, but that seems improbable. I refer to this as the false match hypothesis, if computers change then they seemingly change us too. We have certainly altered the context of living in some ways, children now are exposed to information tools and technologies from their earliest awareness, and this is probably having impact on our cognitive development, but the basics of attention, perception, memory and thinking about the world around us are tied to our being, and we evolve at a pace that is far slower than technology. In many very real ways, we are missing something fundamental about ancient art and life if we assume that people then were very different than us. I contend that they were not. As our ancestors came to appreciate the limitations of their own memories, and the need to keep records using tools to represent numbers, they began the journey in information use and development that has led us to our current age through a slow, accreting process of design. We have got better at building tools to perform information activities, but that does not mean we have radically changed our basic qualities as humans.

This book aims to situate humans as information users across time so as to help orient us to a way of thinking about the technologies of information and their impact in our lives that can inform the design of new and more humanly acceptable infrastructures. We might justifiably worry about literacy, misinformation, loss of privacy and the intrusion of digital mediation in more and more of our daily lives, but we need not be passive in this process. I hold the view that the emergence of contemporary information technologies is a consequence of humankind's extended practice of developing representational means to ease recording and sharing of information throughout history. Furthermore, contemporary concerns with issues such as privacy, distraction, education, are not just a recent issue but have been a constant of human information use. In recognizing this, this book hopefully points to a richer way of thinking about information technologies, one that truly places humans at the center of design and implementation.

We are, at this moment, creating an information infrastructure that is truly global, so I believe we should commit to technologies that augment rather than limit our existence. I use the term "augmentation" intentionally, an acknowledgement to the inspirational work of Doug Engelbart (1962) perhaps best known for the invention of the mouse-style input device we all know, but more importantly, a thinker at the dawn of computer science who argued that our aims should always be higher than greater efficiency or speed of calculation, instead we should leverage the digital world to enhance human existence wherever possible. I share this view and perhaps am railing against a design culture that has tilted so heavily toward the profitable, the consumer-capturing, transaction-enabling interfaces that mine our data in order to exploit our actions. Perhaps some of this is inevitable, but it is not too late to refocus and collectively shape an information world for all of us and more of our needs across our lifespans. To do so, we really must seek to better understand ourselves; we are all users.

How Do We Begin to Tell the Story?

We live in a world of information glut, or so we are repeatedly told. Google allows us to search a universe of documents, images, files, and data sets.

Most text, imagery, video, and audio records are now produced digitally and routinely added to an expanding corpus that is said to double our information resources in the proverbial blink of an eye. Buckminster Fuller proposed the "knowledge doubling curve" in the 1980s, based on an estimate that where once it took a century to double humankind's information resources, it had accelerated to every 25 years by the end of WWII, and would approach a doubling every 12 hours by the end of the 20th century. Well, we might not be quite there, or we may (it really is not simple to measure how "much" information or knowledge exists even if there's many quotable numbers out there which sound impressive) but the hype of accelerating growth is rarely far from the public utterances of industry leaders selling a vision of universal and utopian access in a supposedly new golden age of information technology, all for the price of a simple monthly plan.

While the modern tools at our disposal for searching, reading, viewing and sharing information are unquestionably impressive, I believe it would be a mistake to imagine this is a fundamentally unique form of human existence that has only emerged with the creation of the internet and mobile computing tools. Yes, the power of our cell phones in 2020 would be a surprise even to an early adopter of desktop computers in the 1980s, and probably seem like an idea from a science fiction movie to the average US citizen from the 1950s, but the nature of our information use is more stable than we might imagine from the continual emphasis on acceleration, convergence and network speed. As innovation diffusion theorist Everett Rogers and his disciples have shown repeatedly for waves of different technologies, adoption of any innovation does not necessarily involve dismissal of older products so as to create completely new conditions of existence (Rogers, 1995). Books, for example, are still published in paper and outsell their digital equivalents by considerable margin according to the annual reports of the American Publishers Association (the latest data suggest by as much as 4:1). The digital did not replace the paper format, humans just co-opted e-texts within a broad suite of usage patterns that exploits the usefulness and appeal of the older form for many situations. Similarly, the ability to download movies for home use has not ended the lure of cinema, nor has streaming music entirely replaced CDs (though it has impacted sales considerably) and CDs themselves have failed to replace LPs, again for reasons of how the technology has meanings for us; meanings which rarely, for any complex information system, can simply be reduced to utility (LP sales, in fact, have been one of the few material forms of music that have seen a steady rise in sales recently). It is this range of human responses to our information world, the rational and the emotional ties we form with information objects and practices, that has been and will be a constant in a sea of change. Thus, it is crucial for us to understand these qualities and values of humans if we are to truly make sense of our contemporary and emerging information world.

Much of our communication of ideas and sharing of knowledge relies on widespread literacy and thus the emergence of writing is often taken as a key starting point for understanding human information use. This is temptingly plausible but I fear it is based on a somewhat convenient view of human development. So magical is the written word that for centuries people believed writing was a gift from the gods, with most major religious texts offering origin stories that point to the written word being given to chosen people through divine intervention. Critical study from the Enlightenment onward suggested a more human level of intervention, leading to the belief that writing might have evolved from drawing, as early efforts to depict the world were refined and reduced to create icons and symbols. What came to be termed the "pictographic theory" of writing, which dominated scholarship for decades, was often based on the most spurious evidence (see a pattern here?) and a large dollop of common sense. Pictures presumably represented objects we could perceive, they became stylized or standardized over time, eventually signifying words or names or objects, ordered as necessary to create more elaborate or extended communication of ideas. As an explanation of the wonders of writing, wherein a human can use markings to transcend time and space in order to convey an idea to another human mind, it seems to fit well with how we imagine the process must have developed.

As Schmand-Besserat (1992) argued, the reasoning on pictographic evolution seemed so convincing to all concerned that it could hardly be questioned, even though the link between available traces and the objects they supposedly represented often required a significant leap of imagination. As always, we need to be careful in interpreting the records of the past. More recent analyses of tokens found in archaeological sites across the Middle East by Schmand-Bessarat and others put paid to the simple pictographic theory by the late 20th Century, offering in its place an alternative, richer explanation that suggests we might best view writing as having evolved primarily from counting systems rather than pictographs, with symbols primarily representing quantities rather than objects. With this, the explanation of early information suggests a pattern of human engagement with and through information that has proved remarkably robust over time. By using external markings to convey quantities, we could agree and enable trades, count larger numbers of objects than we could see directly with our eyes, and extend our own memories so as to ensure accurate numerical records over time.

While we cannot claim to know precisely how or why humans first engaged in such information practices, in our efforts to understand how humans learned to exploit the potential of information tools, it is important to consider how our approach to this question might shape our interpretation. We can see in the scholarly treatment of early drawing and evolving writing systems that the data available to us, and the scientific methods we employ for analyzing and dating material culture, are dynamic. Since the de Sautola saga, new records have been uncovered and previously dated or examined artefacts are added to the corpus and re-examined as new techniques and methods are developed. Consequently, there is an inevitable elasticity to estimates of when the human information record began, and there is continual revision of our own sense of the stages that seem present in the long developmental path from scrolls to screens. This is as it should be. The examination of our own history as a species is never-ending and we must always be open to the possibility, indeed the almost certainty, that our current interpretations are not the full story, being subject to change and rethinking as we learn more.

Leaving aside such estimate variability, and the potential for new discoveries to push that date of first record even further back, it should be clear that humans have a long and co-evolving relationship with information. So, while we don't typically frame cave painting in such terms, I am comfortable with the idea that these early images represent something fundamental about us as a species and could be considered one of the earliest forms of an information technology created by and for humans. Indeed, as I will argue in this book, cave art, like any other technology, is insightful not only as a historical record of our own species' activities, but as a lens to understand how we, as humans, exist in the world. In so doing, I take the view that such an examination of information technologies over time is less about history and more about individual and collective psychology. To represent thoughts and ideas externally, which is how art, writing and music essentially function, information reflects our human nature, both as thinkers and as tool-developers. Cave art and computers, separated by millennia, form a continuum of creativity within an ecological niche that also binds our minds to our material and our ideational worlds.

Tracing the Information Arc from Cave to Computer

If we then recast our view of information history as a continually evolving process of meaning conveyance by external representation, utilizing our technical knowledge at any one time to create an expanding infrastructure for our community, then we can learn to see our information history as a process and not as a series of discrete inventions by inspired individuals that presaged distinct eras. Rather than dividing our world up onto phases of cave art, then writing, the rise of printing, and finally computation, informed by the biographies of the "great men" who created this world, as is typical of textbook accounts and best-selling narratives, we might recognize that at any point in our civilization, humans have manifest a natural tendency to represent and share ideas externally using whatever means of expression are at our disposal. It is likely that this type of act is a defining characteristic of the human mind since few other species seem to obviously engage in similar practices, no matter the degree of shared DNA (though of course, we need to be cautious in making such a claim as we learn more about other creatures). In viewing our information uses this way, we weave an unbroken thread throughout our history built on the constancy and invariance of our nature and abilities, embedded within a context of collective efforts.

Viewed this way, we learn to see a more nuanced history and to appreciate that Gutenberg did not, in fact, invent the printing press on his own, though he certainly chased the type of financial rewards for exploiting it as befits a Wall St Journal view of technological progress. We now know that many competitors existed in the 15th century, motivated by the growing demand for religious texts, seeking a means of publishing that would give them the upper hand in producing accurate copies quickly. But that is only part of the story of printing. Centuries before, the Chinese had learned how to use moveable type and it is likely early block printing was developed 700 years before Gutenberg was born. The metal block mechanics and presses of the Gutenberg era were indeed a breakthrough once they were refined and adopted, a process that involved many design efforts and teams. No one person can really claim to be the inventor of the printing press (with apologies to anyone planning to write a leadership guide based on Gutenberg's life) no more than Al Gore (or any one person) invented the Internet. And for the record, Gutenberg never did make his fortune, dying penniless, his presses impounded, in 1468.

Certainly, over our history, progress and shifts in form of information have occurred unevenly but perspective is key. If we focus primarily on the technology and how it has developed over the course of history, we can easily become distracted by isolated revolutionary tools and the shifting pace of change. If instead we examine the human behavior underlying information acts, and concentrate on how communicative and knowledge-sharing practices have been supported, the story seems more stable. For example, if, as we currently estimate, the painting of images began nearly 70,000 years ago, and it was not until 8000 BCE that earliest writing emerged in the form of simple tokens representing counts, then cave art represents a staggeringly durable information form for early humans. Such a stability of representational medium might strike us as remarkable given what followed in the last two millennia when tools and techniques for sharing information have changed rapidly. But over the last two millennia, the basic act of writing has not changed as much as have the media supporting the process. Quill and ink on parchment is in many ways the equivalent of pen on paper, and while most modern writing is created digitally, using a keyboard layout optimized for mechanical devices, there are recurring efforts at enabling old-school handwritten input using digital styli and screens. All to say, if you considered writing solely as a human act, the physical process in which writers engaged over the centuries would seem familiar to most observers, regardless of the tools involved.

Of course, we would be well-advised to allow for new knowledge to emerge suggesting as yet unrecognized changes were crucial during any lengthy period, perhaps from tools that have yet to be uncovered and which might not have been as durable as cave art, but regardless of current estimates, the earliest cave paintings do seem now to be the first flourishing of human information technology. For me, while the timeline is always interesting, the precision of dating is less fascinating than trying to understand what the earliest forms of representation meant to our ancestors and how they shaped their behavior in and understanding of their world.

Since their first discovery, explaining or interpreting the meaning of cave art has challenged the abilities of many scholars. All that we have to go on are a small sample of images, differing in age, often located in isolated areas reachable only with great effort, and devoid of many clues as to means of production. Of the various theories that exist to explain or interpret cave painting, the analysis of patterns, form, and content offers a more rational than artistic insight. Typical images are painted in a limited number of colors, with red and black dominating, which offers some clues as the materials that were employed. The most common images are animals, with some images of human forms and genitalia, but even so, the range is limited. Of all possible animals to paint, the most common are bison, horses, and cattle, which might suggest the utilitarian nature of such images, perhaps as guides to food sources nearby but even then, several scholars have noted that while animal bones, most likely from hunts, point, for example, to ample consumption of reindeer in Lascaux, France, the art so far discovered in this area never portrays that particular animal.

While the representations of animals are somewhat lifelike, often the painting of humans is more symbolic rather than visually accurate, relying heavily in painted form on stick figures. There are numerous hand prints which are realistic, and some images of human forms show signs of violence, perhaps indicating a record of battles or tribal conflict, but as yet, there is little consensus among historians, anthropologists, or archaeologists as to how we are to understand the intent of the original painters. Were they marking territory or sharing sources and warnings? Was there a religious significance or might some images be personal or decorative? That groups separated by considerable distance produced a similar selection of images is noteworthy. This has led some to speculate that the paintings represent highly memorable events that were shared experiences, either emotionally (e.g., close encounters with potentially dangerous animals during a hunt) or psychologically (some have argued that the images represent visions, dreams or altered brain-chemistry induced states, see e.g., Lewis-Williams, 2002).

One curious aspect of early art is its depiction of human form in different media. Earliest cave art presents humans as skeletal, perhaps reducing the human body to its most simple, reproducible and recognizable form: a head attached to a central spine with pairs of limbs sprouting off at somewhat regular points, a form that children worldwide seem to use with little prompting. But by 30,000 BCE, when models and carvings enter our narrative, the depiction of humans takes on an exaggerated form that remains remarkably consistent for another 20,000 years, across locations as far apart from the Russian Steppes to Southern Europe. Carved figures uncovered from these times present humans as heavy, rounded, and often faceless. The shape characteristics seem fairly universal, leading some to suggest that these qualities represent important or desirable goals for early nomadic groups such as signs of plentiful food or ability to reproduce, basic properties that surely had significance for our ancestors We can only speculate on this but the commonality of such representations across time and place strongly suggests that our earliest art had meaning that was intentional (for a good overview of the historical regularities of early art, see Spivey, 2005).

Cognitive scientist V. S. Rachmandran's Peak Shift Principle (the view that our brains react most strongly to stimuli that portray the essence of something desired or valued, has been invoked as a potential explanation for people's reactions to art (see e.g., Rachmandran and Hirstein, 1999). In other words, in a world where food and reproduction are primary drivers of behavior, humans liked and responded most positively to representations that exaggerated these specific qualities, with the consequent effect of such forms being generated more and, if strength lies in numbers, then more likely to survive for us to identify today. In this way, the principle of desirability manifesting itself in art is the constant, even if a culture's agreement on what is most desirable might well, and indeed has, shifted over time.

It will require far more evidence than we currently have to better explain the meaning of early art but by viewing the records we do possess through the lens of cognition, we can at least begin to appreciate that our ancestors were not simply leaving instructions or markings of territory through painting and carvings, it seems more likely they were externalizing deeply held understandings of the world, how they interpreted it, and what they valued in it. Furthermore, if some tendency such as the peak shift principle is in operation through time, it can offer us an at least partial basis for understanding the human need for and response to information. While we tend, in modern terms, to think of information as functional, we would do well to acknowledge that our externalizing of our thoughts has an emotive, affective, and sometimes spiritual purpose.

Within 20,000 years of the earliest statues, roughly around 5000 BCE, archaeological records suggest a shift in representational form away from the extreme exaggeration of bodies toward highly stylized and uniform patterns epitomized in the paintings found in the tombs and records of the Egyptian empire. Where cave paintings depicted stick figures, or carvings emphasized extreme shape, the newer form delivered a more realistic representation, at least in terms of shape and detail of the human body. The Egyptian tomb paintings have particular characteristics that seem to show a break with previous and indeed subsequent depictions, namely the front-on perspective of torso but a side view of the human face, with the eye presented as if looking face-on.

This schematic of representation lasted in Egypt for centuries (or longer) and how it was agreed upon and adopted is itself a fascinating question, but it informed, in turn, Greek efforts at presenting the human body, which took on their own rigid adherence to patterns, and in their case, ideal proportions. As Spivey (2005) notes, it does seem as if humans have continually wrestled with how to convey the reality of the world through external imagery while simultaneously exaggerating particular features or components at any one time. The emphasis on a specific characteristic is easier to recognize than to explain but it is not difficult to imagine that the Venus of Willendorf's exaggerated child-bearing qualities, of great importance to our ancestors 20,000 years ago gave way to the Greek statuary emphasizing physical and athletic prowess that was core to classical Greek culture later. While this type of framing allows us to connect art to meaning and values over time, it raises the fascinating prospect of external expressions and representations being important shapers of culture. And naturally, this asks us to consider how current imagery and styles reflect and shape our own times.

We might argue gleefully over what is and is not art but we cannot argue with the fact that humans have evolved representations of others, of ideas, of data in every society over time. There is seemingly no collective without a form of information sharing, though the mode employed might be unique to time and location. In short, information and collectivism or social groupings co-exist, and perhaps are co-constructive. That is to say, art and creative representations that might best be understood not as the product of primarily settled societies, engendered by the move from hunting-gathering to a more agrarian form of existence, but as a co-occurring reflection and shaper of settlement processes that improved the human condition. If, as seems logical, great numbers of people must have been involved in the creation of some ancient monuments (such as Stonehenge in the UK or Gobekli Tepe in Turkey) then it would seem less that the artefact reflected a move to settlements but that provision of support for a large number of people in one area so as to enable them to build a monument, might itself have been encouraged more agrarian or settled practices. Art then is perhaps less the outcome but the means of co-habitation and co-operation.

All this is the remit of evolutionary archaeologists and historians but it is also of interest to those of us seeking to understand how humans came to make representations of their ideas and thoughts, and externalize these in a form that others can perceive or experience. Rather than a neat and clean narrative that suggests around the Neolithic era, circa 9000 BCE, humans learned to understand seasons, crop cycles, and the value of keeping livestock, and consequently became settled, whereupon we produced more art, it seems plausible that images, representations and external information displays were an instrumental part of the process wherein humans learned to exploit the world collectively to enable a move to agrarian culture. In this way, information is not a simple by-product of human activity, it is an engine and enabler of co-operation that improve the conditions of life.

Psychologist Merlin Donald has made an argument that the history of humankind represents a form of cognitive evolution, as we have learned to exploit external representations to create collective understandings which allow us to build knowledge over time. He argues that there have been moments in our history that represent transitional moves in our understanding of the world and that these have triggered progress. Most interestingly from my perspective, he argues that these stages are tied to our abilities to externalize our knowledge for collective benefit, unlocking ideas and their implications from the private to the public sphere. He suggests four stages in our species development which I summarize in Table 1.1.

In essence, Donald argues that at the earliest stages of cognitive evolution our ancestors first developed the capacity for event memory, which served them well in understanding some aspects of how the world worked, enabled the recognition of regularities, and to determine connections between members in a group. The next stage of evolution, what he terms the mimetic, wherein early hominids developed the ability to copy or model the actions of others, enabled greater skill acquisition and transfer of at least some forms of knowledge. The third great step was the emergence of linguistic capabilities which enabled homo sapiens, now recognizably us, to engage in far richer forms of interaction, share stories, collectivize memories and experiences, and describe the world. The final stage, termed the theoretic, is the breakthrough phase that gives us our current cognitive abilities to engage in symbolic reasoning, a signature ability of modern humans.

Obviously, this is a sweeping treatment of complex evolutionary processes that can only have occurred over time spans that are almost impossible for us to grasp (the timescale of human evolution is measured, or at least expressed in units of a million years, or rather humorously, we speak in units of "mya," which sounds technical but it just an acronym meaning "millions of years ago"). If we consider early hominids to be emerging around 5–10 mya, one can see the challenges in being precise and in trying to map changes given the pace of evolutionary development as understood by paleontologists.

Speculative as it may be, Donald's belief that human cognition evolved, as we assume it must, it is almost certain that culture plays a role both as an outcome and as a driver of human cognitive attributes. Rather than just accept an idea of human evolution where the changing morphology of our brains determined our separation from other species, he posits that our evolving brain structure reflects the context in which we reside, and from this, he argues that increasing socialization led to demands on our mental processing that drove brain development in specific ways. Though he doesn't lean heavily on the term, he very much argues for a situational understanding of human cognition that is in contrast to more dominant theories which point to our minds as computational devices isolated in our heads to handle incoming stimuli.

Donald is mainly concerned with explaining how humans developed and in particular, what was required for us, cognitively, to advance our civilization

Table 1.1 Summary of Donald's (1998) Layers of Culture Based on Cognitive Criteria

STAGE	PERIOD	FORM OF REPRESENTATION	CHANGE	COGNITIVE ASPECT
EPISODIC	Primate	Complex event	Self-awareness	Reactive
MIMETIC	Early hominid	Action modeling	Skills	Variability of customs
MYTHIC	Homo sapiens	Linguistic	Oral records	Lexical, narrative
THEORETIC	Recent	Verbal and non-verbal symbolic	External storage, theory	Institutional

through major transitions. His perspective is engaging and provocative, though far from easily testable, but for the purposes of considering humans as information users, it does draw attention to some key attributes that fit with what we know of the human record as seen in information history. Rather than being an afterthought or luxury, early images, be they seen as cave paintings, statues, stone scratches, or counters, are best seen as the first evidence we have of humans externally representing their thoughts, in so doing enabling us to expand on our limited memory, signal a record to another not immediately present, or to express a mood or desire. These are fundamentally different markings than the traces of presence other animals leave through scent and movement, and they represent a species defining attribute whose timeline we are still discovering.

Evolution indicates that our modern brain did not come about in a single developmental step, so it seems likely that as we uncover older examples of external representation which cause us to revisit our estimates of their origins, we may begin to better appreciate that the act of representing information is woven deeply into our history, not just as an output of our minds but as a possible shaper too. One might well ask then if our current information technologies are also shaping our minds, positively and negatively, at an evolutionary level. The answer is almost certainly yes. However, while the pace of evolutionary change suggests nobody reading this book need worry too much about this, we might ask if the growth in digital reading and writing, with its emphasis on short texts and thumb-written words is going to have any consequences? Certainly our current cognitive architecture is the one we are likely to enjoy for some time yet but we are dynamic beings, change is exceedingly slow but it is not non-existent, and the conditions of our evolving world have impacts. As I will attempt to show in this book, this human mind is well worth studying if we want to help design better information systems so we might as well start with what we have now.

Three Key Themes for Understanding the Experience of Information

Throughout the book, I will reiterate three themes of our lived experiences that are fundamental to understanding ourselves as information beings. These are key to examining broadly what information is to humans, and how the various technologies of information that we have evolved impact the world and our identity and sense of place within it. Only by treating the digital world in this way, I believe, can we begin to design in a truly human-centered fashion for inclusion, acceptance, and ultimately, our own augmentation.

Representation as Cognitive Extension

First, by developing and embracing the means of conveying thoughts and ideas externally, the act of representation enables humans to transcend the limitations of individual minds and of time, and allows for collective consideration and recording of ideas and data. Our own cognitive architecture has capacity and processing limitations which are easily reached in the short term and require continual effort to maintain over the long term. Further, individual memory, no matter how long-stored, is by definition transient and tied to the life of the individual. It is also subject to deterioration and bias as it becomes embedded in our long-term stores. By externalizing and representing ideas, events, images and records, our information technologies support collective and temporally extended communication, which over time has augmented our abilities to act on the world through a sharing of knowledge and experience.

Information as Imagination

Second, by forming external representation of ideas, we demonstrate a capability for symbolic thought that encompasses more than simple description but also the conveyance of synthesis and of possibility. Representation is certainly a precursor to counting, record keeping and basic labeling but it offers more than this, it enables us to engage in mapping the external world to a rendering, locating ourselves in relation to others, allowing for "what if" thinking, planning, checking and comparing, and ultimately enabling the exploration and imagining of ideas over time. This hardly happened quickly, but from the first time a human externalized an idea on stone, in the sand or through small counters, we demonstrated our profound and possibly unique ability to imagine.

Information as Social Infrastructure

Third, immersion in information creates an infrastructure which we, as a species, create and exploit through our technologies. From earliest times, we have manipulated environmental resources to create tools not just for hunting and agriculture but for information sharing. What started with pigments and evolved to paper has brought us to silicon chips and the internet, all products of our continual human drive to develop the means of recording, storing, and sharing information with others. In a practical sense, our thinking and our tools for thought, the information technologies of our time, indeed of any time, are mutually dependent. It is difficult for us to imagine our existence without some infrastructure of information, or to imagine how another species could extract value from our information tools without a particularly human way of thinking.

This embrace and co-construction of thinking and tools is, I believe, such a taken-for-granted, routine disposition of humans that we might consider it a drive or native tendency of Homo sapiens, given choice and opportunity. This last point is important, not only for understanding the evolution of our social and technical infrastructures, but for helping us understand some of the challenges of modern life where information tools compete aggressively for our attention and even economic resources. We seem disposed to adopt what we can to enable our expression of ideas, opinions, facts, thoughts, and emotions. But in doing this, we give rise to environments that did not exist a priori. If so, then the mass adoption of social media should surprise no one, it's simply the latest manifestation of our habitual tendency. But since adoption gave rise to a new space, we see behaviors that few predicted when first imagining mobile phones, discussion forums and Facebook. Further, since modern technical service is priced commercially, there are inequities in access and availability that are sadly inevitable under current cultural and political realities, and problematic in terms of ensuring quality and reliability in our information infrastructure.

So why does it matter that we conceive of information technologies in a deeply human and long-term sense? While it is hard to know if there were benefits received by the earliest information technologists for their carvings, sculptures and art, there is no doubt that in our contemporary world, the financial rewards for being a successful technology innovator are potentially huge. The image of new college graduate (or better yet, drop-out) who produces a world-beating app or device has given us the iconic modern CEO who leaps from bedroom to boardroom in months, wowing venture capitalists and gaining untold wealth and an army of followers. This success story encapsulates in its purist form a view of technology innovation resting on the twin axes of technical expertise and market incentives. I call this the Wall St model of innovation and it is part of the ongoing myth foisted on us by business schools and compliant politicians, that our successful future rests on reducing any obstacles to such individuals and trusting the unfettered and supposedly "free" marketplace to give us the best technologies at the lowest price.

I take exception to this view as it fails to address explicitly the most important part of contemporary concerns with information technology, the human. Given a free hand and open market we've seen how Facebook captures our data and sells it for profit, and how Amazon's Alexa can place our orders, answer our vocalized queries and perhaps even without our realizing it, record parts of our private conversations. We know we are now targeted endlessly by companies based on our online behavior, that we are forced to bundle services when we only want a fraction of what is on offer, that our data streams can be throttled, cable services packed with forced advertising, and perfectly serviceable products allowed to become obsolete when there's a new version to sell. We might vaguely be aware of nudges in messaging and interaction that cynically encourage us to spend more, give more, or stay longer than might be good for us. To assume that the market will just work this out over time to produce fairer, cheaper, and more healthful information interactions is to adhere to a political belief over market reality.

In the Wall St model, there are consumers, customers, and clients. We are indeed, most of us, a consumer some time, but that is a particularly narrow part of our existence and a greatly reduced usage context, or "use case" as people love to say, for many of our information acts. Without putting human needs, capabilities and preferences directly into the discourse on technology innovation, we will not create more healthful, constructive, and user-centered information infrastructure. As the rest of the world's population gets to join us online, I believe this simplistic, innovator-friendly model of design and development that reduces humans to customers and interactions to monetizable events is never going to deliver what we want or need. What we must consider is how humans create, use and care for information in their full lives, over time, so we can leverage design that is truly user-centric.

So Where Are We Going?

Humans and information are inseparable. It is common to call us an information processing species, or to speak of information as the meaning humans add to data, and neither of these claims is wrong. However, I believe they are insufficient for helping us wrestle with the design challenge we face with our emerging global information infrastructure. It is somewhat of a cliché now to speak of being user-centered in our attempts to design new information technologies but I believe we have not achieved this yet. What passes for user-centered design (where it is really practiced rather than just claimed) is, I argue, still based on either a narrow view of what a human is doing when they use information, or on a flawed division of human psychology into time-based processes that dominate our theories and models of human action. I want to value and apply what we know from science but in a form that speaks more directly to the challenge of designing our information world.

This book continually reminds us of key tenets of our natural history that I believe can usefully inform our current thinking about digital technologies. First, let us consider that information traces and outputs are a product of our nature, that we have learned to use these and rely on them for tens of thousands of years and as such, these may have induced or shaped out culture. If this is so, we might want to pay more attention now to how our culture is moving and being shaped by the technologies we are developing that mediate so many of our endeavors on the planet.

Second, let us question the dominant model of human cognition with its modalities and processing limitations as key to interface design. As I will argue, the way we view people in scientific terms drives much of our approach to technology design (though I am sure many of my colleagues would argue that this science needs to be more not less applied). It is not that our current models are wrong (well they are, in the sense that every theory of human behavior is to some extent wrong and we are in a Popperian battle to just be less wrong as we progress) but that the rather fixed views we inherit from social science of human activities existing a multiple independent levels (physiology, perception, cognition, etc.) has been accepted unquestioningly in human factors engineering and user-centered design, with some cost to our appreciation of the nature of use, behavior, and intention.

Finally, if we trace the history of key technologies, we likely find that after we created images, we learned the representation of numbers, words, and the co-opting of resources to create and share these – portable artifacts and permanent monuments, temporary records of trades and cherished narratives of myths and deities. In so doing, we should be less concerned with the form of technology employed, but learn to understand that today's tools are just the latest step on the continuum of tools we have developed to serve representational purposes. As such, the social media mutterings and self-promotional postings of Facebook users are just natural outcomes of a species that needs to communicate, to represent, to share, and has continually sought effective technologies for doing so. What is most interesting therefore is how this ongoing process might have impacted us and how we can leverage what we know of ourselves and our history into shaping the process going forward. It is this that I consider the ultimate expression of user-centered design, a topic that I address directly in the next chapter.

References

Cartailhac, É. (1902). "La grotte d'Altamira. "Mea culpa" d'un sceptique". *L'Anthropologie, 13*, 348–354.

Clarke, S., and Madariaga de la Campa, B. (2001). *Sanz de Sautola and the discovery of the Caves of Altamira: Some Observations on the Paintings*. Spain: Fundacion Marcelino Botin.

Cloudnine eDiscovery Blog Here are Some More Up to Date Fun Facts on Big Data: eDiscovery Trends https://cloudnine.com/ediscoverydaily/electronic-discovery/date-fun-facts-big-data-ediscovery-trends/ (Downloaded July 21 2022).

Donald, M. (1998). Hominid enculturation and cognitive evolution. In C. Renfrew, P. Mellars, and C. Scarre, (eds.), *Cognition and Material Culture: The Archaeology of External Symbolic Storage* (pp. 7–17). Cambridge, U.K.: The McDonald Institute for Archaeological Research.

Engelbart, D. (1962). Augmenting Human Intellect: A Conceptual Framework. Summary Report, Stanford Research Institute, on Contract AF 49(638)-1024, October 1962, 134 pages. http://www.dougengelbart.org/pubs/augment-3906.html (downloaded July 27th 2022).

Hoffmann, D., Standish, C., Garcia-Diez, M., Pettitt, P., Milton, J., Zilhao, J., Alcolea-Gonzalez, J., Cantalejo-Duarte, P., Collado, H., de Balbin, R., Lorblanchet, M., Ramos-Munoz, J., Weniger, G., and Pike, A. (2018). U-Th dating of carbonate crusts reveals Neandertal origin of Iberian cave art. *Science*, 359(6378): 912–915.

Lewis-Williams, D. (2002). *The Mind in the Cave: Consciousness and the Origins of Art*. London: Thames and Hudson.

Ramachandran, V., and Hirstein, W. (1999). The science of art a neurological theory of esthetic experience. *Journal of Consciousness Studies*, 6(6–7): 15–51.

Rogers, E. (1995). *Diffusion of Innovations*, 4th ed. New York: The Free Press.

Schmand-Besserat, D. (1992). *Before Writing, Vol 1: From Counting to Cuneiform*. Austin: University of Texas Press.

Spivey, N. (2005). *How Art Made the World: A Journey to the Origins of Human Creativity*. Oxford: Oxford University Press.

The Emergence of User-Centeredness

2

We All Live in a Designed World

City planners and architects commonly suggest that the 21st century marks the first time in history when most of the world's population will live in an urban environment. No longer scattered unevenly about the earth's habitable space, the emergence of population centers results from our human tendency to cluster together and to shape the environment around ourselves. Demographers now predict perhaps as many as two-thirds of all citizens on the planet will be residing in an urban environment by 2050 (UN Dept of Economic and Social Affairs, 2018). Contrast this with the dominance of rural living for much of our time on this planet. As recently as 1800, for example, only one in ten people lived in an urban space, and in some areas of the world, rural living has dominated up until that late decades of the 20th century. Undoubtedly, this is a pivotal point in cultural evolution, a moment when living environments seemingly converge in terms of typical infrastructure and form, but I suspect even this moment of shift lags behind a more dramatic one that we are witnessing in the information realm.

This century will witness the first time when everyone on the planet can be present in a designed, networked, global information space that affords any individual the opportunity to access the same information or connect with any other person regardless of geographic location. Of course, we need to emphasize the theoretical aspect of this claim, the potential for universal accessibility and participation rather than its inevitability given some predictable economic and political constraints that operate less equitably across the globe than we may desire. Obviously, such constraints cannot be ignored but the pace of adoption and coverage of our

DOI: 10.4324/9781003026112-2

information infrastructure is rapid, outstripping the shift to urbanization, and though some parts of the planet may prove challenging, we are on the cusp of an age when the world's citizenry and collective knowledge is within reach of everyone, at the push of a button, the swipe of a screen or the utterance of a vocal command.

This possibility has, in historical terms, occurred breathtakingly fast, from the first connected computers of the 1960s to the early web browsers of the 1990s, onward through the spread of social media, we are seeing, in the span of a single lifetime, a profound transformation in human abilities to reach and to communicate with each other, independent of time and space. The world's largest retailer did not exist 30 years ago yet today there are few countries in the world where Amazon.com does not sell and ship products (at the time of writing this list only included Cuba, Iran, North Korea, Sudan, Syria, and the Crimean region of Ukraine). What started as online competition for local bookstores has become a total transformation of the global retail market for all goods, and in the process changed longstanding manufacturing, warehousing and consumption practices in a few years.

While the Wall St model of technical innovation paints a rosy picture of progress and profit, more recently there has been a collective questioning of how we might best design this expanding information infrastructure to do more than improve business efficiency or accelerate data capture but to create technologies that serve health, education, and government services, ultimately augmenting people's lives in an equitable and positive manner. If we are truly building a new world, maybe we can make it better than the world it is replacing. But as quickly as this information age has hit us, many of us have noticed that technical progress is not always positive, that user benefits are not inevitable, that the advantages of speed and access can carry a cost in terms of accuracy or enjoyment. As we are beginning to realize, commerce cannot guarantee the promised improvements will be available to all. More clearly, we are beginning to see that any designed structure carries with it assumptions about use, and these assumptions are rarely true for all possible users. The campaigns of misinformation that sully political discourse, the potential of artificial intelligence to deep fake video evidence, the spread of outlandish claims about COVID-19 vaccines involving a chip being inserted in your body, or the brutal shaming of individuals through viral postings show us all too often the downsides of our information age. We do not even need to pick such extreme examples. We can easily observe instances of smartphone addiction, the dopamine push for endless refreshing which sucks our attention from meaningful activities, the wasteful investment in poorly conceived educational technology that rarely delivers better learning, or the push to provide customer support only through impersonal bots and chat features. All around us, the downsides of information tools are not hard to find. For many of us, our everyday interactions with even some of the most basic information technologies in our homes, our cars and our workplaces remind us continually that exploiting the power of the digital infrastructure often involves learning, error-recovery and a good deal of patience.

When we consider the nature, form and impact of information technologies in our world, our natural human tendency is to tell this history to ourselves through an account of breakthroughs, landmark products, and personal need. "Home" computers emerged in the 1970s, mainly for hobbyists who wanted to build and assemble them, gaining a broader foothold in domestic life through gaming and word processing in the 1980s. Whether or not Ken Olsen, the CEO of Digital Equipment Corporation really said "there is no need for anyone to have a computer in his home" around that time is debatable, but the quote is often used as evidence of how little expectation there was for the home computing market in industry at the time. Similarly, when mobile phones were first developed for general use, those brick-sized devices were thought to be useful only for people working outside of the office, or when driving (a somewhat foolish idea given the potential for distraction we know handheld communication devices pose in such an environment). Few people really imagined needing a mobile phone, it was considered a luxury or specialized tool (an early 1983 version by Motorola cost close to $10,000 in today's money). Now, children expect them, schools might require them, and parents comply, seeing the benefits of connection for safety. From functional tool, the mobile phone has grown to be a fashion accessory, with top models selling themselves on size, color, and form factor as much as coverage.

In truth, the emergence of most technologies has a long and sometimes complicated history which we mostly ignore. Instead, we mythologize important individual figures who we associate with key inventions or technical innovations. Clive Sinclair is a name many in Europe associate with home computers in the 1970s, and Martin Cooper is identified with the first mobile phones in the 1980s. In our current time, we think of Bill Gates and Steve Jobs as the inventors the modern PC, of Jeff Bazos as the creator of online retail, or Mark Zuckerberg for conceiving social media. But such attributions are about as accurate as claiming Johannes Gutenberg invented printing; they provide a convenient shorthand for history that springs from a blindness we have to seeing technical progress in our world and a bias we have toward personalizing cause and effect.

This tendency to view progress through the lens of individual innovators, the so-called great-thinkers who changed our world, is in fact an extremely reductionist interpretation of technical progress. Not only does it downplay the efforts of many people who were involved and the powerful shaping effects of context, the great thinkers label is frequently narrowed down further to a few "great men," as if women such as Ada Lovelace and Hedy Lamar were not also instrumental in the history of information technology. But even if we can balance the gender inequity in this telling, the reality of design progress in our world is, I will argue, less tied to individual "great thinkers" than it is to an evolution of social practices resulting from opportunity, necessity and trial and error. Such practices are typically worked out within a group or community, leading to new ways of communicating, calculating, and co-operating that make sense to the collective. This is not new, such technology evolution takes a form that our ancestors understood and practiced in improving their material conditions. In short, someone might claim an idea (and our economic incentive system certainly encourages this) but delivery and adoption of any technical innovation is largely a team sport.

A more nuanced history of information technology's evolution might be gained by recognizing the emergence of "user-centeredness," a design philosophy with associated methods as an important driver of new technologies, and a view of advancement that sits somewhat at odds with competition for profit as the energizer of development and innovation. Examining user-centeredness as core driver offers of view of our species as engaged in a continual process of adapting our world to ourselves, obviously constrained by nature and politics, but with the best outcomes determined by the collective benefits that obtain. From this perspective, it would be almost impossible for one person, no matter how "great," to accurately envisage and deliver a perfect technology for the rest of us. User-centered design is a collective effort and key to our building a better digital world. The trouble is, like pornography, we might know it when we see it, but defining and delivering user-centered design is more complicated than it might seem.

The Turn to User-Centeredness

Everyone seems to believe "user-centeredness" is a good thing. Advertisements might frequently put the term "client" or "customer" in place of "user" but whether it's "client-centered financial advice" or "customer-centered retail," the claim is common, every organization wants you to believe they are acting in your interests, meeting your needs, designing experiences you will enjoy, in effect being user-centered. This ubiquity may eventually render the term meaningless as one could hardly imagine a company openly admitting its products were anything less, and no designer would take pride in delivering software that paid little or no regard to the needs of its intended users (although some designers apparently still believe they know intuitively what a user needs so they don't actually need to ask). But overuse aside, what does it really mean to design in a "user-centered" manner? And how did we get to the point where faith (or at least the claim of faith) in this idea has become commonplace?

The principal claim of user-centeredness in the digital realm is that any device or application which requires a human to operate it in order to exploit its functionality, should be designed to render the interactive experience a positive one. As information technology evolved from a narrow use in scientific, military or industrial environments operated only by experts into general office life where non-specialists might engage them, there was increased recognition of the need for the control interfaces to be "user-friendly." That latter term, less common now in contemporary user-experience design, came to prominence in the 1970s as a challenge to system designers of the day to consider the needs of the person who would end up using their design (see e.g., Stevens (1983) for a historical and amusing review of this term in the computer industry). The actual suffix "-friendly" is frequently employed now as a marketing label, attached to every manufactured product or experience from "buyer-friendly" packaging and "drinker-friendly" cups to "wearer-friendly" hats and "driver-friendly" cars. While it might sound like advertising fluff, "customer-friendliness" speaks directly to a core concept of user-centeredness, the belief that operating or engaging with a product or service should not require special skills or involve significant effort on our part. Instead, a well-designed, "user-friendly" product should offer a means of control that the user can exploit effortlessly and quickly.

Of course, we can identify some products in particular use contexts that will necessarily involve learning or training (the car used to be the classic example of a design that involved significant user learning to exploit but that hasn't prevented design efforts aimed simplifying much of that process too). There will likely always be some products and processes that involve user experiences dependent on specialized skills, but even here, we can append the "friendly" adjective to them when some thought is given to reducing the learning effort even slightly e.g., "pilot-friendly cockpits" or "surgeon-friendly operating theaters." The essential point is that there is now a widespread recognition, or at least a frequently stated belief, among those responsible for producing our information technologies that we should pay close attention to what people want when using a device, putting user needs or preferences at the center of the development process. In this way, we tend to view "user-centeredness" as a core value or driver of information and product development in our world. Thus, we find the idea of user-friendly information technologies crossing all sectors, from the design of phones to the interior of cars, from domestic appliances to the payment processes on website stores. Maybe before long, we might even see this movement improve one of the most annoying routine interfaces remaining in modern life, the label instructions on medicines (a simple pain reliever I buy requires me to unpeel a tightly folded label full of warnings and pharmacological details in order to locate the recommended dosage, a requirement I have learned to by-pass by just scribbling "1 × 6 hrs" on the outside of the lid in sufficiently bold letters to be easily read at the point of need). We can do better!

Obviously, user-centeredness in design is much easier to claim than to deliver, and consequently there are still many products and services which some designers intended to be "user-friendly" but for a variety of reasons ended up being difficult or unpleasant to operate. There is an extensive literature from studies of design processes, techniques, exercises, management interventions and investments that result in poor products. Even mega-corporations are not immune to messing up. Google seemed to bewilder more than a few people with its "Google Glasses" a few years back, a truly innovative, wearable, computing device that resembled spectacles but added various intelligent features such as voice activated functions and smartphone-like internet access. The product was less than positively received. According to McEleney (2019), users looked "like Dorks" and most people seemed unsure what problems these $1500 glasses were intended to solve. Multiple software glitches went unaddressed and once word got out that wearers could record what they were seeing, privacy concerns among the public created a backlash against the glasses and those publicly wearing them which the designers clearly had not anticipated. Some organizations, not only Las Vegas casinos, banned them on their premises. Russia outlawed their sale and use, leading to Google essentially retiring the product from the consumer market. The idea of smart glasses is not without merit, particularly in industrial and medical use, and I expect consumer versions of alternative designs to receive wider acceptance in due course as lessons are learned. Virtually anything we wear on our bodies is a potential space for digital enhancement, that much seems obvious. But as Google found out, a successful "smart spectacle" design will require a better sense of what people want and will accept. And it's not just about the direct or end-user, others in the environment of users also have a stake and their needs must also be considered. Clearly, common sense is not enough, user-centeredness requires continual and significant effort.

Competing interpretations and missteps aside, user-centeredness has become a dominant philosophy in many design fields, but it was not always so. Design historians tend to view this emphasis on user needs as a 20th-century phenomenon, tied to the explosive growth of products and goods that occurred after the industrial revolution and with the emergence of a consumer class. In this telling, as technologies evolved so did our thinking, shifting from the dominant view of operators being always trained to fit a machine's design to a recognition that any machine might be designed so as to suit the user. Today, there is even recognition that ease of use might be a market differentiator. While it's true that views of the operator or user have evolved significantly with new design theories, I believe it is worth noting that the rapid development of digital technologies has co-occurred with, and as a result of, the emergence of symbol and language-based interfaces for operating our devices. Where technology design was once about physical artifacts and material objects, manipulated manually through switches, levers, buttons and physical actions, our 21st century world of virtual, digital environments has added a layer of interactive experience that relies on software, resulting in a symbol-intensive, non-material environment in which we work and play through the exchange of data over networks. Our interactions are not limited to the physical control layer but incorporate linguistic and visual modalities. We exchange images, sounds, animations and text, not just simple commands or constrained instructions. The design challenge of the digital realm raises new complexities related to comprehension and action sequences that can be quite distinct from the physical or tactile interactions that have dominated much of our technological history.

Of course, the material world still exists and many if not most contemporary information devices, at some point, still require some form of physical contact, but the forms of physical manipulation that characterized usage in the pre-digital realm are less prevalent with current information technologies. We have entered a realm where interaction is reliant on images and language as much as or even more than physical movement or strength. This morphing of materiality does not change everything about human activities, people manifest behaviors in the digital realm that mirror aspects of engagement and ownership of objects that are almost identical to physical products (for more on this, see Dillon, 2019) but the rapid adoption of interactive technologies, where a staggering range of routine human activities are supported by a quite restricted form of interface usually involving screens, keyboards, and touchpads, has forced attention onto the representational aspects of user interfaces. This focus has at least coincided with, and in my view might even be thought of as instrumental in, the rise of more user-centered thinking since the need to understand people's reasoning and mental experiences has become crucial to delivering successful products, services and artifacts. Whether we intended it or not, user-centeredness has become unavoidable.

While recognizing that digital technology has accelerated this focus on users, I do not share the view of many that we can draw a hard and fast distinction between late 20th- and 21st-century technologies and all that went before. The idea that a human operator's needs might be important for ensuring a product's successful deployment certainly did not begin with digital tools. We have numerous accounts of design challenges faced by our ancestors, not just in creating superb architecture that paid attention to how people lived or worshipped, but in addressing with the practical problems of their contemporary worlds. We know, for example designers paid attention to optimizing wheels for horse-drawn carriages to withstand the demands of terrain (Sturt, 1923) or to developing the grooved inner bore on early rifles for improved shooting accuracy (Kauffman, 2005). Such examples reveal even in earlier times a concern with and for the intended users of these devices. The dished cartwheel example is particularly interesting in that we are still not sure how and why that design became the norm but it is almost certain it came about as a result of observing the problems of non-dished wheels in use and determining how to develop, in modern vernacular, a more usable design. So, while user-centeredness is clearly a central theme in contemporary design, humans probably always considered at some level what we now refer to as the user experience (what use, for example, would be a spear that was too heavy for a typical person to throw accurately?) even if they did not use or possess such language to describe this orientation in pre-digital designs.

Making Design Methodical

What did preface the formal concern with user-centeredness and enabled its clearer articulation as a key design value is the emergence of more systematic design methodologies, an effort initiated in the 1920s but more forcefully pursued from the mid-20th Century onward, to frame design as an intellectual discipline which could be taught and studied formally. During the Second World War (1939–1945), as countries embarked on a massive program of manufacturing and deployment of military technologies, the management of design processes became a vital part of the war effort as nations sought to maximize productivity, protect precious resources and leverage the skills of available labor. Byazit (2004) notes that there was a recognition among the industrial design community in the decade after the war that the large-scale production efforts of those years might offer lessons that could be applied to civilian projects. Chief among these was the belief that the process of design could and should be systematized for better management and more efficient outcomes. If appropriate exploitation by users was one desired outcome then somehow this needed to be built into any design process.

In her history of design since the 1940s, Vardouli (2016) examines how ideas about "users" have both driven and been shaped by some of the evolutionary tensions in contemporary design education. She notes that the last century witnessed repeated efforts at developing a more formal or systematic methodology for design as a conscious act or process. The goal was to formalize our understanding and teaching of design as a formal discipline, while juxtaposing it with science, which had itself evolved a recognizable approach to problem solving largely understood and shared by fellow scientists. Of course, the notion that science had a uniform identity and agreed methodology is a contestable claim, but Vardouli's main point is less that science is cohesive but that design seemed to compare poorly when it came to agreement amongst its practitioners and that this was a weakness design educators were motivated to address. Obviously there may be some questions raised over how uniform any design methodology can be, but Vardouli highlights the efforts of the Design Research Society in the UK to describe design in more disciplinary-wide terms, to bring a sense of cohesion to definitions and education of design professionals. Of particular note for those in user experience design, Vardouli reveals how the Design Research Society made deliberate efforts to build connections with the emerging human factors and ergonomics discipline as awareness increased of the importance of designing beter human-machine interactions for emerging industrial technologies.

This recognition of studying and designing for the "human in the loop" cannot be overstated. Rather than assuming a generic human (or user) of a designed product or artefact who could simply be modeled and accounted for once appropriate training was provided, this newer framing conceived of design as the determination of a complete system, one in which a living being with physical and behavioral tendencies forms a contingency on successful operation. Such a recognition led to a fundamental shift in thinking about how to design for successful outcomes. While it is true that there were earlier efforts to address human involvement in the system, these typically emphasized the selection of particular humans, operators with certain physical or dispositional characteristics for specific industrial activities. Taylor's (1911) Scientific Management approach was one such early effort, built on the belief that science could help us design better and more efficient work processes through the optimization of the technology and selection of the best workers as determined by time and motion analysis. Crude as Taylor's work might seem to us now, it was considered a breakthrough in industrial management. But like many other person-attributed innovations, we can trace the idea that some humans might be better suited than others to particular tasks at least as far back as the biblical Book of Judges, where only soldiers who drank water in a certain manner were deemed suitable for service in Gideon's army. Such approaches are more about personnel selection and hardly fit our current understanding of being "user-centered." The early human factors movement that Vardouli describes represented a distinct advance on such ideas, explicitly arguing that technology should be designed to accommodate the physiology and psychology of users, with a view to making the resulting "human-machine system" more productive. User-centeredness was becoming a cornerstone of modern design methods.

By the 1960s, two decades after the end of World War II, this idea of designing with a user foremost in mind was not limited to industrial design. Architects were actively considering how humans reacted to space and designed environments, even if they did not employ the word "user" as frequently. Alexander and Poyner (1966) spoke of "human tendencies" as a key component for understanding and structuring architectural design choices. Engineers were embracing the models and outputs of ergonomic research on human fit in determining machine design and Licklider (1960) spoke of "man-computer symbiosis" as the way forward for the emerging (but as yet unnamed) field of computer science. The 1962 conference on *Systematic and Intuitive Methods in Engineering, Industrial Design, Architecture and Communications* (Jones and Thornley, 1963) brought many of these disciplines together to explore design methodologies, one of the first scholarly acknowledgments that design was a key interest of many disciplines, and further, that appropriate consideration of the human as part of any design solution should be universally acknowledged.

Writing about this meeting some 40 years later, Bayazit (2004) acknowledges its landmark nature. He suggests that too many of the conference participants were content to propose their own way of working as a putative design method that others might emulate (an approach that has not entirely been eradicated in our current world, further perpetuating the "great man" notion of design practice) but goes on to say that it was also clear to the participants that "interest had to be shifted from hardware and form to the consideration of human needs (which) required a new look at the subject of design methods." (Bayazit, 2004, p. 18). Now, rather than just claiming that the user was important, the design world was starting to acknowledge that users were key, and it was essential to find the means of formally incorporating better understanding of users into emerging design methods, and thus user-centeredness came to be seen as a requirement, not just a claim

An agreement on one approved design method for every situation, or even for each design discipline, has never been reached, and it is unlikely that it ever will, but in the intervening decades, user-centeredness has become a descriptor for various approaches intended to address the problem of meeting human requirements or incorporating user input into the design process. With the adoption of user-centric approaches, or at least the acceptance of user-centeredness as a design philosophy, has come an emphasis on usability, accessibility, acceptability and so many related terms that are best considered values or qualities of a designed experience that we should aspire to or aim for in development. While user-centeredness often seemed like a rallying cry for designers of all stripes, the convergence of agreed methods to deliver on this idea has proved challenging, as witnessed in the many methodological and theoretical disagreements that continually surface when design researchers and practitioners attempt to explain and justify their preferred methods.

Within the human factors tradition, and particularly so in its early focus on human-machine interfaces and systems, there has always been a strong quantitative orientation which seeks to leverage the science base of physiology and psychology to determine a design's "goodness of fit" for any specific task. Ergonomics, for example, has established population norms on human characteristics such as height, reach, strength, reaction time and so forth to generate estimates of "typical" users on certain dimensions in order to constrain design choices on the machine side. With the emergence of scientific cognitive psychology in the 1950s onward, further predictive estimates of perceptual acuity, processing speed, memory load and skill development added to the strong quantitative modeling of users within certain parameters. The strength and popularity of this type of theoretical approach advanced a particular form of design that involves specialized analysis and laboratory testing of user interfaces.

Such a scientific approach to design has not been widely accepted across all disciplines. Within the architectural tradition, for example, there is frequently greater emphasis on more qualitative aspects of the user experience. Here, designers want to understand how people experience and make sense of the built environment. Where human factors professionals emphasize statistics and test results, the architectural emphasis is often more on the emotional and phenomenological responses of people. This distinction is regularly discussed in the design literature of the 1970s and 1980s, reflecting the tensions between design traditions, each side claiming to advocate user-centeredness but presenting slightly different understandings of who and what users are, and which characteristics of humans were most important to understand.

And these distinctive orientations are not only between design disciplines. If we consider only the development of information technology, many have traced the evolution over time of distinctive user-centered approaches just within the field of human-computer interaction (HCI). Harrison et al. (2007) identify three different paradigms across the history of HCI, reflecting a dynamic set of methods and theories that deal with the challenges of designing for the moving targets of digital technologies and shifting user demographics. Thus, in their telling, we see the early ergonomic emphasis on the physical human-machine interface slowly giving way to a more cognitive focus on the way users think about tasks and seek to optimize their interactions for effectiveness and efficiency. More recently, Harrison et al posit a situated emphasis that is concerned more with values, and qualitative aspects of people's real-world experiences of using technologies in their everyday lives (one not entirely dissimilar to the user discussions in the architectural models of earlier years).

There are likely alternative versions of HCI's evolution which see this history differently, and we can certainly debate if any of the waves labeled by Harrison et al really constitute paradigms or just topical concerns driven by the technology of the time, but for our understanding of what it means to be user-centered, the key point is that one agreed definition did not and still does not exist. While we might all accept that "user-centered" does imply the ideal of designing to accommodate human tendencies and to deliver positive benefits for people when using a designed product or environment (and this is no small achievement in the history of shaping technologies in our world) there is less agreement on how to achieve these aims or how to determine our success in doing so. In part this reflects the methodological stances of distinct disciplinary traditions (e.g., cognitive psychologists employ models and lab-testing; anthropologists employ field studies and observations etc.), but it also reflects quite directly the fundamental understanding each contributing discipline has of the human for whom we are all designing. When an ergonomist speaks of a "user" they hold a view of a human operator that can be different in key ways from the view held by an architect imaging their "users" of a built space, or by a social-psychologist who is concerned with "users" in an organizational setting. No wonder then that the term "user-centered" is hard to nail down with a simple definition as it has to cover such a range of meanings.

So What Then Does It Mean to Engage in User-Centered Design?

While acknowledging the ambiguous and sometime confused uses of the term, there is, I believe, a core emphasis we can recognize and exploit in our efforts to design in a more humane, person-focused manner. User-centeredness is fundamentally an orientation to design that acknowledges the quality of a human's experience with an artefact is important. In this way, designing in a user-centered manner means placing emphasis on the needs, abilities, and preferences of intended users when exploring design options. This much we can all acknowledge, regardless of discipline or field of practice, but it is really not a strong definition that neatly distinguishes user-centered from other processes. All design problems carry constraints on cost, time, and related resources, so it is not simply the case that being user-centered means the designer can ignore those aspects while focusing on user preferences, or that a designer who is working to a budget or a deadline cannot be really user-centered. Instead, we might best think of user-centeredness on a spectrum, along which a designer or team might be placed depending on how much emphasis or proportion of available resources they allocate to addressing the human interface within the process.

This is somewhat easier to appreciate when we examine the types of processes that user-centered design is thought to have arisen in opposition to, according to design researchers. The traditional management of software design hardly ignored users but sought to establish their requirements early, often in a form that fixed them in place, with minimal change and even less checking, so the process of delivering a product could proceed in a controlled fashion. Royce's (1970) classic "waterfall" model of software development (see Figure 2.1) which offers a linear sequence of activities that run from requirements to maintenance, reflects such a high- level management view and is usually criticized by the user-centered community, amongst others, for

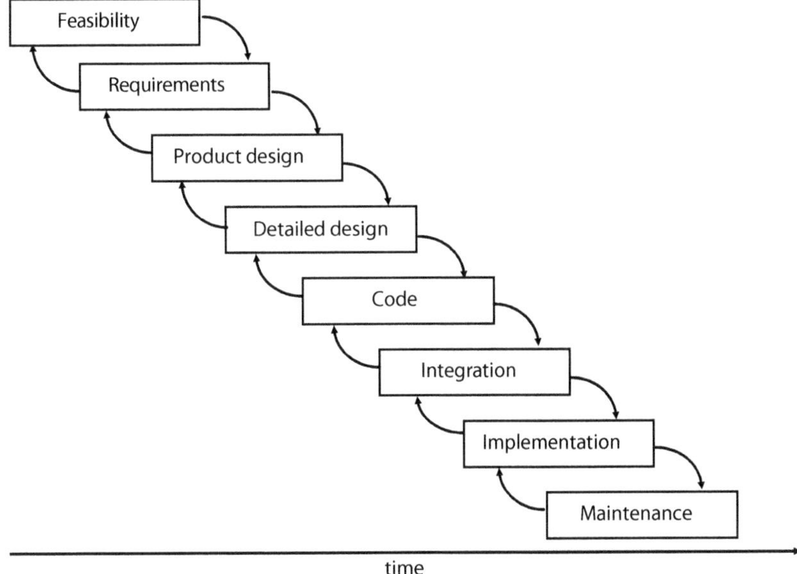

Figure 2.1 Simplified waterfall model of software design

being too inflexible, targeting strategically sequenced steps of delivery on a path to final product in a manner that made revisiting or iterating earlier steps difficult or impossible. While the criticisms might be justified in theory, it should be recognized that the waterfall approach, or the more interactive spiral model of Boehm (1988), itself a reaction to the criticisms of the classic waterfall approach, are not primarily intended to to guide the designer, they more appropriately provide managers with a framework for allocating resources as needed to ensure budgets and deadlines can be met.

The primary criticism emerging from the user-centered design movement, and perhaps a key differentiator between its philosophy and traditional design management is not just the emphasis placed on establishing user-requirements, which the waterfall and spiral models certainly also consider, but a belief that determining user needs is necessarily iterative and can rarely if ever be fully articulated early on in the process. User-centered designers thus commit to cycles of prototyping and testing potential solutions with users in a continual fashion, considerthing thiisa necessary step in accurately establishing what people will find most beneficial or appealing in a final product. In other words, user-centered design acknowledges that requirements may not be easily established up front and might only be teased out through the act of building and testing candidate solutions.

This distinction highlights two aspects of design, and the development of user-centeredness, that are fundamental to this book. First, we should not consider traditional and user-centered design processes to be distinguishable purely by their degree of interest in users. While it is common in textbook treatments of human-computer interaction to place these approaches in opposition, leveraged apart by some imaginary emphasis on the system (traditional) or the person (user-centered), in reality, this is a straw man argument. It makes for convenient pedagogy but fails to acknowledge that both approaches acknowledge that users' reactions to a final design are important determinants of success. Rather, it is the manner in which the determination or establishment of user requirements is made that characterizes the distinction The commitment to growing our understanding of users *throughout* the process, employing iterative examinations of the emerging user experience to check progress, the suggesting and subsequently testing of potential solutions, and the use of these evaluations to generate newer and hopefully better designs, which in turn are tested with real users, that is the hallmark of the user-centric method of design.

In contrast, the belief that we can establish user requirements without iteratively generating and testing potential design solutions, perhaps relying on marketing data and customer feedback from earlier versions or competitor products, putting undue faith in one-time interviews and task analyses at the front end for which a design solution can be determined, is characteristic of more traditional, less user-centric approaches. In both approaches, users are certainly considered, sometimes in great depth, but it is the ongoing and empirical checking of these considerations against real user experiences, coupled with the willingness to accept that new data might force us to reconsider or question earlier understandings of what is required, that singles one approach as genuinely user-centered, as I apply the term.

The second aspect of importance for this book is the emphasis within user-centeredness on empiricism or data. User requirements, preferences, needs, attitudes, abilities, and so forth have all been studied extensively, and we now possess decades of results on such matters that can be found in libraries of conference papers and academic journals. This work can be overwhelming to navigate but it is important, and it provides a solid educational grounding for those who wish to learn about designing for people. Even so, when it comes to estimating the likely response of users to any design, for all our research literature and theoretical understanding, we continually rely on and recommend testing, gathering data from representative users trying to complete relevant tasks with our proposed interface designs, having them tell us what they do or do not understand, what menu items they would select if faced with choices, or what they like and do not like about using the proposed design. When we usually want to know if a user can operate a device or application without support from others, if a new version of our design is really easier to learn than the last version, or if it offers a better experience than a competitor product, the most reliable and valid answers to such questions invariably are gained empirically. Testing the design with people who are given sample tasks to perform while we observe what transpires, how long it takes them to reach the goal, or what steps they take en-route to reaching their goal is more informative to a design team than anything else we can use. Even if only confirming what we know, such data are always insightful, but more frequently humbling as we learn that something we believed simple is confusing to some user, or that a much admired feature created by the design team is useless or unappealing to actual users. In short, while we have a mountain of design tests and experimental results to call upon, and rich theoretical and research findings to inform many of our initial design choices, codified knowledge is almost always insufficient. If we want to be confident that one design alternative is better than another, we continue to need real test results.

Taken together, these two aspects highlight a great challenge facing user-centeredness as a design approach. It is neither easy to define nor is it theoretically sufficient to ensure a satisfactory design outcome. Understanding the research base of UX can certainly help narrow the design space at the front-end, or suggest ways in which the problems found in a usability evaluation might best be overcome in a re-design. These remain two very important applications of theory that those lacking knowledge cannot provide, but user-centered design embodies a commitment to engaging with users continually, using appropriate methods, so as to improve the chances of delivering a humanly acceptable outcome. In short, theory can shorten the process, but only data can assure us of hitting the target.

The spirit of user centeredness underscores professional education in multiple fields or sub-disciplines committed to information design. In fact, it is this spirit that serves as the bridge between often-distinct forms of disciplinary education and training for UX professionals. While we are beginning to see the emergence of formal degree programs in user experience design or human-computer interaction, the reality is many professionals working in this space often come from quite difference educational backgrounds, with theoretical and methodological orientations that can make communication among them sometimes confusing. Ritter et al. (2014) offer an historical view of user-oriented design that suggests it has drawn on the following disciplines:

- Cognitive and social psychology
- Linguistics
- Mathematics
- Computer science
- Engineering
- Human factors and ergonomics
- Socio-technical systems design
- Scientific management
- Work, industrial, and occupational psychology
- Human relations
- Organizational behavior

This is almost certainly not a complete list as the impact of technology in many other domains now draws in scholarly interest from the humanities and arts disciplines which justifiably argue for the applicability of their own field to understanding user experiences, particularly in the context of immersion, and engagement. Attempts then to define user-centeredness through a bounded set of intellectual or professional disciplines are, in my view, neither easy nor particularly helpful. We've seen turf battles in the field of human-computer interaction and design that reflect academic labeling more than meaningful distinctions, e.g., I don't believe it is fruitful to argue endlessly about the lines between "user-centered" or "human-centered" approaches, or to posit that interaction designers focused on usability must be overlooking the broader contextual concerns of people for collaboration and communication. In one sense, the similarities of approach and the shared belief of each community of practice in serving the user, in being data driven, overwhelms the putative distinctions of disciplinary approach and label. Further, the range of use and adoption of technologies in our lives means that there is always going to be a need to spend time at one level (e.g., the task or the team) sometime at the expense of another level, temporarily favoring one discipline or one method of analysis, but the ultimate success of a design usually is determined by how well it works across all levels of experience, from the physical to the cultural, as I will show in later chapters. In short, user-centeredness transcends current disciplines; it is a both a philosophy and a suite of methods, and while we may aspire to being a discipline of design, it does not make too much sense to me to think of user-centeredness this way at this time.

From Definition to Design Method

While disagreements about the exact definition of user-centeredness will likely continue, there is value in exploring what it is that designers who profess to being user-centered actually do. Obviously working UX professionals have unique positions and operate in diverse organizations so a complete list of work responsibilities and tasks is not going to be too useful but we can distill the commonalities. The Interaction Design Foundation, the world's largest online school for HCI and UX professionals, characterizes a four-phase effort behind any instance of user-centered design work, synthesizing a consensus view of what user-centered designers actually do. They present the role in four broad steps as follows:

1 Investigate the context in which people will experience or use the design
2 From this, generate some requirements that the design must meet to succeed
3 Propose a potential design solution to meet these requirements
4 Test the solution on users to determine how well the requirements are met.

While the steps are distinct, there is the expectation of iteration as needed, a belief that feedback from the test for example, not only offers guidance on the design proposed in step 3, but might also reveal any important gaps in the set of requirements generated in step 2, or they can help improve the design team's understanding of the context of use initially established in step 1 (see Figure 2.2).

This generic form of staged, iterative process, with arrows and boxes, or circles and cycles, is invariably found in many books and papers on design. I usually encourage my students to seek out such models online and then to determine the similarities and slight differences among them to learn if there is a core set of ideas or any unique additions that might be made. Generally, upon completion of this effort, they report that the commonalities are high, that wording and labels might vary, and that some models might break down the number of steps further, perhaps, for example, adding development as a stage after a conceptual design, or unpacking the context of use analysis into separate analyses of users, tasks, and environments. Regardless, the essence of the user-centered approach remains: iteration around requirements, generation of possible solutions and user evaluations to determine goodness of fit.

It is important to recognize that from a user-centered perspective, any artifact that is being designed might be used within multiple contexts.

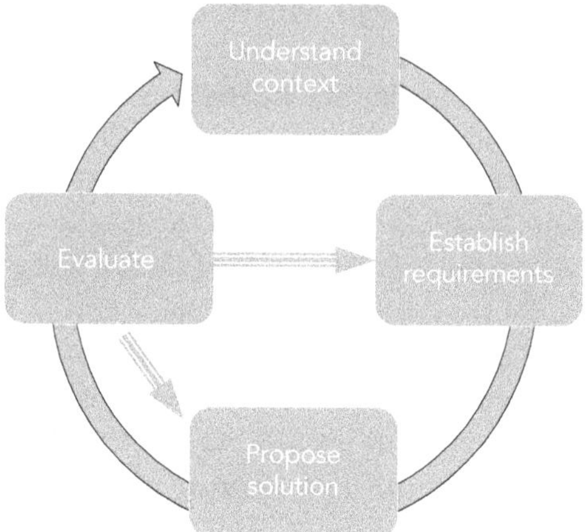

Figure 2.2 Generic model of user-centered design process

Consequently, it is necessary to determine the requirements and solutions for each context independently. While there likely will be overlaps, it is possible that distinct contexts require different design solutions or that a final design might offer a range of interaction possibilities with which only some users ever engage. In this way, we sometimes speak of *instances* of UCD within this phased process, and a complete design process might involve multiple, different instances, all aimed at delivering an acceptable final design for all intended users and environments.

Considered as a phased process, we can see that when engaged in user-centered activities, the work involves considerable effort on activities that are not, perhaps, stereotypically thought of as design acts. Studying use contexts involves a form of enquiry that is grounded in social science methods of observation and data solicitation. This is more the type of activity associated with anthropology than computer science, where the focus is on determining how people work or understand their tasks, and how the information tools we design will fit in with or change the flow of working practices. Even when committed to engaging in such user-centered methods, it is far too easy to conduct this type of work superficially and hence poorly, using sparse or inappropriate data to generate a set of requirements that turn out to be wrong. As Dourish (2004) notes, context is dynamic and emergent, tied to a person's construction of their social world, not simply a statement of given conditions in the environment. As such, understanding the context of use for any designed artifact involves careful observation and interpretation of the meaning that people make of their world as it is constructed during use.

Similarly, when considering people's responses to proposed designs, a trained evaluator knows that biases can easily influence results or user responses, that the wording of questions or interview prompts can lead people to certain answers that may not truly reflect how they see the design. There is always the problem of people not being able in advance to know what type of innovations might best suit them or being impressed enough with a quick examination of a proposed option to state a view that no longer holds when they are using it on their own later.

The point here is that while defining and explaining user-centeredness as an agreed, phased process seems relatively straightforward, conducting user-centered design appropriately requires a set of skills and analytic abilities that are not common or routinely provided in information technology or computer science education. Being user-centered involves more than just considering "user-friendliness" to be valuable, it involves a combination of theoretical and methodological skills that must be developed through education and experience. A comment often heard from those not educated in these theories and methods is that user-centered design is "just common-sense," or a set of "ask-the-user-what-they want" techniques that anyone can apply. Obviously, such comments tend to irritate, or at least amuse, those in the UX profession who have spent years developing and applying their understanding of human behavior to the challenge of creating better systems and who recognize the complexity of translating observations and theories into actionable and relevant design outcomes. Generations of poor user interfaces around the world attest to the difference between claiming and really completing user-centered design.

Is remains true, however, that user-centered design is very easy to do poorly, and can appear very expensive to do well, especially if one does not actually count the true costs of delivering a poorly designed interface that results in frustrated users, increased demands for support, or outright rejection. A contemporary variant of user-centeredness, design thinking, has gained traction in recent years espousing something close to common-sense married to brainstorming, reducing the complexity of user-studies and making a case that it can yield efficient results. In its most basic form, design thinking represents an approach to group problem solving that is based on rapid and continual idea generation, usually in a context of divergent thinking that resists early judgement so as to encourage participation and discussion among stakeholders. While there is no formal or even agreed definition of design thinking, like user-centered design, a common set of steps or activities is also found in many descriptions. These generally include the following:

- Empathy – an effort to learn about the users for whom you're designing and their context of use in the real world
- Definition – a phase of establishing user needs, clarifying the problem,
- Ideation – Generating ideas for potential or innovative solutions
- Prototyping – Developing these possible solutions and new ways of working
- Testing – Trying out the ideas on real users to gain feedback

Touted increasingly as a general method for innovation, design thinking has now gained currency among organizational theorists and popular culture as a means of harnessing creativity to serve business ends. Jeffrey Tjendra (2014) stated that design thinking was a necessary response to the logic-dominated educational system of 20th-century America, which led to companies whose leadership was distrustful of creative thinkers. Thus, as technologies started to shift dramatically, industry needed a way to harness value from changing consumer demands and behaviors. By rendering the design process more comprehensible to business leaders and accountants, design thinking offered a somewhat orderly process that could be managed and understood without specialized knowledge, promising to produce outcomes that could be assessed in traditional business terms of value.

More than a UX design process, design thinking has been touted frequently as a way for any organization to harness the power of "out of the box" thinking to solve difficult, or in the rhetoric of design thinking, "wicked" problems. It is now commonly applied in education, healthcare, business, and manufacturing as part of management efforts to improve processes, to engage participants and customers, and to encourage change and innovation. As such, it is less a formal method than a domain-independent approach to targeted problem solving, based on a philosophy of trial and error, collective input, imagination and synthesis.

Design thinking typically presents itself as an antidote to lock-stepped, overly rational approaches to designing systems and services and it has been adopted by diverse practitioner communities. Along the way, critics have claimed it has been over-hyped and representative of a business school orthodoxy that pushes it as a tool rather than a form of reasoning and thinking (Wylie, 2017). Jen (2017) went viral for her talk entitled "Design Thinking is Bullshit" at that year's 99u Conference, specifically pointing to the weak level of informed criticism in the outputs of typical design thinking exercises which she said were overly-reliant on "Post-it note" reactions and uninformed input from participants. For Jen, this was largely due to the underlying belief in design thinking that "everyone's a designer," part of the feel-good marketing of this approach as a cure-all to to business audiences.

As noted in Dillon and Sweeney (2022), other critics have questioned the claims for design thinking's impact, and the lack of a theoretical basis for informing decisions throughout the process. We point to the lack of sufficiently reported case studies of design thinking's value, with typical accounts offering little more than snippets of participant or client feedback as evidence. Norman (2018) points out that we continue to lack reliable comparisons between most design methods, which is a weakness in the UX discipline and particularly so given some of the claims made for the value of one method to the exclusion of others. However, the avoidance of theoretical consideration within design thinking probably encourages inclusiveness and uptake although in so doing, it enocourages a view that all inputs from participants in the process are equally valid, and without theoretical guidance, this offers little assurance that anything other than popularity guides the outcome of design thinking methods.

In its favor, design thinking has raised awareness among many that innovative solutions to problems might be enhanced by considering the needs and experiences of users impacted by a product or service. The lack of conformity to a disciplinary theory or method set might be beneficial in some contexts to encourage diverse inputs. That said, design thinking cannot ensure successful outcomes in all areas of application, and it is hardly a unique formulation of how groups might problem-solve or develop new ideas, but in placing a strong emphasis on users and user-experience at emotional as well as behavioral or rational levels, it aligns with the spirit of user-centered design as traditionally understood and practiced by UX and human factors professionals. The key difference however, is in the depth of understanding of people we really want to attain if we are to design in a truly user-centered fashion. As I'll attempt to show in subsequent chapters, there is a lot we know about people that can really benefit our attempts at designing well for them. It is perhaps less important how we label the steps we follow than it is to ensure valid and reliable user input to the process.

So Can We Really Define User-Centered Design?

Iiavari and Iiavari (2006) provided a thematic analysis of the term "user-centered" as well as synonyms such as "human-centered" in the design literature and suggested there are ultimately four general ways in which this term is employed by researchers and scholars in their writings:

1 User-centeredness as user focus
Here, the user as an individual is the core focus of the design effort. Effort is made to understand how each person thinks about the system and its operation. Theories from user psychology and anthropometry are applied to allow for some generalization of needs to similar users and where gaps in knowledge remain, prototypes or experimental tests can help determine the best fit among competing design suggestions.

2 User-centeredness as work-centeredness
A secondary application of user- or human-centeredness is found in work that emphasizes the organizational or social context in which activities are situated. In this approach, the individual is not the focus as much as the structures and process within which individuals of this type operate. Much attention is given to power, authority, change, and routines that are impacted by a new design.

3 User-centeredness as user participation
It is a tenet of user-centered design that people who will be using a product or service should be involved in the process, and there is work that examines how to enable this and what sort of problems such involvement might entail. Such work has helped us recognize the problems of changing designs, the use of power to interpret different inputs to the process and the challenges users face in articulating needs and preferences at different points in the design.

4 User-centeredness as system personalization
A fourth use of the term user-centered is observed among advocates of adaptable or personalized system design. In this framing, a design is considered to be user-centered if it incorporates tailorability, the potential to be adjusted or configured by the user for their particular needs and preferences.

Some fifteen years on, this clustering of terms still seems to reflect the academic literature on "user-centered design" although I suspect some re-weighting of the clusters might now apply. The sharp distinction between a user and work focus is one that is not drawn as firmly since our technologies of information have rapidly expanded into many non-work aspects of life, and personalization has moved from a somewhat optional to almost assumed level of design in many information products and services, at least at some levels. With the growth of interest in user-experience across many areas of human activity, there has been explosion in data capturing how people view or rate particular designs, with everything from mobile phones to dishwasher interfaces now subject to user studies, online reviews, and customer ratings and ramblings. This is mostly a good development, indicative of the general acceptance that in a world of choice, the user's perspective is valued. However, beyond the business argument, I feel we have not made sufficient progress in our conception of user-centeredness as a value Determining what people prefer among commercial products is merely one level of design, understanding how we can create information products that augment or enhance our lives, across the full human lifespan, is definitely more challenging.

We can perhaps best understand this by considering the many ways in which we have become reliant on information tools for many routine activities. The look-and-feel aspects of a design surely matter and will influence choice and adoption, but some aspects of design are not easily determined by tests of interface appeal or usability. Privacy is one vital area of design that user-centeredness struggles to accommodate, not least because it is hard to evaluate in trials, and the infrastructure for protecting data can be complicated and non-transparent in a design. Certainly, there are simple user-centered issues related to how people set up and use password protections (and in this most critical aspect of interaction, we seem poorly served by user-centered input) but for many users, beyond the interface, there are issues of trust in information technologies that are difficult to examine or evaluate in the design process, no matter how iterative or data-driven it might be.

Such concerns scale to cover so many more aspects of contemporary life. Health information and treatments, transportation, education, entertainment, financial planning, interpersonal communication, political discourse, and decision-making, all are now mediated by information technologies that embody very real design choices. The challenge of delivering user-centered products and services has arguably never been greater. We may still struggle to define exactly what we believe being user-centered means, but this struggle reflects the ongoing nature of UX design, and ultimately must be based on trying to determine what methods and theories best offer us the insights needed to deliver a global information infrastructure that serves all of us well. In the remaining chapters I will cover what I believe are key ideas that will help us in achieving that goal.

References

Alexander, C., and Poyner, B. (1966). *The Atoms of Environmental Structure*. London: Ministry of Public Building and Works.

Boehm, B. (May 1988). A spiral model of software development and enhancement. *IEEE Computer, 21*(5), 61–72. 10.1109/2.59.S2CID1781829

Byazit, N. (2004). Investigating design: A review of forty years of design research. *Design Issues, 20*(1), 16–29.

Dillon, A. (2019). Collecting as routine human behavior: Personal identity and control in the material and digital world. *Information & Culture, 54*(3), 255–280.

Dillon, A., and Sweeney, M. (2022). Adding rigor to advance design thinking. In Y. Ericsson (ed.), *Different Perspectives in Design Thinking* (pp. 22–41). London: CRC Press.

Dourish, P. (2004). What we talk about when we talk about context. *Personal and Ubiquitous Computing, 8*, 19–30. 10.1007/s00779-003-0253-8

Harrison, S., Tatar, D., and Sengers, P. (2007). The three paradigms of HCI. CHI'2007, Sessions of the SIGCHI Conference on Human Factors in Computing Systems. San Jose CA: ACM, pp. 1–18.

Iivari, J., and Iivari, N. (2006). Varieties of user-centeredness. *Proceedings of the 39th Annual Hawaii International Conference on System Sciences (HICSS'06), 8*, 176a–176a. 10.1109/HICSS.2006.530

Jen, N. (2017). Design Thinking is Bullshit. https://99u.adobe.com/videos/55967/natasha-jen-design-thinking-is-bullshit.

Jones, J., and Thornley, D. (eds) (1963). *Conference on Design Methods: Papers Presented at the Conference on Systematic and Intuitive Methods in Engineering, Industrial Design, Architecture and Communications. September 1962*. London: Pergamon Press.

Kauffman, H. (2005). *The Pennsylvania-Kentucky Rifle*. Morgantown, PA: Masthof Press.

Licklider, J. (1960). Man-computer symbiosis. *IRE Transactions on Human Factors in Electronics, HFE-1*, 4–11.

McEleney, J. (2019). 5 Epic Consumer Product Design Failures. *Onshape Blog* https://www.onshape.com/en/resource-center/innovation-blog/5-epic-consumer-product-design-failures (downloaded July 28th 2022).

Norman, D. (2018). Rethinking Design Thinking. https://jnd.org/rehtinking_design_thnking/ 12/10/20. Accessed July 21 2021.

Ritter, F., Baxter, G., and Churchill, E. (2014). User-centered design, a brief history. In F. Ritter et al. (ed.), *Foundations for Designing User-Centered Systems* (pp. 33–54). London: Springer-Verlag.

Royce, W. (1970). Managing the development of large software systems. *Proceedings of IEEE WESCON, 26* (August), 1–9.

Stevens, G.C. (1983). User friendly computer systems?: A critical examination of the concept. *Behaviour and Information Technology, 2*(1), 3–16.

Sturt, C. (1923). *The Wheelwright's Shop*. Cambridge: Cambridge University Press.

Taylor, F. (1911). *The Principles of Scientific Management*. New York: Harper.

Tjendra, J. (2014). The Origins of Design Thinking. Wired, April issue. https://www.wired.com/insights/2014/04/origins-design-thinking/?mbid=email_onsiteshare. Accessed July 28th 2022.

UN Dept of Economic and Social Affairs. (2018). *68% of the world population projected to live in urban areas by 2050, says UN*. https://www.un.org/development/desa/en/news/population/2018-revision-of-world-urbanization-prospects.html (downloaded July 28th 2022).

Vardouli, T. (2016). User design: Constructions of the 'user' in the history of design research. In P. Lloyed and E. Bohemia (eds.), *Future Focused Thinking-DRS International Conference*, 2016, 27–30 June, Brighton U.K. 10.21606/drs.2016.262

Wylie, I. (2017). Design Thinking: Does it live up to the hype. Financial Times, Oct 11th 2017 https://www.ft.com/content/a961cada-a520-11e7-8d56-98a09be71849 Downloaded Dec 11th 2020.

Designing Our Information World: Craft or Science? 3

For all the arguments about what constitutes true user-centeredness in a design process, it is also important to recognize that term "design" is itself open to competing definitions and interpretations. I tend to use the term broadly and consider design a form or method of problem-solving and solution generation which, when coupled with user-centeredness, is the basis of human-computer interaction studies and user experience (UX) design. Within the recruitment process however, a distinction has recently been drawn in industry between "UX researchers" and "UX designers" which attempts to draw a separation between those who study people to identify their needs and preferences (the researchers), and those who translate these requirements into the look and feel of user interfaces (the designers). How valid this distinction really is might depend on organizational politics, or even current intellectual fashion, but in attempting to separate user research from design implementation, we can sense that the use of the designer label, even within the UX community, is not without complications.

The traditional literature on design as a human act leans heavily on the suggestion that it embodies a form of craft knowledge manifest in the close coupling of materials and outcome. Clay potters, for example, use a wheel and their hands to shape the raw material into a vessel; carpenters cut and shape wood into furniture; smiths pound and polish heated metal into a sword or utensil. Our cultural history is filled with the efforts of humans to work with, on, and through materials to give form to our imaginations. We can and do mark history through reference to materials (e.g., "the bronze age") and

DOI: 10.4324/9781003026112-3

products (e.g., "the steam age") we have created. Skilled craftspeople have long been admired for their special abilities, the knowledge and skills behind specific crafts often being a closely guarded form of knowledge that was passed down through generations. Even now, in an age of mass production, a premium is typically placed on luxury discretionary goods that are made by hand. In a stereotypical manner, when we use the term "design," it is these forms of practice that many people imagine.

In reality, much of what now is encompassed under the term has become less tied to the image of traditional craft. The industrial revolution enabled and amplified the provision of cheap copies for many of the desired and needed products in society, and in so doing led to a separation of design and manufacturing processes. Consumer goods are rarely the output of one individual shaping a unique product but the result of a machine or operator replicating some designers' or design team's intent to deliver identical copies. This represents a relatively new stage of our history in relation to material goods. As this gulf between the idea of, and the manufacturing of a product emerged, a new form of engineering knowledge evolved that constituted the basis for mass production. In so doing, this formalized for many products the separation of the designer from the act of building or delivering the goods. Craft-based practices certainly remain in niche areas, but for most of our manufactured goods, the designers have a circumscribed role that rarely involves them directly in the production of the final item.

That being said, in contemporary user experience design, there exists a tension between craft- and science-based design practices and this might partly explain the distinction some draw of UX professionals as either designers or researchers. I do not care much for this distinction as it tends to reduce the complexity and interrelated nature of design reasoning into convenient steps (research then design, or perhaps science first to capture data but then hand over to craft for generation of the solution, maybe returning to science for the evaluation stage) and in so doing perpetuates what I consider to outdated and incorrect understanding of what good UX design entails. Studies of designers across multiple domains repeatedly highlight the commonalities of problem solving and reasoning involved, suggesting a process for design that is both rational and empirical, a mix of theory and practice. In the pursuit of more user-centered information technologies, we likely will do better by recognizing the mutuality of craft and science and educating new design professionals accordingly.

What Are We Doing When We Design?

There is general recognition that we all live in a largely designed world. From packaged food to living spaces, the majority of our goods and services are created for us by other people. In short, the outputs of design are everywhere in our lives. Simply put, a designer is someone who plans the form, workings or appearance of an object or space before it is built. Any list of designer types would be lengthy and likely unsatisfactory though that has not prevented some from trying to quantify them (there are 11 types according to Brooks (2021) though Spacey (2017) reckons there are a least 16). In our modern world the label "designer" also carries connotations of value. Bespoke consumer goods are often tagged with the label "designer" to suggest they are unique, or of higher quality because of some special expertise involved in their development, all testimony to the power of the word "design."

While we might quickly acknowledge the presence of design in our world, at least part of the difficulty of defining and quantifying types of designers springs from our rather limited understanding of what humans are doing when they engage in this process. In any model of design, certainly in the kind discussed in the previous chapter, there is a point at which the identified requirements and recognized constraints must give way to the act of generation, the articulation of a proposed solution upon which the subsequent stages rest. While requirements help reduce the potentially infinite range of solutions that might be proposed, or the results of a test on a prototype can identify weaknesses in a proposed solution, there remains a moment (or more likely many moments) in every design cycle where a leap of imagination is required. At some point the designer is expected to propose a solution, a suggested embodiment of a product or service, which then needs to be given sufficient representational form to enable its serious consideration by others.

Unlike a standard mathematical problem for which there is typically one correct answer, any design challenge can usually be resolved in multiple ways, some of which will likely prove more appropriate than others but more than one of which might be acceptable. Just consider the wide range products designed to perform essentially the same task in our kitchens or living rooms, a shared context with similar user needs, and yet different products are proposed by various design companies as a solution. So, we can know this much: different designers, faced with the same problem space, will likely suggest a range of possible solutions, any or all of which might be satisfactory but only one of which will likely be selected for implementation. This is a rather unique aspect of design which we probably would not find so acceptable in medicine, mathematics or even classical music.

Although design has been a routine human activity for millennia (and as I write this, I am reading an article in the news about common designs for stone tools that seem to have been shared by our ancestors more than 60,000 years ago), the formal study of design as a cognitive and physical act is comparatively new. Bryan Lawson, an architect and design theorist has made a lifelong study of the manner in which humans perform design tasks and his research posits a view of design as a form of human problem solving that accompanies many activities, many of which we do not even think of as design. In *How Designers Think* (Lawson, 2005), a classic text on the psychological processes underlying design reasoning, he states: "the very word design is the first problem we must confront since it is in everyday use and yet given quite specific and different meanings by particular groups of people" (p. 3). As he notes, the rather precise and procedural form of design we might observe, for example in a precision engineering context, can seem quite different to the apparently spontaneous and less predictable process adopted, for example, by a fashion designer. Yet both practitioners would surely describe their work as "design," and few of us would argue otherwise, suggesting that a unified or definitive representation of the act is certainly not easily obtained.

Paradoxically, while there are endless job openings for designers in our economy, relatively few schools or departments of design exist on their own in academia; they are more typically found as specialized units or programs within engineering, architecture, or art colleges (Dillon and Sweeney, 2022). It seems that for most of its history, at least in academic circles, design is best thought of as a general process that is conducted across application areas rather than being a unique intellectual discipline. There have been several proposals over the years to broaden the education of professional designers and to develop a common core that treats design as domain-independent but, according to Lawson, such a dream is rarely actionable given the traditions and barriers to entry in many professions that require distinct preparation for membership, often before a student is even admitted to an educational program.

Why does this matter you may ask? I believe it results in confusion over labels and credentials that make it difficult for user-centeredness to gain a strong intellectual foothold in education. Though we are now observing an increase in the number of degree programs with "design" in the title of the degree or the academic home, the reality is such programs often provide a narrow or idiosyncratic focus so that a student in one program is not necessarily sharing much at the curricular level as a student in another. A quick examination of the various degree programs in the US that claim "design" as their focus will yield education in a range of possible subjects such as landscape design, architectural design, graphic design, interior design, industrial design, stage design, fashion design, sustainable design, urban design, museum design and more. This diversity renders difficult any attempt to construct a representation of design through a synthesis of distinct literatures, each with terminological traditions and recognized outputs that reflect a specific and sometimes narrow professional identity.

We are required, therefore, to step outside and across disciplines and domains if we wish to make sense of design as a human act and attempt to articulate a shared view of the act of design that can be applied generally in education, regardless of professional venue. Thankfully, some thinkers have gone before us on this path and helped frame an answer to that central question: just what are humans doing when we design?

The Limitations of Craft and the Emergence of Design

While humans have developed a material environment of increasing complexity over centuries, the knowledge utilized to create the artifacts of each era was rarely formally articulated, and the practice of design has been characterized in a manner that is often described as craft-like. In other words, practitioners learned through tradition and apprenticeship to an expert, the ways of building or making objects. In educational terms, the skills and knowledge needed to craft material objects for utilitarian or aesthetic purposes resided in the maker and was usually passed on through demonstration and practice rather than being codified in written form. Also spoken of in terms such as "folk design" or "blacksmith design" to reflect the act of designing while making, craft practice embraces the co-occurrence of design with manufacture, shaping through doing, adjusting, and refining the form or innovation while constructing it rather than following a menu of external instructions or executing steps of a formal plan.

We should not underestimate the power of this form of design activity. Communities have survived at length exploiting craft-based knowledge handed down over generations, indeed most of our civilization's material history is dominated by such practices, many of which still exist to this day. Just ask most designers "what are you doing?" at the moment of solution generation and they may have a difficult time expressing their thoughts clearly and may still see their work as a form of crafting. Aristotle recognized the importance of such craft (or "techne" as he described it), considering it a form of knowledge, important for the functioning of a society and the basis for producing objects used by its members. For him, the quality of craft knowledge could be measured by the product, the objects that resulted from its application (see e.g., Massingham, 2019). However, even with its recognition by philosophers as foundational and our historical record of technological evolution through this, the craft approach came to be understood by design theorists as having significant drawbacks.

First, craft knowledge resides in the individual, therefore it is heavily reliant on the unique skills of the practitioner. Consequently, the outputs of craft designs can be inconsistent. While uniqueness is highly valued in some contexts such as jewelry or artworks, it is less appropriate in others, for example developing reliable weaponry or vehicles, where consistency of quality and factors such as the reproducibility and interchangeability of parts are important. Not only might a practitioner's own outputs vary, but any two practitioners tasked with the same design goal might also produce quite different results which can render production at scale variable at best and impossible at worst.

Second, by virtue of its internal or mental representation, the knowledge base of crafts, that is, the understandings that practitioners have of why their products work or how they might be improved, is often constrained. New practitioners learn by emulating, copying the existing forms, and duplicating them under an apprenticeship-type model of learning. While this ensures a degree of continuity, and the formation of identifiable traditions or schools of design, the process offers little room for innovation or even deviation from the master's approach. Historically, apprentices were expected to learn by copying, then embarking on their own career (as referred to in the somewhat outmoded term "journeyman"), with relatively few ever becoming a master designer in their own right (a process that not only involved the production of a "masterpiece" but usually the payment of funds to a guild for consideration of membership). In such a world, the formal representation and articulation of the master's thoughts was not of paramount importance, it was the output that was rendered visible, not the skill or knowledge that underlay it.

Third, if an especially skilled craftsperson or master designer dies, parts of their knowledge and skill can be lost to the group. With sufficient numbers of apprentices trained over time the loss of any one might not matter but where skilled practitioners are limited, this can be problematic for a community. Further, since the type of craft skill transfer is thought of as more procedural than declarative, that is based on doing rather than acquiring articulated knowledge, there is no way of ensuring a master practitioner's knowledge is fully expressed in the apprenticeship process and it is not hard to imagine that with the loss of any master designer, some parts of their expertise might die with them.

A classic example that is often invoked in design texts to highlight the limitations of craft-based knowledge is case of the dished form of cartwheel, originally outlined at length in George Sturt's *The Wheelwright's Shop*, published in 1923. In his book, Sturt outlined his experiences trying to understand why cartwheels evolved their distinctive saucer-shape from the original flat form, an elaborate construction that required specialized skills to build. The case and underlying rationale have been examined in many other books, including Lawson (2005), but the main point is that the practitioners Sturt studied seemed to have little real understanding of why the wheels were shaped as they were, and instead concentrated on building them to conform to that shape without undue concern for explaining it. Subsequent authors have speculated on the advantages presumed to result from dishing the wheel, ranging from it allowing for overhanging loads that might be otherwise restricted by a flat wheel to it allowing for smoother response to the swaying induced by a horse's gait when pulling the cart. Each explanation has some face-validity, plausibly explaining a motivation for this form, but none has yet fully explained why dished wheels became standard. As Lawson (2005) suggests, there are probably several related advantages to dishing which defy a single explanation. In essence, this example has come to epitomize the critiques of craft-knowledge as a means of advancing design, we might build better but never know why, highlighting the gap between practice and rationale that limited the opportunities for knowledge to drive advancement.

But rationalizing improvements is not the ultimate problem with craft-based design. Given enough time and practice, solutions can be generated and optimized through trial and error, or through refinements and feedback, even if the craftsperson cannot formally articulate or calculate why one particular design is better than the other. This might be perfectly acceptable in some contexts, though the error issue should not be underestimated. Trial and error is a time honored approach that has served humanity well except in situations where the cost of an error (user injury or death, accidental damage, major disruption or cost to those relying on the design etc.) is particularly high. As we might imagine, in such cases, trial and error thinking can encourage us toward sticking with the tried and trusted, slowing innovation and rendering some communities vulnerable to the advances made elsewhere.

Conservatism aside, the greatest limitation of craft knowledge seems to lie in its inevitable slow response time, or even failure to respond at all, when circumstances or contexts change. If a craft person knows only how to fashion one type of output, and spends a lifetime developing the skills to refine this, a group reliant on that design is vulnerable when outsiders with a more advanced technology arrive. This is easily recognized with weapons or hunting tools as whole peoples throughout history can attest with the arrival of guns, but it can as easily apply to food production and storage, modes of transport or construction methods, and in our current time, digital information tools. Crafters typically learn through a process of emulation not innovation. Such a process is intrinsically slow and not always conducive to adjustment. In economic terms, when a market changes, or a new technology threatens an existing one, it would be better to understand why one design is better suited than another to a particular task so as to quicken the process of reacting and countering a competitor's offerings instead of simply copying them. For this to be possible however, the crafters (for want of a better term to describe designers wed to such practices) should possess more than the ability to replicate an object but also to know how and why it is better, from its material construction to its fitness for purpose.

The Separation of Design from Manufacture

The industrial revolution in Europe is usually seen as a critical turning point in evolution of design practice and thinking, representing a shift from the dominant model of craft practice toward a new approach built around the evolving understanding of engineering. Design theorists such as Christopher Alexander (1964) make the case that the rise of mechanization was pivotal, threatening the existing craft-based practitioners by delivering a machine-enabled form of manufacture that could manipulate materials much as a crafts person might but at a greatly more efficient and profitable rate. As mechanical devices improved, an irreversible shift followed in our understanding of how material goods should be produced. Mechanized manufacture necessarily involved detailed examination and articulation of the processes used to weave, for example, so as to enable James Hargreaves to build his "Spinning Jenny" in the 1700s, a machine for lining up and spinning threads at rate that dramatically outperformed the pace of even the best traditional weavers. The Jenny (popularly thought to be named after one of his daughters, though evidence for this is scant) had a dramatic effect on production and lasted until such time as it was further improved by the invention of the next generation machine, James Crompton's "Spinning Mule," the shift from a personal to an animal name certainly seems symbolic of the advancing dehumanization of workers in the industrial revolution. While the line between *knowing how* and *knowing why* in design is surely blurry, the rise of industrial production induced the formal separation of design from making or manufacture, which has subsequently become viewed as a characteristic difference between craft and engineering-based modes of production. Now, with machines to deliver the goods, quite literally, a new emphasis was placed on identifying, analyzing, and automating some of the physical actions that previously only humans practiced in a craft could perform.

This shift from craft to a more scientific form of knowledge for design was not, however, a simple and unilateral step. Machine-aided design did not just emerge, it predated the industrial revolution by centuries (wood lathes for example were used in Ancient Egypt as far back as at least 1300 BCE) but early use was mainly individual. Developments in the 18th century amplified machine use to a level beyond any previously seen. Major shifts occurred in how human labor was employed, and where machinery triumphed, as in agriculture and the textile, mining and glass making industries, wholesale change followed. As demand for workers spiked, large swathes of the population were drawn together around factories, creating new urban spaces and a commensurate requirement for new infrastructure. But the nature of work also changed in the factory system, workers became tied to machine operations, directly or indirectly, which divided labor into specific roles for parts of the manufacturing process that required little human skill or judgment (for a fascinating history of this period, see Landes, 2003).

Not every craftsperson was immediately displaced or rendered obsolete, at least not without a fight. In the early 1800s, General Ned Ludd and his followers, upset at the deskilling and inevitable lower pay for factory workers, raided factories and destroyed machines they believed threatened their livelihood. The so-called Luddites were ultimately unsuccessful, and the name became synonymous with those who would willfully stand in the way of some imagined progress. Mass production has thrived, spread globally, and for most industries has become the dominant model of production but there remain highly valued design skills to this day that represent specialized craft practices or alternatives to mass-produced goods that some people are willing to support. While mechanical production has many positives in terms of scale and reproducibility there remain niche areas where the human touch is still deemed vital, so craft practices live on, not least in software design.

The impact of industrialization fits with the broad view of social evolution proposed by Robert Wright in his book, *Non-Zero, The Logic of Human Destiny*, published in 2000. He argues that over time, civilization has progressed by harnessing technological developments through a process of social adaptation, driven by a human desire to engage in what he terms "non-zero sum game" activities that benefit all participants. In his view, humans have slowly learned that collective action in the pursuit of shared goals such as safety, nourishment, and shelter yields more positive results than individual competition, and, in the course of history, we have designed new technical solutions that ultimately serve this aim (obviously with a few backward steps where negotiation and co-operation took a back seat to some baser human motives). According to Wright, as new tools are adopted within a community, they often lead to new social structures which serve further non-zero sum pursuits within the group, community, or society, binding individuals together in a manner that offers shared benefits beyond any one product or user. A common example he uses is the emergence of agrarian practices which allowed for crop production that was stable and sufficiently productive to encourage trade and bartering with other groups who wanted and became reliant on the goods produced. This type of engagement set up a form of economic co-operation between groups that built and extended networks of mutually beneficial relationships, raising the quality of life for all.

While this theory paints a somewhat rosy picture of social progress on the surface, Wright acknowledges that it's rarely straightforward. When major competing technologies or practices occur a period of instability in the social structure seems inevitable as groups transition to new technologies. Clearly, the industrial revolution was precisely such a period. Nevertheless, for our interests in the emergence of design as a human act, this transition set in motion a broad move from so called "cottage industries" to factories, and with itemerged a conception of design as a form of professional practice that could be decoupled in some meaningful ways from the actual hands-on making of any material object. In due course, the meaning of design shifted from making to planning, from the manipulation of material as epitomized in craft practices, to the representation of a desired, manufactured outcome using such information techniques as drawing, calculating, and modeling to convey the goal to those charged with the building or assembly of a product. In this refining of human abstraction and conveyance of design targets or solutions, we see the emergence of design as a professional practice in a form we consider routine today.

All of this, however, leaves us still pondering the question of what is happening in the human mind when a person makes that leap from problem situation to potential solution. When we consider design to be a human act and allow for it to be represented abstractly through plans or recipes, we can draw a distinction between processes that are real-time, material-contingent, and emergent to those that allow for conceptual and representational form, offering an instruction-set for others to use in production. Rather than observing designers in action as they shape and form a physical output we recognize, we are forced to examine their thinking and reasoning more than their actions as they deliver a different kind of output. This leads us to ask what are the properties of such a process, are they similar for all designers, or across all domains, and how might we educate or train people to perform or engage well in the act of design? In an era where we find ourselves living out our existence in human-made environments, virtual and physical, better understanding how we design both types of space and how we might improve the outcomes seem to be of vital importance to our collective well-being.

Understanding Design as an Intentional Act

While the scholarly study of the design act has roots in the mid-20th century, as outlined in the previous chapter, the early interest focused primarily on better understanding how to manage the design process for greater efficiencies or to ensure effective outcomes. Certainly there were explorations of how architects worked or what the nature of creative thinking entailed (see e,g., Doherty's (1963) overview in the 1962 *Conference on Design Methods* for an examination of design as a psychological process, or Alexander's (1964) prescription of the design process as a sequence of steps involving interacting requirements) but these early efforts relied heavily on introspection by one or two designers of their own working practices, or on general theories of creativity and problem solving drawn from early psychological writings.

In the last quarter of the 20th century, however, attempts to understand what designers were doing as they worked on problems became the focus of scholars outside the traditional design world, greatly influenced by the publication in 1969 of Herb Simon's *Sciences of the Artificial*. The book represented the output of a series of public lectures delivered by Simon at Harvard, covering a range of subjects from economics to social planning, thematically linked by his key argument that in a world now largely created by humans, there was a need for a new kind of science dealing with the artificial rather than natural world. In his words:

> "for most of us … the significant part of the environment consists mostly of strings of artifacts called "symbols" that we receive through eyes and ears in the form of written and spoken language and that we pour out into the environment as I am now doing by mouth or hand. The laws that govern these strings of symbols, the laws that govern the occasions on which we emit and receive them, the determinants of their content are all consequences of our collective artifice."
>
> (Simon, 1996, pp. 2–3, all Simon page numbers are from the later third edition)

One lecture, and subsequent chapter in his book, dealt directly with the act of design. Here, Simon made a series of strong claims about the need for greater understanding and teaching of design to address the challenges of our age. He traced a series of requirements for a curriculum of design education that situated it as a cognitive act of problem reasoning which combined an understanding of logic, the mathematics of utility functions and optimization, with a set of skills that humans could use to apply such knowledge reliably since the calculations involved in the former would exceed our cognitive powers. Simon extended his analysis of this proposed new science to include a taxonomy of representation that he argued was necessary for understanding which forms, for example visual or mathematical representation, might prove optimal for certain types of design challenge. Since he was a proponent of the view that many life decisions cannot be optimized in advance using algorithmic methods but rather relied on an ability to recognize the conditions of what he termed "satisficing" alternatives, he recommended that we should also study how people decide on their choices and what kinds of analyses might yield outcomes we can accept.

Simon posited a view of humans as relatively simple organisms operating in an environment of complexity to which we adapt by use of our mental resources. All design, in his view, was a series of refinements intended to reduce a problem space, reliant on our memory, our knowledge, as well as inputs we receive and constraints we identify from the world around us. For Simon, design was everywhere in our lived experience, a natural act of human existence.

> "Everyone designs who devises courses of action aimed at changing existing situations into preferred ones. The intellectual activity that produces material artefacts is no different fundamentally from the one that prescribes remedies for a sick patient or the one that devises a new sales plan for a company or a social welfare policy for a state".
>
> (Simon, 1996, p. 129)

Given its routine presence in our lives, Simon felt design to be a curiously overlooked area of studyin the sciences. One of the best known expressions emerging from Simon's work was his claim that natural science was concerned with how things are, but that design was interested in what ought to be, and accordingly design needed not only to be studied but taught more, especailly in higher educationif humans were to continue shaping the world for collective benefit.

Criticized as positivistic and overly rational by some in the design community, Simon's views have proved extremely influential and durable. Roozenburg and Dorst (1998) described Simon as a dominant force in the literature and reported that his work was cited more than any other scholar in the annual Design Thinking conferences even 30 years after the original lectures. That said, it is not clear that any education program has ever fully implemented the curricular ideas he advocated, part of the continuing problem of design education being driven primarily by professional interest groups, but his visionary push for design to be considered a core educational need and a subject worthy of study has resonated across the decades in many fields.

Yet the criticisms prevailed, and to some extent continue, among some in the design scholarship world who feel that Simon's call was an attempt to "scientize" design, offering it up as a form of rule-bound problem-solving strategy that reduced the mysterious and creative act to a somewhat algorithmic or mechanical process. Over the years, even as Simon refined his ideas, he was peppered with criticisms that he did not really understand how designers worked, that he had an overly selective emphasis on some design fields at the expense of others, or that, most pointedly and personally, since he himself was not a qualified designer, he could not fully appreciate the act of design with all its nuances and complexities (see You and Hands (2019) for a review of the critical response to Simon's ideas).

As an alternative, many in the design world found greater resonance in the work of Donald Schon, a contemporary of Simon's, who developed an alternative description of design that rested on his observations of how skilled practitioners in various domains, not just those we might traditionally label design, but also management, engineering research, and psychotherapy, thought through their work in situ. Schon starts from an assumption that skilled professionals in any domain are not easily able to articulate what they do or why they make the choices they do. Instead, they engage in a form tacit, intuitive knowledge application that is very grounded in the immediate context of their work and which is guided by what Schon describes as a "conversation" with the problem space.

Schon coined the phrase "reflection-in-action" to describe the underlying reasoning and problem-solving approach of designers. Presented with a design challenge, Schon argued that designers do not start their activities from a blank slate but call on a repertoire of skills, knowledge, and experience that allows them to identify the unique properties of the current challenge. From here, designers engage in reframing, considering potential changes or options, which Schon terms "moves," which stimulate further reflection on consequences or changes to the problem. In this way, the situation or problem "talks-back" to the designer, highlighting other aspects to consider that were not immediately apparent or considered in the initial reflection. As Schon puts it:

> "In their problem setting, means and ends are framed interdependently. And their enquiry is a transaction with the situation in which knowing and doing are inseparable. These inquirers encounter a problematic situation whose reality they must construct. As they frame the problem of the situation, they determine the features to which they will attend, the order they will attempt to impose on the situation, the directions in which they will try to change it. In this process, they identify both the ends and the means to be employed. In the ensuing enquiry, action on the situation is integral with deciding, and problem solving is part of the larger experiment in problem setting."
>
> (Schon, 1983, p. 165)

The main axis of distinction here seems to be the extent to which an approach might be viewed as rational – Simon on one side, Schon and critics on the other. However, while this might make for a convenient pedagogical dichotomy, it is not as firm as is often presented. Most reviews of Simon, particularly in comparison to Schon, acknowledge Simon's good intentions in advocating for greater understanding, but ultimately fault him for insufficiently acknowledging the "special" nature of design, and, to use Cross' almost mystical description, failing to appreciate sufficiently "designerly ways of knowing." Yet, one can read both Simon and Schon and find far more similarity in their depiction of design than is usually acknowledged. Certainly, Simon casts his description in the technical language of cognitive science, using terms such as representation, resource allocation, means-end analysis, and declarative logic as essential components of a design curriculum he believed should be developed. But in his attempts at definition, Simon remarks that perhaps the best way to describe design is as an act involving "the generation of alternatives and then the testing of these against a whole array of requirements and constraints" (p. 149), a description that would not have been out of place in Schon's outline of how reflective practitioners proceed to have conversations and make moves.

When design theorists such as Nigel Cross criticize Simon while lauding Schon, they tend to do so by describing the latter as offering a "clear account of a typical fast-moving, thinking on your feet live design example" (Cross, 2011, p. 25) that employs a kind of knowing not found in textbooks. But this is hardly a weakness of Simon's work where he frequently argued that we simply do not have textbook knowledge for design and we must develop the type of curriculum that might impart an improved and useful education for new designers to solve problems in the real world.

This forced dichotomy between the work of Simon and others such as Schon seems to me rather limiting and possibly results from a straw-man picture of Simon as embodying a stereotypical model of science, pushing a hyper-rational form of epistemology that demands clear goals, logical methods of discovery and quantified evidence to produce a straight answer to a specific question (all the while presumably dressed in a white lab coat). Even if Simon was primarily one of the fathers of cognitive science, few critical examinations of scientific practice suggest its adherents are so methodologically rigid. Indeed, innumerable studies of how routine science is conducted reveal a far looser, hypothesis-testing, and review cycle that relies heavily on insight and experience by its practitioners (see e.g., Chalmers, 1976). Even Schon's main contribution, his book *The Reflective Practitioner*, contains numerous examples of scientific and engineering practices that comfortably fall within his depiction of problem-solving as situated, interpretive, and conjectural. As Schon says, the best scientists and engineers "learn to model unfamiliar problems on familiar ones and build new theory by reflecting on perceived but as yet unarticulated similarities" which, he goes on to write, embeds "technical problem solving in relevant and, in its own way, rigorous reflection-in-action." (Schon, 1983, p. 203).

In fact, in the empirical literature on the working practices of designers, perhaps the most scientific of terms, "conjecture," is routinely employed to describe how design professionals posit potential solutions. This term, popularized by philosopher Karl Popper in his model of scientific enquiry *Conjectures and Refutations* (Popper, 1963), refers to the continual trial and error process underlying scientific practice and knowledge accretion. Problem solvers, be they designers or scientists according to Popper, continually suggest possible or hypothetical solutions based on current understandings, and then subject these to tests in order to determine empirically their utility. These hypotheses or "conjectures" are a hallmark of the scientific process, and that term is similarly employed in many research studies of design. Indeed, one of the most influential descriptions of the design process, Jane Darke's Primary Generator model (Darke, 1979), derived from her detailed examination of architects, posits that most designers latch on to a key part of the problem, their "primary generator," which they then attempt to solve through the process of conjecture and analysis, using the outcomes of each attempt to continually refine their ideas and potential solutions. In this way, design can be thought to involve multiple cycles of conjecture and analyses, a general problem-solving process that mirrors much of how Popper describes the work of scientists.

Darke's basic finding came from fieldwork with architects but it is supported by lab-based research also. In one study that has gained significant attention in the design literature, Lawson presented students with a block assembly puzzle with a set of constraint that had to be met, some but not all of which were made explicit (e.g., they were told to maximise one exposed color on one face of their solution but not informed in advance that some combinations of blocks could not be employed), a scenario expressly intended to mimic real world design problems where all the variables in play are rarely known in advance. Lawson examined how each group proceeded to generate solutions. Most interestingly, he compared students majoring in architecture with those majoring in science, noting there had long been arguments and firmly held beliefs that each group's problem-solving approach must be quite distinct. In general, Lawson did see a difference, reporting that the architects tended to try out multiple solutions in their efforts to maximize the color requirement, using feedback on the solution's suitability to narrow down their options. The scientists seemed more determined to uncover the hidden constraint on allowable combinations first and then proceed to maximize color in any proposed solution. This led Lawson to generalize that designers could be considered more solution-focused while scientists were more process-oriented. This does not surprise too much given the typical charge for designers to derive a solution with less concern for how they do so, while scientists are expected to document a clear and ideally reproducible method for any research answers they propose.

However, not content with this simple distinction, Lawson wondered if education played a part in how each group proceeded to solve problems so he devised a further test. Here, he compared a graduating class with incoming students for each group. Most interestingly, now he found that there was little meaningful difference between the problem-solving approaches of either group at the start of their studies, rather it seemed that immersion in a program of education inculcated a distinctive pattern of problem solving that the graduates in either design or science professions were expected to follow. Of course, this should not surprise us. Practitioners and professionals in any field manifest and adhere to behavioral norms and competencies they expect of each other, and membership of such a community involves the socialization, if you like, of new practitioners into the ways of thinking and working that the established members consider appropriate. Through education, these norms are reinforced and reproduced. But these differences do not naturally reflect a particular form of problem solving that is innate or normal for people prior to education. As Lawson later summed up his many years of studying what design involves, he concluded that "design is a form of thinking, and thinking is a skill … (which) can be acquired and developed" (Lawson, 2005, p. 303). In fact, design thinking is acquired and developed, over time, through some very distinct educational and training programs. Small wonder then such differences and commonalities exist.

In this light, we can begin to appreciate the argument of Simon for a more universal curriculum in design, since the evidence we have of problem-solving approaches suggests there actually is a strong core of commonality between various fields of design practice, marked by differences that reflect education and context. If your goal is an output that can be used, the explanation for its value or its theoretical contribution to knowledge is perhaps not necessary. If your goal is to determine the correct solution to a defined common problem, then documenting efforts which both fail and succeed so that others can learn from your efforts and interpret your findings might be considered essential. In this way, it would seem that in the course of a project, a problem-solver (be she a designer or a scientist) might engage in multiple behaviors involving idea generation, conjecture, analysis, synthesis, evaluation, reframing of questions, and so forth. Further, depending on the type of problem being tackled, one might need to immerse oneself in prior efforts, or to investigate the broader context in which the problem is situated, perhaps gathering more inputs from stakeholders, and invariably reflecting on what you are learning as you go.

Does this mean that all design is the same? Of course not. As humans we have carved up the professional world into domains of authority and expertise, driven by demands for services and outcomes. Different people are likely drawn to different domains by a variety of factors, not least their own interests, so that some naturally feel more engaged with architecture than zoology, but even within architecture, they may be drawn more to interiors than exteriors, to housing than landscapes, or to historical restoration than innovative structures. All to say, there are very different types of designers, whether we view the differences in terms of application areas or by the types of outputs (products, buildings, services etc). But if we can resist the urge to carve up the act of design by application area, and instead look at the mental processes underlying the act of design by humans regardless of field, it would appear that there is far greater commonality than might be otherwise acknowledged.

So What Is Design Really?

Making sense of design is, as noted, problematic when even the very word "design" is used so loosely. This is exacerbated in our modern digital world where the ease of software production means that relative novices can produce interactive tools and websites that reaches potential users located anywhere with internet access thereby taking on the mantle of experience designers Qualifications for "digital design" are extremely vague with self-labeled "designers of user experience" appearing almost overnight in large numbers, regardless of education or training, claiming to understand what users need or prefer. In one sense this represents a tremendous democratization of information design but it also makes any serious determination of who is a designer and what this label entails in terms of knowledge and qualifications largely impossible.

Herb Simon postulated that all of us are ultimately designers, in that no matter our professions or positions in life, we continually engage in activities that aim to close the gap that exists between the current state of our world and some desired alternative. In this sense, many routine daily activities for most of us involve some attempts to shape outcomes from current situations using whatever resources we can call upon in that context. This is obviously a remarkably broad conception of design acts, effectively including any problem-solving process that we engage in, from cooking a meal to driving our cars. In a very real sense, Simon is committed to this view, positing the act of design as quintessentially human, indicative of our intentional engagement with the environment in the search for solutions. Since he notes that contemporary life is largely lived in artificial (that is, human-made) environments, we must continually evolve our practices, and thus are engaged, routinely, in design acts that reflect our needs and problems of the moment.

Simon's view of our innate design skills rings true in the digital age and is acknowledged by other thinkers in more recent work. Lawson and Dorst (2009) summarized their view of what constituted design in the 21st century identifying three distinct framings which reflect a concern with design acts (formulation, representation, moves, evaluation, and management), design levels (the project, the process, the field of practice and the profession), and types of thinking (convention-based, situation-based or strategy-based). These authors argue that each framing reflects a particular language within which we talk about design, leading to somewhat disconnected discourses, perhaps explaining some of the confusion that exists in the literature and popular use of the word "design" (e.g., those talking about the problem-solving practices of engineers are using a different framing than those discussing the education of architects etc.) In mapping the conceptual space of design along these axes, Lawson and Dorst consider these discourses as kinds of expertise that manifest themselves in different contexts.

Their work offers a rich sense of what it means to talk about design. They acknowledge that when unpacked, design is a mix of creativity and analysis, involving problem solving and the generation of solutions. They suggest designers are compelled to learn while doing and that solutions rarely emerge in the stereotypical "Eureka" fashion of popular myth but more often evolve from exploring and studying the problem space over time and within a context of meaning that is not immediately apparent at the outset. Ultimately, like Simon, they conclude that design is a fundamental human activity, countering the idea that design is a special or exclusive skill that only some people have.

Now this last point is important and more nuanced than it might appear when so boldly stated. To say design is a basic human activity is not to lump all design work together or to imagine that there are no qualitative differences between acts of design or between designers. Like many other general human activities (communicating, thinking, moving, etc.) there are important individual differences. Further there are significant competency differences introduced by education, practice, motivation, and ability. While it is natural for all humans to move, the physical movements of a trained dancer or gymnast offer a level of refinement and technical achievement that few humans ever attain. This is the result of practice, effort, and willful desire to improve or reach certain targets, supplemented by education from experts with an understanding of the building blocks of skilled performance and the methods of communicating these effectively. Similarly, within design, it is one thing to say we all design, but it is important to recognize that the very best designers manifest a level of skilled performance that is also the outcome of dedicated practice and education, resulting in qualitatively deeper and richer skills and likely better solutions when solving problems. Acknowledging this means we must then determine how best to encourage the development of the next generation of great designers.

The Challenge of Educating User-Centered Designers

We might then wonder, if design is really a general practice of humans, why is design education in the academy so divided. While some areas of practice such as architecture have attained wide acceptance as a discipline that belongs on the finest university campuses, others, such as software design or industrial design, do not have similar standing. Partly this reflects the dynamic nature of disciplines in a changing world. I remind colleagues that Computer Science did not exist as a recognized discipline in the US academy before the formation of a Computer Science department at Purdue in 1962, and we might imagine a time when it no longer exists as a separate academic field (not to pick on computer science in particular, my point is simply that erecting buildings and departmental structures to house a discipline should not be confused with its permanence as an intellectual subject). The educational delivery of knowledge is ultimately dynamic, disciplines evolve, sometimes growing, sometimes fading away, as attention and interests evolve. We might still be wed to classrooms and lectures, and the university library might still house shelves of books, but the courses of study available to a student in the 21st century do not overlap with those offered a century ago. Times and topics change, so what will be the disciplinary structure in the next century? This is more than just labeling, the disciplinary structures of a university reflect our current understandings and concerns; it is in their nature that these are not fixed.

Software Engineering has long struggled to establish itself as a legitimate academic field, and depending on the university we examine, it might be seen as part of Computer Science or as a branch of Engineering. Indeed, Berry (1992), in attempting to make a case for the discipline as the academic equivalent of any other engineering branch, suggested that the weakest parts of this academic field were those dealing with the psychology, sociology, and management of users. One might read Berry as suggesting such human or social aspects should be jettisoned in the interest of making software engineering more rigorous, thereby, presumably increasing its chances of being seen as an equal among the broader computational sciences. In this light, it is hardly surprising that user-centered design has struggled to gain any foothold in academic programs where we might imagine its relevance. But let us be clear. n this century, do we really want to produce more computer scientists or software engineers with no education about people?.

The challenge of academic status and intellectual boundaries might seem somewhat divorced from the everyday concerns of creating better user experiences with information technology but these issues are deeply connected. In as much as society values the creation of new information tools and technologies, it at least partially sanctions and enables this through education and credentialing. Our current technical evolution is driven largely by market forces and the innovations they incentivize, but as the technology impacts every aspect of our lived experience, other interests must be engaged, from governments and political organizations to rights groups and employers. As data about our activities in the world is captured, shared, and monetized, questions come to be asked about how we are designing and implementing our information technologies, who has ownership of what information, what kinds of traces we are leaving on our digital paths, who is responsible for security and reliability and to what extent our internet should be considered a basic civic utility treated more in the manner of our water or power supplies than as an optional consumption choice like entertainment or convenience goods?

Couple with this is the increasing recognition that no matter how innovative or affordable a new technology might be, it will rarely achieve widespread adoption among its target audience if it is not designed in a manner that enables easy and successful use. Further, the user experience of any design is increasingly seen as a differentiator in the market, with products and services that deliver better engagement with users being more likely to succeed than those which simply try to differentiate on price. As the population of information technology users grows, it continues to embrace people of wildly different abilities and levels of expertise, so it is not acceptable in most usage scenarios to expect people to invest significant effort in learning to use every product. And where some learning is inevitable (for example in complex data modeling software or new gaming control handsets), the experience of learning must be considered part of the process of adoption that also needs to be designed well.

To this end, there has been a continual push over the last 30 years to treat the development of user interfaces as a form of design that requires its own educational programs. Lawson and Dorst (2009) suggested that design education is "pretty well sorted out" (p. 218) for traditional disciplines (a curious line of reasoning that might have been echoed at all points in our history), and while they acknowledge user interface design is a growing area of concern, the examples of design programs explored in their book rarely touch on that topic of education. If one searches online for degree programs or diplomas in related fields such as human-computer interaction, user experience, or user-centered design, you will quickly find a mix of lists, usually generated with no clear principles (except of course, for profit), representing often the biases of those who are studying in or providing one program. Unlike more established fields such as architecture or industrial design, the state of education in user experience design is largely in the realm of university extension courses (meaning it is not a degree program affiliated with an established department or school) or of private programs run for profit, promising practical job-skills and career opportunities. I frequently see adverts for such programs, promising a highly employable credential as a "digital designer" or "user experience analyst" in as little as 12–24 weeks of part-time study. Without oversight or accreditation, the educational route to a meaningful credential poses a challenge for anyone seriously interested in studying or pursuing a professional career in user-centered design. The situation also makes it difficult for recruiters to know what they are getting when they hire and surely generates a certain cynicism over time about the value of user experience designers.

There has been some recognition in academia that designing for users of our global information structure requires deep understanding of people but progress is slow. The eary attempts at programs in the 1980s saw isolated efforts, usually graduate professional degrees offered under various labels such as "human factors" or "ergonomics" either in programs of applied psychology, cognitive science or sometimes in more far-sighted computer science programs. In the US, Carnegie-Mellon University offered the first formal HCI degree starting in the early 1990s which stimulated the development of other such titled degree offerings across the country, including such universities as Washington, Indiana (where I served as that program's original director), Georgia Tech, and others, to the point that there are more than a dozen programs offering a degree with HCI in the title and dozens more that cover this area under related titles of "UX design," "Interaction Design" or such. We are even witnessing the growth of undergraduate degrees in user-focused design, though a formal count of such is hard to establish given the diversity of terms and lack of details in many program listings.

So, given the growth, why do I believe user-experience design education is not "well-sorted" yet? The answer to this lies in what we know, what we agree about what we know and how to pass this on to new practitioners. As I've attempted to show here, design knowledge is complex, a mix of theories and methods from traditional disciplines bridging social and technical science, and rooted in practices that sometimes can only be learned by doing. Academics, naturally, have not always agreed what constitutes a robust and valid curriculum for such programs, consequently, there can be quite a range of differences across educational offerings. This need not be fatal, and indeed might be a typical birth pang of any field. However, as the technology we aim to design continues to evolve at a rapid pace, user-experience education seems to continually chase to catch up. Focusing on the individual user was seen as insufficient when collaboration and collective use became common; systems design was impacted when the internet arrived; web applications demanded new technical knowledge, and currently we're concerned with understanding how AI and machine learning might alter the nature of any number of human-computer interactions. All this when we still don't seem to agree on something as basic as menu design.

It seems unlikely that we will soon resolve the curricular content fully, and this may not be crucial, most professional fields evolve a set of expectations over core components while allowing individual educational programs to deliver them as they chose. Further, beyond the core offerings, any one program may have a specialty focus that makes their program unique. While many professions rely on accrediting bodies to recognize and acknowledge such variability across programs seeking recognition as reputable degrees for entry to a field, I do not share the view that accreditation is the answer, particularly as that process is currently practiced in some parts of the information field. Disciplines such as Computer Science have successfully evolved collective understanding of core competencies and quality without embracing formal accreditation and it's certainly not hurt the recognition or public value placed on that discipline.

So why might be the greatest challenge to a well-sorted design education in information systems? I suspect part of the problem stems from what Simon (1996) argued about our own knowledge, namely that the principles for good design are just not sufficiently well known for us to devise the appropriate education fully. Further, universities embody the historical path we've taken since the Renaissance of intellectual specialization that instantiates a fragmentation of knowledge, first into science and humanities, and then into ever greater divisions by subject and methodological distinction which privileges certain kinds of problem identification and solving. Kim Vicente (2003) explored this phenomenon in his book, *The Human Factor*, arguing that technology-oriented studies have always been the province of mechanistic thinking, of the kind found in engineering and science disciplines, lacking appropriate acknowledgment of or reference to the humanistic insights of social science or the arts which are crucial for understanding how people actually think, feel and behave. Consequently, as he argues, our knowledge practices have followed the classic divide and conquer approach that has been very successful in enabling humans to develop new technologies while leaving us somewhat blind to our own relationships with them.

A true discipline of design would cut across or bridge existing disciplines, serving as a unifier that complements existing natural and social science approaches to problem solving while recognizing the shared connection with arts and humanities in studying how we live in this world. Simon makes the point repeatedly that humans are basically quite simple creatures that display complex behavioral responses due to the environments in which we exist. Because the outer world of contemporary existence is increasingly human-made, that is, we live in a designed space, then the proper study of human existence is the study of design. I would like to extend Simon's thesis. Since increasingly our lived experience is within an information space, then the design of information technologies is fundamental to our quality of life. No wonder Simon concluded that design should be seen "not only as the professional component of a technical education but as a *core* discipline for every liberally educated person" (Simon, 1996), p.159, emphasis added).

Forty years on from Simon, we may well question if we have made the progress he hoped for in this regard. We see multiple usability problems in everyday technologies, the implementation of user-centered methods in product development remains spotty, despite the oft-claimed belief of many in putting user needs at the forefront of design. Not only are rapid development approaches such as Agile constraining the role of user experience professionals (a classic complaint of the traditional human factors community since the 1950s) but any division between so-called "user experience-researchers" and "user experience-designers" perpetuates the old narrow view of design that pushes research and design apart. Further, this division only exacerbates the long-recognized problem of conducting appropriate user research early and often within the design process. Writing for the Nielsen-Norman Group, a consulting firm named after two of the early and influential thinkers in user-experience design, Loranger (2014) presented case studies of design teams seeking to create usable designs but failing to engage appropriately in user research, noting that "unfortunately, most teams don't conduct user research on a consistent basis, if at all.

People cite tight deadlines and staffing shortages as reasons for deficiencies in user-centered activities."

What will it take to change this? Despite the marketing and advocacy of the user-centered and design thinking movements, UX professionals still face the same old challenges reported for decades. Kelkar and Ratcliffe (2020) surveyed professionals over several years to establish trends and challenges in the field and reported that the number one problem, as reported by 64% of respondents, was getting user research into the product development process. Half the respondents also reported challenges related to having sufficient resources or budget for UX, and getting buy-in or support for UX from senior leadership. If there's genuine progress here, perhaps it lies in the fact that the other half of respondents felt otherwise about resources and budget. Either way, these data hardly paint a convincing picture of UX as a regular and assumed part of typical design and development processes and mirror many of the findings from industry surveys on practices from decades earlier (see e.g., Dillon et al. 1993).

This situation shows little prospect for change if we fail to educate those responsible for the design of information systems how to reliably address user issues. I am not convinced we are making sufficient progress here. Even if we could agree on a core curriculum for interaction design, and we were able to standardize this across sufficient educational programs, the number of UX designers we are producing would likely still be insufficient to meet the needs of commercial developers in our digital world. As the push for rapid development seems relentless, we must convince those controlling the resources and costs for system development that an appropriate user-centered process, with suitably skilled UX professionals, is key; as essential to the delivery of a viable product as the professionals handling the coding. Until then, those long-standing complaints of generations of user-oriented professionals, of being involved "too little and too late," or having "research" treated as distinct from "design," will remain a significant stumbling block.

At the end of the day, the answer to our contemporary design challenges cannot rest only in the practices of professionals who employ a method. The act of design is not entirely methodical, it relies on a creative leap, the translation of requirements to interface form, guided not just by data or experience but by an understanding of people. This understanding is a form of knowledge that comes from many sources, among the most important being the research findings of social science. We have accumulated a rich body of knowledge about how people think and behave. Some of this has been directly studied in the context of human-computer interaction and information activities. Simply following a method involving user trials can gain you invaluable insights into where the problems lie with a design, but knowing then how to improve it, how to optimize the interaction between a person and a computer, how to identify problematic design choices before they are implemented, is what really matters.

On its own, there is currently insufficient knowledge to ensure one always makes the right decisions in design, but in concert with a truly user-centered method, such knowledge of how people think and reason, respond and adopt (or reject) new information tools will more efficiently move the process forward to the desired outcome. It is such knowledge that improves the conjectures any designer makes, and the better the conjecture, the potential solution proposed by the designer or design team, the quicker we will be to ensuring the results that best meet user needs. It is step we start to take in the next chapter.

References

Alexander, C. (1964). *Notes on the Synthesis of Form*. Cambridge MA: Harvard University Press.

Berry, D.M. (1992). Academic legitimacy of the software engineering discipline. Technical Report, Software Engineering Institute, Carnegie Mellon University ESC TR-92-034 https://resources.sei.cmu.edu/asset_files/technicalreport/1992_005_001_16115.pdf

Brooks, A. (2021, April 16th). The 11 common types of designer. Upwork https://www.upwork.com/resources/what-type-of-designer-do-you-need

Chalmers, A. (1976). *What is This Thing Called Science?* Cambridge MA: University of Queensland Press.

Cross, N. (2011). *Design Thinking: Understanding How Designers Think and Work*. London: Zed Books.

Darke, J. (1979). The primary generator and the design process. *Design Studies, 1*(1), 36–44.

Dillon, A., and Sweeney, M. (2022). Adding rigor to advance design thinking. In Y. Ericsson (ed.), *Different Perspectives in Design Thinking* (pp. 22–41). London: CRC Press.

Dillon, A., Sweeney, M., and Maguire, M. (1993). A survey of usability engineering within the European IT industry-current practice and needs. In *People and Computers VIII, Proceedings of the 1993 BCS-HCI Conference*. Cambridge: Cambridge University Press.

Doherty, E. (1963). Psychological aspects of the creative act. In J. Jones and D. Thornley (eds.), *Conference on Design Methods: Papers Presented at the Conference on Systematic and Intuitive Methods in Engineering, Industrial Design, Architecture and Communications. September 1962* (pp. 197–203). London: Pergamon Press.

Kelkar and Ratcliffe (2020). Four top challenges faced by UX teams in 2020 and how to solve them. https://www.userzoom.com/ux-library/four-top-challenges-ux-teams/

Landes, D. (2003). *The Unbound Prometheus: Technological Change and Industrial Development in Western Europe from 1750 to the Present*, 2nd ed. Cambridge: Cambridge University Press.

Lawson, B. (2005). *How Designers Think: The Thinking Process Demystified*, 4th ed. New York: Architectural Press.

Lawson, B., and Dorst, K. (2009). *Design Expertise*. Abingdon: Architectural Press.

Loranger, H. (2014, May 16). Doing UX in an Agile World: Case Study Findings. Nielsen Norman Group. https://www.nngroup.com/articles/doing-ux-agile-world/

Massingham, P. (2019). An Aristotelian interpretation of practical wisdom: The case of retirees. *Palgrave Commun*, *5*(123), 1–13. 10.1057/s41599-019-0331-9

Popper, K. (1963). *Conjectures and Refutations*. London: Routledge Kagan and Paul.

Roozenburg, N., and Dorst, K. (1998). Describing design as a reflective practice: Observations on Schon's theory of practice. In E. Frankenberger, P. Badke-Schaub, and H. Birkhofer, (eds.), *Designers: The Key to Successful Product Development* (pp 29–41). London: Springer.

Schon, D. (1983). *The Reflective Practitioner: How Professionals Think in Action*. New York: Basic Books.

Simon, H. (1996). *The Sciences of the Artificial. Third Edition*. Cambridge MA: The MIT Press.

Spacey, J. (2017, March 18th). 16 Types of Design. Simplicable https://simplicable.com/new/types-of-design, https://www.nngroup.com/articles/doing-ux-agile-world/

Spacey, J. (2017). 16 types of design. https://simplicable.com/new/types-of-design

Sturt, G. (1923). *The Wheelwright's Shop*. Cambridge: Cambridge University Press.

Vicente, K. (2003). *The Human Factor: Revolutionizing the Way People Live With Technology*. Toronto: Knopf.

Wright, R. (2000). *Non-Zero, The Logic of Human Destiny*. New York: Pantheon.

You, X., and Hands, D. (2019). A reflection upon Herbert Simon's vision of design in the sciences of the artificial. *The Design Journal*, *22*(1): 1345–1356, 10.1080/14606925.2019.1594961

Humans and the Vertical Slice

4

Seeing Some of the Picture, Some of the Time

There's a well-known Indian parable of the blind men and the elephant. None has ever been close to an elephant before, so when they finally have an opportunity to examine one, they eagerly reach with their hands to touch this wonderful creature. Each man utters a reaction to what they experience, so when one feels the tusk, he comments how sharp like a spear is the elephant. Another pressing the animal's side states it is solid like a wall, one man holding the tale suggests the elephant is like a rope, while the blind man who handles the trunk suggests that an elephant really must be like a snake and so forth. Among themselves they argue what exactly is an elephant, unable to reach agreement.

Variations exist in the precise number of the protagonists or if they are just operating in the dark rather than being blind, but the essence is the same and this story has been employed in multiple contexts to highlight various problems we have in trying to understand the world. We all seem unduly convinced that our own sense data are reliable and the ultimate guide for explaining the world. Some use the parable to highlight how subjectivity and objectivity are easily confused, or that people are slow to acknowledge their understanding might be enhanced by collective or further observation. Clearly, it is the nature of a good parable to be sufficiently flexible to suggest several lessons, but the elephant and the blind men come to mind for me every time I try to explain the challenges social scientists face when seeking to understand humans and their lived experiences.

The science base of human behavior is rich and has provided us with ever-more refined understandings of how we think, reason, behave, and co-exist with others in multiple contexts. However, this knowledge base can be highly

DOI: 10.4324/9781003026112-4

technical, rooted in theoretical constructs that require significant preparation to interpret correctly, and exists piecemeal across a diverse, scholarly literature that few can fully survey. Rather like the elephant touchers in the parable, most social scientists spend their time examining one narrow part of the full problem space and rarely have the chance to step back and study the full human.

Beyond its obvious vastness, there is a particular problem with the science base that seems to trip us up when we try to derive guidance from it for design. Put simply, this is its supposedly natural division of our research enquiries into time-sliced or temporal units of analysis, which on the surface seems to make sense but in practice has created a framework for examining ourselves that does not easily map to everyday activities. Where we see ourselves writing a letter or preparing a meal, the science base has us engaging in a cycle of physiological, perceptual, cognitive, and social or cultural acts that might suit theoretical framings and make sense to other social scientists who study similar phenomena but would seem quite odd to an ordinary person. This is not just a matter of terminology or the specific theoretical language games of academics, it is a matter of time, or more directly, the units of analysis social scientists have accepted as forming the boundaries of their specific enquiries.

Collectively, the social sciences specialize in facets of human experience that range from the micro-second level (such as how quickly can a person perceive or react to a signal) through actions involving several seconds (e.g., decision making or conversational discourse) to minutes, days and longer (e.g., planning and managing a team project). The research at each level tends to exist independently, engaging with ideas and concepts predominantly of interest to other scholars or scientists working at that level. This makes complete sense on the one hand as it allows us to agree on the specifics of a question and compare findings across research studies, to derive mutually comprehensible terms and constructs to explain what we are examining and to encourage generalization through theory-building. On the other hand, this time-sliced division comes with a significant cost in terms of piecing together the puzzle of human experience when we ask questions that don't easily fall into these neat temporal divisions or when we try to reconcile concerns that seem to bleed over from short-term to medium or longer-term concerns. But such concerns are usually the very ones faced by designers.

Decades of research and education on human experience have produced a deep understanding of some essential aspects of our mental lives but along the way, we seem to have partly lost our recognition that all humans are a combination of each of these temporal levels and that to understand ourselves, we need to piece together a science of experience that recognizes the multiple temporalities within which we engage and mentally construe our actions. In the current chapter I propose approaching the science base differently, invoking the idea of the "vertical slice," a framing of human activity that recognizes every human as being a physical, perceptual, cognitive, and social creature at one and the same time across the multiple activities that they engage in daily. Rather than trying to narrow the design challenge to one level of social science, I see the value of vertical slicing across all levels as particularly useful in understanding and designing information artefacts. Viewed this way, I advocate a form of user theory for experience design that draws on the extant science base but rotates the viewing angle to shift perspective from one layer to many, so as to present all users as multi-leveled beings who manifest qualities across the full range of parameters, from physical to cultural.

The Vertical Slice and the Social Sciences

Social science, in a very simple sense, refers to the application of the scientific method to the study of people. We think nowadays in terms of psychology, sociology and anthropology as formal disciplines focused on generating this knowledge but for generations, humans have observed themselves and each other to better understand how and why we behave as we do. It is impossible to definitively date the origins of social science, but we can certainly trace this interest in self-understanding back to the Greeks and their examination of how states function and the role of morality in social life, most famously dealt with by Socrates, and written about by Plato almost 2400 years ago. The Islamic Golden Age (between the 8th and 14th Centuries) might have yielded the first anthropologist, Al-Beruni, who in the early 11th century even conducted what we might now describe as field work when he sailed to India to study the region's culture and religions. While theology and religious thinking, along with politics and medicine dominated the writings and examinations of human nature for much of our history, a significant advance in our approach to self-examination is attributed to Rene Descartes, writing in the mid-17th Century, for suggesting that the human mind was key to understanding our nature, sparking a revolution in our rational consideration of human existence. Descartes made the case for adopting a critical approach to studying ourselves, and while he is best remembered for his argument that mind and matter should be considered distinct but interacting substances, summarized pithily in the legendary phrase "I think, therefore I am," it is perhaps his rules for enquiry, outlined in his *Discourse on Method*, that have most relevance in shaping the time-sliced nature of contemporary social science (Descartes, 1986).

According to Descartes, it is important that we proceed in our study of human nature by never accepting as true anything that is not self-evident; that we decompose the research problems we study into their simplest parts; solve these in order by proceeding from the simpler to the more complex; and finally, we should recheck our reasoning to be confident in any conclusion we draw. Perhaps radical at the time, in the centuries that followed variants of these rules have guided scientific thinking about all areas of enquiry, and these rules have been invoked repeatedly by many thinkers or scholars wishing to bring a greater rigor to our efforts in studying humankind. The idea of being a somewhat detached observer of the problem space so as to see it most clearly, making as few assumptions as possible, is a natural derivative of Descartes (though the possibility of detached observation has been seriously questioned within social science in the intervening years). Similarly, the value placed on forming research questions that are tractable through data, and, ideally, answerable using agreed methods springs directly from his rules. Indeed, Descartes' final rule, to recheck our reasoning at the end is the basis of everything from blind reviewing of scholarly papers to the reliability checks of interpretation employed in many qualitative and increasingly quantitative methods to this day.

It is important to note that the prefix "social" in front of sciences is employed typically to distinguish them from other disciplines, most typically the so-called natural sciences of physics, chemistry and (for some but not all) biology, which as the name suggests, deal with the fundamental study of nature as we understand it. There is of course the waggish use of "natural" here to suggest other sciences, namely those dealing with people, are somehow unnatural, but that's part of the general running joke among scholars that some disciplines are more "scientific" than others, which gives rise to the further pejorative labels "hard" and "soft" when discussing sciences. Second, I use the term sciences in the plural here intentionally, there is really no single social science, there are at least four and maybe even ten, depending on who you ask, ranging from anthropology and economics through psychology and sociology (for the record, those four are invariably included in all such lists which can be expanded with the inclusion of politics, history, law, linguistics, geography, and archaeology, some or all of which are added in other lists). The "social" prefix reflects the emphasis in each on studying people, usually in some sphere of behavior where they are actors, perhaps in markets, or in organizations, or as individual decision makers. In recent decades, the term "behavioral sciences" has been used as an alternative to social sciences to highlight the role of human activity, from the single actor to members of a culture, and even as citizens of the globe, but I will use the term social sciences inclusively, to embrace all relevant disciplines and emphases.

Regardless of what is included under the heading "social sciences," one particular outcome of the Cartesian framing is likely now so engrained that we rarely notice it. We might be interested in people as members of a group, or as individual decision-makers, or as economic animals, as childhood learners, and so forth. The breadth of our existence and experience yields endless questions about how people live, behave, think, communicate, believe, choose, give, and receive influence over time, and so forth. Our enquiries into ourselves are as diverse as we are, and different researchers have approached these facets of existence in different ways. Over time, as students of the human condition shared impressions or findings, and found common areas of enquiry, it perhaps comes as no surprise that clusters of interest tended to form around particular subject matters, giving rise to the variety of disciplines we now include under the social sciences label.

Now what is most interesting about this disciplinary structure is that our carving up of the social sciences has led to very specialized practices within the scientific community, with equally specialized groups of scholars forming communities of practice who invariably speak a technical language shared primarily among others within their area of concern. If you are a sociologist, you largely read papers and books by other sociologists, you attend conferences where other sociologists go, and you present your own research to similar people who routinely use words like "anomie" and "endogamy" in casual conversation. The same is invariably true of psychologists, economists, or archaeologists and so forth. In fact, it is generally seen as a strength of a discipline that it has its own conferences, journals, membership groups, and academic departments where only like-minded scholars speaking the same technical language are employed. For sure, there can be distinctions within the discipline, so that one sociologist might study penal policy while another examines family and kinship, and each talks primarily to similarly focused members of the larger tribe or discipline, but even if these individuals employ different theories and methods for their research, they both likely feel some connection to their parent discipline and can recognize, if not appreciate, each other's research outputs in a way that reinforces the boundaries of their shared domain.

If, given the variety of disciplines that have evolved from our enquiries into ourselves, we ask a particular question about humans, such as "how long does it take a child to learn to read?" or "how does a rise in the minimum wage effect employment rates?" then one is pushed in the direction of a specific discipline within which such questions are more typically asked (psychology in the first instance, economics in the second). This makes sense in as much as each discipline has its own focus and tends to claim certain types of question as its excliusive concern and its findings as most directly providing the answers. If you want to understand organizations, you consider social psychological perspectives on people as collective actors within a constrained context bound by membership rules and expectations. If you want to know what types of material possessions are valued in a culture, you read anthropologists who examine the meaning of objects in people's lives and so forth. While there are emerging fields that evolve in response to new types of questions, they tend to pull in theories and methods from existing disciplines, sometimes dragging the remaining parts of the discipline along with it or becoming a specialized sub-area within a discipline (see, for example, the recent excitement about "data science" or "machine-learning" which are vectors of such influence in computing and information sciences they are not just magnets for funding and hiring, but are recognized as having important social impacts that require non-computational forms of examination). Yet for all the talk of interdisciplinarity, the basic structure of the social and natural sciences has remained fairly robust for a century, and this is enshrined in the departmental divisions of our universities, which despite their often-claimed desire to break boundaries, usually find it hard to overcome the inertia of established disciplinary identities.

The existence and durability of disciplines serves a purpose, allowing for the development of shared knowledge over time and the education of new scholars to sustain a field. Primary literature is recognized and prescribed, enshrining a collective sense of what is relevant work, allowing new scholars to find their space within the community and to signal their own contributions in due course. For young academics seeking tenure and promotion, an ability to articulate their fit within the shared and recognized structure of their discipline is vital, ensuring fit and continuity for a field of enquiry over time. This can be very important for building knowledge in a domain but where this type of structure lets us down, however, is in trying to piece together a fuller picture of a human experience which by its very nature is not so easily reduced to the structures of disciplines. This is particularly important in our current world where the rapid and continual spread of new information technologies has reshaped many areas of our lived experience, altering our behaviors, changing our consumption patterns, re-structuring education, and changing the nature of work for many. So rapid, in evolutionary terms, has the technology of the few decades been adopted and amplified, that those looking for answers to how digital information is impacting human life are given few pointers by the research perspectives of the extant social sciences.

So what is it about information technology that challenges our existing ways of knowing about ourselves? I believe that in a very real sense, the emergence of a global information infrastructure has rapidly and fundamentally changed the possibilities and indeed the actualities of life as it is now lived. Where once it was virtually impossible to connect with a stranger from another country without making strenuous efforts of travel or engaging in a pen-pal style exchange of letters, one now only needs go online and find the opportunity to communicate, person to person, across the globe in a matter of seconds. If nothing else, this alone would be a significant development in human communication, challenging the very ideas of connectibility, community and physical location as a constraint in profound ways.

Commensurate with this new reality of connection is the ability to work without ever sharing the same physical space as one's fellow organizational members, to shop without leaving home, to widen one's channel of communication so as to locate the narrowest viewpoints that match your own, and to monitor your own existence with a steady data stream of measurements, photos, and comparisons. Everywhere we look, information technology has not only reduced physical barriers, but it has opened up the opportunity for new markets to emerge which service the needs of distributed peoples, to reach them directly, to let them reach and exchange with each other. The technology provides real time updates on the status of the world, and of one's Amazon delivery, allows us to watch live events occurring continents away or to hear obscure favorite songs on demand, and to access rare materials from special collections and libraries that you could never physically visit. Ideas (good and bad) spread rapidly, and in this new world there are jobs and services that people perform which did not exist even a decade or two ago (blockchain analyst and influencer are two that currently spring to mind but no doubt there are and will be many others). Yes, it is a cliché to state that information technology is changing our world, but it is no less true for that. In connecting and in amplifying routine and original human acts regardless of proximity, our existence, the real, lived human experience of people alive on the planet now can be thought of as radically different from that of our ancestors, or even our parents. It also means that the experiences we now have will likely only hint at those our children and grandchildren may experience in the coming decades. This is truly an extraordinary time in the history of humankind.

The speed and nature of change poses a challenge for our own studies of ourselves. How are we to answer questions concerning information behavior and experience if the science base for considering our existence has been developed to tackle the questions of a different world? In particular, how do we approach a consideration of information use that accommodates the full representations of human experience in the digital realm? What in our current social science helps us deal with the loss of privacy that springs from an interconnected world? How do we understand work and leisure when both now occur in the same space? And what does it mean to design for a new user when the idea of new covers a range of people from those who have grown up with digital technology and those whose first introduction to telecommunications is a cell phone? One way is to start by outlining the disciplinary emphases we have inherited and how they have been applied so far in user-centered design, identifying both the strengths and limitiation, before suggesting a key shift to this framing that might enable us to leverage value while acknowledging the incompleteness of each.

Carving up the Enquiry Space on Humans

The social sciences each contain one or more theoretical models of humans that reflect their account of the important questions and how they might best be studied. Put another way, the basic picture of a human that emerges from say, sociology or anthropology, is a little different that the picture we get from economics or political science. It is not that any one of them is more or less correct than the other, but by emphasizing certain human qualities and actions for study, each discipline has painted an incomplete picture, offering a partial understanding of humans that focuses on some, usually small, aspects of our existence and experience.

For user-centeredness generally, and specifically so in the case of designing the emerging global information infrastructure, the derivation of suitable guidance from our science base can seem daunting. Organizational theorists explore the impact of new IT on a company or a group. Cultural theorists consider the impact of new digital texts on literacy. Cognitive scientists seek to understand the mental steps taken in searching for answers to a query. Ergonomists consider how form factor and size constrain use of mobile devices. Since our new information technologies mediate more and more human endeavors, it's hardly an exaggeration to say that the range of concerns for social scientists now extends to every aspect of lived experience, with published studies overwhelming any individual's ability to synthesize and integrate meaningfully. For a user experience designer, the amount and depth of reading required to claim a solid understanding of social science can be off-putting.

Of course, as Vicente (2003) noted, the Cartesian divide and conquer approach has both been useful and harmful. On the positive side, the breaking apart of a large problem space into smaller, more tractable challenges has enabled collective progress through individual shared effort. However, Vicente suggests we have created a division in knowlesge between the mechanistic and the humanistic ways of understanding, which he sees as the primary source of difficulty in modern design as the technologists who primarily build are ignorant of the ways non-technologists (i.e., most of the rest of us) think. While we certainly have bridges to build between the technical and humanistic tradutions, we have also allowed the divide and conquer approach to fragment the social sciences, further weakning our own understanding of human nature. By enabling a focus on one area (e.g., the collective or group by sociologists), others can turn their focus to another area of interest (e.g., the individual by psychologists). In this way, social scientists have set boundaries around areas of concern and allow scholarship to proceed within a proscribed,bounded space without having to deal with all the issues that arise in other areas or spaces of enquiry. Accepting such boundaries can lessen the load for designers too as they attempt to select meaningful guidance from the science base but it comes at a cost.

Over time, the divisions between disciplines tend to reify certain ways of thinking, any one of which might work well within its limited enquiry space, but which increasingly makes it difficult when speaking to researchers in other areas. Vicente highlighted the lack of communication that occurs between technical specialists and humanists, with the result that our technologies, built by those of one orientation, historically reflect a limited understanding of humans and can prove difficult to use by all but other technical folk. The results are found in accidents, errors, and ultimately rejection of innovations. As Vicente puts it:

> "We are so used to defining people this way that it's easy to forget that the traditional humanistic and mechanistic world views are both abstractions of convenience; nobody has ever seen technology without people or people without technology."
>
> (Vicente, 2003, p. 32)

I am a great admirer of Vicente's perspective on bridging traditions but I would extend it further. In my view, the divide-and-conquer mentality has been so unquestioningly adopted within the social sciences themselves, the humanistic side of Vincent's divide, that principles and findings of one specialist area (e.g., sociology) are barely recognized or considered by scholars from another area (e.g., cognitive psychology). What this means then is that social scientists, all ostensibly studying humans, even humans in a technological environment, have made it difficult to share ideas among themselves and thus to generate a cohesive or holistic understanding of ourselves that has application for technologists building our information world.

For user-centered design, this carve-up of social science manifests itself in varying approaches to the nature of the human beings as "users." Ergonomists tend to consider users to be mostly physical or psychophysiological beings. Consequently, much attention within ergonomics focuses on physical interface controls and layout, with design being a process intended to ensure that a user can see, reach, touch, leverage, handle, and manipulate the affordances of the workstation, device or space being created. There is no doubt this is vital when we consider how common activities such as driving rely so heavily on reach, touch and combinatorial physical behaviors. But it's also true for real and virtual keyboards, that ubiquitous input mechanism we use on everything from laptops and phones to microwave ovens and remote controls. Who needs to stop and think about pressing keys when you want to communicate and share information?

Social psychologists, on the other hand, consider users primarily as members of a team or group and focus their attention in design on the communication patterns, actor relationships, collective behavior and responses, so as to facilitate shared understanding and contextual awareness of what shapes engagement with the technology on mutual tasks or goals Again, how important that knowledge might be becomes clear when you experience an information system at work where you wonder who thought to use those odd terms and commands for the revised platform everyone is now required to learn? Since any working group tends to develop a shared language for referring to the structures and processes in their niche community, surely an appropriately designed technology should reflect this language rather than impose a new one? Who has not felt the stomach sinking sensation following the realization that you sent that tossed-off, somewhat sarcastic email to the group rather than the single intended recipient because "reply-all" is now the new default when, with the automaticity honed from years of repetition, you push that familiar "send" button on the mailing app?

Both the ergonomists and sociologists involved in a system design would identify their particular focus as user-centered but in operating largely independently, not necessarily ignorant of each other's work but rarely engaging in meaningful discussions or considerations of each others' perspectives and activities, the results for a user can be ergonomically smooth but socially embarrassing! The holds true for all areas of human design, there are those more interested in visual properties of interface design, those concerned with learning or error analysis, or those with an interest in the cultural differences in user responses and preferences around the globe. There is simply so much to know in each area that it is too easy to specialize and too difficult to step back or outside of the disciplinary blinkers to recognize that the actor in each case, the user for whom we are all trying to design, is the same person.

In classic divide-and-conquer style, each area of emphasis within user experience design tends to have its own scholarly journals and conferences for research findings. User-centered designers of a particular flavor or level identify with particular associations and gatherings of fellow level-dwelliers, present their ideas only to those, receive new ideas from such peers, and risk forming a worldview of typical users that is inevitably partial. If and when members of such groups do recognize the limitations of their view, the practices of user-centered scholarship are inflexible and might be thought of as encouraging this narrowing rather than expanding the focus of user-centered design knowledge. In the course of my own career I have been a member of multiple groups all of whom, in theory, share a similar area of concern with user-centered design (SIGCHI: the Special Interest Group on HCI of the Association for Computing Machinary (ACM); UXPA: the Usability Professionals Association; and HFES: the Human Factors and Ergonomics Society being the three who are most closely related in coverage, but I could add at least several more which would not exhaust the list). What always struck me was how little overlap there really seemed to be among the people involved, most of whom saw one and only one of these groups as their primary community and as such, they engaged only with fellow tribe members. Once we extend the focus to groups or associations interested in graphical design, information architecture, socio-technical studies, informatics, media studies and more, the ties are looser still, and we find entire groups that may have no awareness of related communities also engaged in trying to answer similar questions. Certainly, the work of some leading thinkers in UX might transcend the divisions due to their popularity or media visibility (think Don Norman or Ben Shneiderman) but such people are a rarity, for the most part each user experience design group lives happily within its own independent space.

It is worth noting that the divisions of social science that we are heir to are neither immutable nor inevitable. There is no law of nature that determines we frame our study of human experience in this way, logical as it might seem to those of us so used to it that we find it difficult to envisage any alternative. The study of people as thinking and behaving organisms can also divide us by modality (visual, auditory, tactile, etc.) or cluster us by age (infant, child, youth, adult, senior, etc.) and in so doing, frame questions around these facets of our existence. Such groupings certainly exist within the social sciences as a further level-of subdivision, but they are subservient to what I refer to as the primary "fault line." Whether by principle or convenience, the divisions we do see everywhere in our familiar social sciences are predominantly based on an axis of temporality or duration.

There are many reasons we might have ended up with this division once we adopted the Cartesian approach to social science but in a very direct way, we can tie this framing in the field of human-computer interaction and UX design to Newell and Card (1985). In their classic paper, "The prospects for psychological science in Human-Computer Interaction" they argued that we can map the various scientific responses to the study of humans in terms of the time duration of all basic activities that we wish to study. Human behavior ranges from the neurochemical to the cultural, and so, the phenomena we examine can be thought to manifest themselves within bounded time spans. Thus, at the most rapid level, where the particulars of interest are of short duration, we are dealing with millisecond neural responses in the human nervous system. At the slowest level, where the particulars we are interested in might occur over decades or centuries, we are in the realm of culture and social history. These timespans form the ends of the continuum of social sciences, particularly as they relate to designing technologies of information. In between, there exist studies of phenomena that involve minutes or hours of activity, such as balancing a financial statement, or that involve weeks or months of human activity, like learning a new skill or writing a book.

Newell and Card offered a precise carving up of the range of human activities as outlined in Table 4.1. It is not so important that we agree completely with their time estimates (e.g., their general category of "task" is so broad it covers a timespan of a minute to a month) but what is most interesting for our discussion here is how it broadly maps theoretical orientations within social science to temporal concerns; and how neatly these map onto the various research agenda of groups within user-centered design.

Table 4.1 The Breakdown of Social Science Theories Based on Temporal Concerns, after Newell and Card (1985)

TIME		ACTION	MEMORY	THEORY
Secs.	Common units			
10^9	Decades	Technology	Culture	Social and Organizational
10^8	Years	System	Development	
10^7	Months	Design	Education	
10^6	Weeks	Task	Education	
10^5	Days	Task	Skill	Bounded rationality
10^4	Hours	Task	Skill	
10^3	10 minutes	Task	Long-term	
10^2	Minutes	Task	Long-term	
10	10 seconds	Unit task	Long-term	Psychological
1	Seconds	Operator	Short-term	
10^{-1}	Tenths of second	Cycle time	Buffers	
10^{-2}	Centiseconds	Signal	Integration	Neural and Biochemical
10^{-3}	Milliseconds	Pulse	Summation	

Broadly, Newell and Card suggest a four-level distinction within social science on the time axis between the neural and biological level, the psychological level, what they term the "bounded rationality" level, and the social/organizational level. Each level reflects activities of a particular duration, certain actions of interest, the form of memory process involved, and a shared broad theory.

While they suggest research in HCI or UX is dominated by work at what they call the "psychological" level, theories and insights need to be delivered in a form that speaks to the level of bounded rationality where skilled designers try to shape interactions over task-length activities. However, we might argue this is too narrow and that the range of relevance at least extends from what Newell and Card term the system level within the realm of social and organization theories to the short-term memory sub-task level of psychological theory. I would further argue that neural level processing is also pertinent since the growth in neuroinformatic research has been advanced by the development and use of tools to capture rapid eye-movements and fixations of milliseconds durations which enable us to study user experience in detail at this level (see e.g., Gwizdka, Zhang and Dillon, 2019).

Newell and Card's framing of social sciences across the temporal spectrum was the backdrop for their forceful argument that the best way for social science to inform design practice is through models of task performance that can yield calculational tools for estimating user task completion times with various interface configurations. They argued that only by developing such models could user-centered design achieve the status of what they termed "hard science," providing quantitative models based on fundamental human operations and processes,to influence design (an example of what this might look like is provided in chapter 6). They contrasted this approach with (in their words) the "softer," more traditional user-centered methods, those that rely on testing of instantiated designs as part of an iterative process, which Newell and Card considered too weak or time consuming to ever infuence design practice sufficiently. The specifics of their formal modeling are less important here, it has received considerable criticism from others in the field (see for e.g., Carroll and Campbell's (1986) rejoinder to the original paper from the same issue). However, we should acknowledge that their argument echoes a concern that many of us in the UX field share, namely that we cannot just propose a continual process of design-test iterations and assume it will be sufficient or even workable for many situations. It would be far better if UX professionals could shape the initial generation of possible design solutions through more formal or theoretical means so as to optimize our inputs or enable the derivation of improvements in design alternatives at the earliest stages in the process without the need to prototype and test every conceivable solution.

In the intervening years, the argument over formal modeling has largely been settled in favor of the critics as the model human processor and its family of calculation tools pushed by Card and colleagues has never been widely accepted within the design world, and only infrequently applied in scholarly work on user-experience or human-computer interaction. Regardless of one's stance on the need for, or even the possibility of a "hard science" for interaction design which Card and his colleagues claimed was crucial, I believe their carving up of social science along the temporal lines is perhaps the more important legacy of their approach. While we might argue about the boundaries of the time bands or the theoretical framings in Table 4.1, it is important to acknowledge their existence as I believe it can help us understand important recurring challenges we face in improving user-centered design. I believe we should even embrace these divisions as an accurate reflection of the science base we draw upon so as to be more clear-eyed in cutting across them to enrich our view of what it is to be a user of technology, thus pivoting our viewpoint to gain a perspective I term "the vertical slice."

Carving in a Different Direction: Users as Multilayered Beings

If the intent of the user-centered design community is to create and implement more humanly acceptable information technologies, then surely, we need to conceive of the user as a real human, with the full range of responses, physically, emotionally and cognitively, that define us as experiential beings. So, what parts of our human nature are not fully attended to when we employ a typical view of people as users? It is certainly true that we are physical, material beings, but we are also perceiving, thinking, and reasoning beings. We sometimes behave and respond emotionally and not entirely consciously, rationally, and deliberatively to the world around us. We might use technology on our own but we also live, work and play in groups. We communicate and share ideas, facts, opinions, experiences, memories and stories across distance, within and beyond organizations, and our expectations for communication, behavior of others, and norms of interaction are shaped by and reflected in our cultural immersion.

This much seems self-evident when we stop to think about our own lives and the existence of those we know and love, yet it is not really the way we have considered user-centered design or educated our interaction designers to view the users of their products. Instead, our research emphasis and curricula precisely enshrine the time-sliced distinctions Newell and Card outlined decades ago for HCI, which echo the centuries old divisions initiated by Descartes. Ergonomics characteristically treats the human as an "operator" engaging physically with systems for which we incorporate our knowledge of population norms for reach, finger strength, target size, posture etc. The cognitive or psychological layer dominates considerations of interface design with its emphasis on task completion, human perception, interpretation, choice-selection, and error-recovery. The combination of theories and models from these two layers, within a loose methodological framing of prototyping and testing forms the substance of most UX design education. If we wish to consider issues beyond the actual design style, such as will a user adopt this technology, or how can we increase the likelihood of a user community collectively shifting to a new platform, our UX education tends to hand-off the problem to socio-technical or organizational theorists who emphasize motivation or incentives to use, inter-group relationship dynamics, collective cognition and decision making or how to manage the implementation process. Further, once we seek to understand how cultural forces might influence the manner in which new technology is viewed or used, another set of ideas and theories, related to behavioral or attitudinal norms of regions and nations are invoked, by which time we often find ourselves dealing with a set of concerns that maintain only a loose tie to the types of design questions that initiated our user analysis.

Obviously, this is a limitation of our knowledge and research. A human and a technology are present in and common to each temporal layer, but when we separate out the questions asked at each, we introduce a forced separation that can isolate crucial shared aspects of the design challenge, encouraging us to view the problems as isolated rather than interconnected. It is certainly important to understand if people *can* use a design, but this question is not independent of whether they *will* use it, given whatever constraints exist for them. It is useful for us to know that certain color combinations support faster grouping or visual parsing of a display, but it is also important to understand that cultures vary in what they consider colors or images to symbolize or convey. And yes, it is crucial to recognize that we might be adjusting working practices in an organization as a function of new information technologies, but whatever system is introduced, it must also meet relevant usability or ergonomic standards for the groups impacted. Divide-and-conquer has given us a set of problem spaces and suite of methods and findings, grouped along disciplinary an, theoretical lines, but if we are to design in a rich, truly user-centered manner, we will need to cross these lines openly and fluidly rather than be locked into them professionally and methodologically.

In an earlier work (Dillon, 2004) I first considered this problem for user-centered designers in the context of digital documents and the new practices of handling, navigating and using large text corpora that exploded with the rise of the web. In this design area, the psychological research on reading was often invoked to help us consider what users were doing and how them might best be supported. I invoked the term "vertical slice" to describe a multi-layered analysis of human reading that did not limit itself to the standard time-sliced approaches of HCI. I argued that insight might be gained by viewing "readers" experiences across multiple layers rather than within each layer. In particular, I attempted to show how a vertical slicing across the temporal layers Newell and Card (1985) described could help us understand how a range of factors, from interface manipulation facilities to people's understanding of genres and collective forms of discourse, each play a role in determining the overall quality of readers' interactive experience and performance. So, while we might consider the act of reading to be perceptual and cognitive predominantly, and that is certainly how it is frequently represented in the psychological research literature, we need also recognize that readers usually handle and physically manipulate both paper and digital document. Furthermore, the manner in which readers move through a document as they read or search for target information reflects long-established conventions of form which have evolved over decades, or sometimes longer, in particular language or cultural communities.

By construing digital document interactions in this more holistic manner, I wanted to encourage user-experience designers to draw on the relevant knowledge base from each layer and to weight these while considering the steps a user was taking to complete whatever they considered their reading act. Since we knew from many excellent studies that image quality certainly is a determinant of reading speed (see e.g., Gould et al., 1987, Dillon, 1992) so is the way we enable readers to scroll or page through a lengthy text. Further, the structure around which we organize large documents can determine how well any reader is able to comprehend or locate information in the text, and this structure is often tied to communication norms within a group. By vertically slicing the act of reading across all layers, we can encourage a broader treatment of questions related to how digital documents might be adopted or resisted in certain contexts. So while it is popularly believed that digital documents will inevitably replace paper (the earliest prediction for this was made i by Jonassen (1982) who confidently estimated the transition would be complete within a decade), it was always more likely, according to the vertical slice approach that some aspects of reading were tied inextricably to characteristics of genre forms that would likely prove much longer-lasting and possibly difficult to improve upon with digital text, no matter how well the image quality issue was resolved or the paging and scrolling mechanisms were designed. In short, the act of reading is a multi-layered user experience and solving for one layer alone is never going to result in an ideal design. The continual survival of paper books and related documents certainly suggests the human experience of reading is richer than many digital designers imagined. What goes for reading is true for so many of the information activities humans engage in routinely, they are multilevelled, interwoven manifestations of our full nature as humans.

Thinking Vertically as a Design Requirement

The challenge then for those interested in user-centered information design is to get outside the traditional tramlines of disciplines and learn to think *across* the layers of temporal duration on which nearly all of the social sciences are based. This, however, runs counter to the divide and conquer principle that has yielded so much success for human enquiry for centuries.

I want to emphasize there that I am not suggesting our science base is wrong to have proceeded as it has, that would be a foolish claim given what we have learned about ourselves over the last centuries of social scientific enquiry, but it does point to a specific need for those who want to leverage this research into actionable guidance for the design of our information world.

The interaction between a human and a designed interface cannot simply be reduced to a constellation of individual moments, each of which is isolated from the preceding moment, analyzed independently, with a resulting design suggestion based solely on one appropriate temporal framing. Rather, the unfolding of typical interactions involves the simultaneous activation of the multiple components of our physical and mental processing, within a specific context that partially shapes the choices and responses we make. When immersed in use, a human is actively engaged in a dynamic sequence of communication that involves their continual application of all layers of physical, psychological, and sociocultural processes. When it works well, when the interaction is well-designed, any user will effortlessly switch their attention across layers as needed, effectively acting as a physical input provider and a cultural being *at the same time*. Inputs from fingers will typically affect a change in the display state of the device under use, leading to the rapid perception and interpretation of the user, in a back-and-forth cycle of interaction which cannot easily be treated or understood a single layer of the temporal divide, except in the abstract manner we might employ for purposes of scientific classification. This is the challenge a designer concerned with truly improving the user experience through a research-based approach must face.

As researchers, we can specialize, concerning ourselves only with the interaction at one layer, but it is unlikely that we can ever ensure good design by restricting ourselves to this. An aesthetically pleasing form factor certainly impacts the user experience, but it will be ultimately wasted if the interaction sequence violates expectations for layout and induces continual errors. But more importantly, the form factor or the dialog or the visual display, indeed any specific feature of the design, can never constitute the full experience any user has of any interaction. For us to even begin to understand user experience, we cannot treat the layer of immediate attention as isolated and sufficient for our analysis. Rather, at each moment of interaction, the user's attention carries with it the multiple layers of physical, perceptual, cognitive and sociocultural processing that characterizes us as living, physical, human beings, members of a species, a culture, an organization, a group and yet always still an individual. Certainly, we can

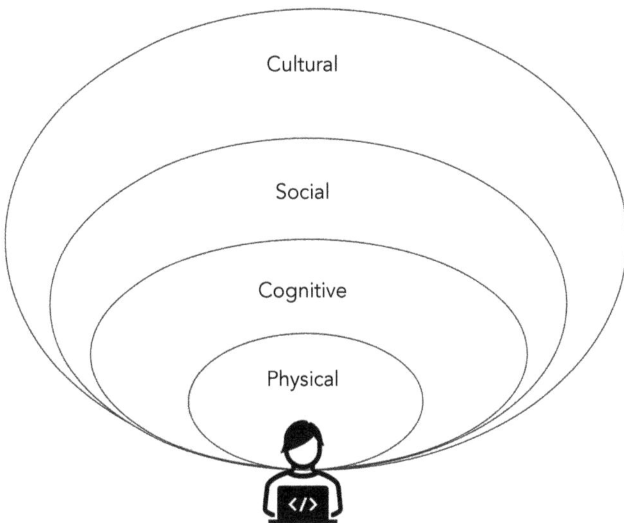

Figure 4.1 The user experience as multi-layered interaction

isolate specific features or input-output states we wish to focus on, and this can be vital in a formal usability test as we try to dive deeply into what people are thinking at a particular step of the interaction, but we cannot maintain this perspective to obtain a full examination of the user experience we wish to understand. Routine use of technology involves more than a sequence of standalone states, all of us are multi-leveled in our engagement with the world and we need to slice vertically to view the user fully (see Figure 4.1).

One implication of this pivot is educational. A user-centered designer needs to be able to understand users *across* rather than within the layers presented in the scholarly literature. Of course, awareness of human physiology is important when thinking about handheld devices or wearable computers, but so is an understanding of perception, memory processes, group behavior, and many other topics that are framed within apparently separate research literatures. But the unique challenge for a human-centered designer is to develop the facility to see the user as engaging at all layers. Some might interpret this as my arguing for designers to be generalists rather than specialists, but that is not my intent, though I am not overly concerned if that is intended as a criticism. Indeed, what I recommend is a very different kind of specialism, one that operates vertically across the traditional divisions of social scientific understanding. The key to this is creating a form of social science for design that turns the existing temporal model around and considers its subject matter to be the experience of humans across layers.

Consider the analysis of users when designing a keypress sequence. Perhaps one point in the interaction might be a locus of error that we could remove by dialog re-design. For sure, we want to improve the flow but while doing this, we might ask how the dialog sequence reflects other tasks, how the users learn and remember this and other keyboard sequences, if the dialog builds on knowledge or experience of other interfaces one typically observes in this user community, and so forth. At the opposite level, when considering how a new system implementation will fit into the shared work practices of organizational members, a classic socio-technical concern, we might also check for basic usability concerns related to effective and efficient task performance so that we can be confident the new system is not making tasks harder or slower to complete. To do this, the user-centered designer cannot just be an expert at one layer of human behavior, but must be capable of recognizing the continual interplay of all aspects of user experience in determining the quality of a proposed design solution for any given context.

Practically, any field that builds on even an introductory understanding of humans tends to borrow the layers handed us by social science, and UX education is no exception. Even when we do cover the range of layers across a broad curriculum, we tend to offer coursework that parcels each out separately. Students learn the basics of perception and perhaps gain an introduction to human cognition in on or two modules. They will learn about group and organizational effects through a separate course on social and cultural psychology. Students subsequently tend to specialize in one or other and rarely stop to think that these different theories and research findings are interwoven in the very users they are professionally committed to serving. Within a design curriculum such courses might focus directly on the applications of this form of knowledge for shaping user experiences so that, for example, students might learn the Gestalt principles of visual form, the efffect of group size on communication, or how Fitts' Law (Fitts, 1954) estimates how quickly a user can select a target on screen. This is all essential knowledge, but what will be missing, what most students in such programs will never receive, is an explicit treatment of how these layers co-exist within each human user and how to think about user experience in its fullest sense, not just as a physical or perceptual, an organizational or cognitive phenomenon but as a combined, multi-layered process that does not deconstruct simply or sequentially to one type of process.

There is obviously considerable room for improvement in education. Frascara and Noel (2009), in a critique of contemporary design programs noted that even basic coverage of the literature from cognitive psychology is missing in many schools, with guidance reliant more on explanations or justification of best practices rather than theoretical grounding. In their words,

> "these 'best practices' might be the best, but might also be not good enough. Imitation is not really a reliable strategy to arrive at excellence in design or in design education."
>
> (Frascara and Noel, 2009, p. 43)

Their recommendation is to be more user-centered, evidence-based and results-driven, a call for putting human and social needs to the center, to study deeply what is known already about people, and to evaluate designs based on how intended users respond to them, not how the instructors or other designers view them. These would certainly be a move in the right direction but it leaves unaddressed, I fear, what a deep study of "what is known already about people" might actually entail (the layers of social science most likely being invoked and taught again).

It is certainly troubling that more than a half-century of advocacy for user-centeredness has produced so little change in design programs, but at least part of the challenge, I believe, lies in the difficulties we have in translating the social science knowledge we possess into a form that makes application to design easier. Simply mimicking the structure of the science base, offering piecemeal snapshots of human behavior in the hope of tying an experimental finding to a design principle might be part of this problem. While a rule such as "don't offer users more than 7 (or 5, or …) choices at a time as it taxes their short term memory" might seem plausible, out of context this conveys a highly simplistic view of a user, and one that is not particularly useful for contexts where a range of choices in excess of the "magic number" 7 could better serve the user by reducing a need for sub-menus (see e.g., Kent Norman's (1991) groundbreaking work on menu design which clearly challenged that simplistic interpretation of cognitive theory). Understanding that a user comes to an interaction with a life-history of experiences, habits, skills, preferences, and knowledge, and quite possibly in a particular emotional state, makes a simple claim about short-term memory capacity perhaps less useful than it seems, and certainly suggests a more nuanced interpretation and application of the principle is often warranted. Sensitizing user-centered designers to this, enabling them to appreciate and consider the fuller workings of the human mind and the importance of context in understanding how any human might view the interaction being designed is crucial.

Getting There from Here

Clearly, we are required to represent the science base appropriately and that does mean that designers must be sensitized to the way research has carved up the study of humans. So, while we do want to explore ergonomics, and mine cognitive psychology as well as cultural studies, we need to combine these in one learning environment. My personal belief is that an overview of user-centered design must take these layers, explore them, but turn them on their side, so to speak, so that no single layer can ever be considered standalone in the context of designing interactions. To do this we must continually push students to connect these layers through their evaluations, their prototyping, their task analyses, and contextual enquiries. In the next few chapters, I'll present what I see as important in each of these layers and attempt to show how we can extract appropriately from the science base without losing sight of the multi-layered nature of user experience.

References

Carroll, J., and Campbell, R. (1986). Softening up hard science: Reply to Newell and Card. *Human-Computer Interaction*, *2*(3), 227–249.

Descartes, R. (1986). *Discourse on Method*. New York: Macmillan.

Dillon, A. (2004). *Designing Usable Electronic Text*, 2nd ed. Boca Raton: CRC Press.

Dillon, A. (1992). Reading from paper versus screens: A critical review of the empirical literature. *Ergonomics*, *35*(10), 1297–1326.

Fitts, P. (1954). The information capacity of the human motor system in controlling the amplitude of movement. *Journal of Experimental Psychology*, *47*(6), 381–391.

Frascara, J., and Noel, G. (2009). What's missing in design education today. *Visible Language*, *46*(1,2), 36–53.

Gould, J.D., Alfaro, L., Finn, R., Haupt, B., and Minuto, A. (1987). Reading from CRT displays can be as fast as reading from paper. *Human Factors*, *29*(5), 497–517. 10.1177/001872088702900501

Gwizdka, J., Zhang, Y., and Dillon, A. (2019). Using the eye-tracking method to study consumer online health information search behaviour. *Aslib Journal of Information Management*, *71*(6), 739–754.

Jonassen, D.H. (1982). *The Technology of Text: Principles for Structuring, Designing, and Displaying Text*. United States: Educational Technology Publications.

Newell, A., and Card, S. (1985). The Prospects for Psychological Science in Human-Computer Interaction. *Human-Computer Interaction, 1*, 209–242.

Norman, K. (1991). *The Psychology of Menu-Selection: Cognitive Control at the Human-Computer Interface*. New York: Ablex.

Vicente, K. (2003). *The Human Factor: Revolutionizing the Way People Live with Technology*. Toronto: Knopf.

The Physio-Tech Layer 5

The User as Physical Being

An old philosophical conundrum first documented by the ancient Greeks requires us to think carefully about what makes a material object consistently identifiable. Typically referred to as the Ship of Theseus challenge, it poses a relatively simple sounding question as a thought experiment, that is, if a ship embarks on a long voyage and enroute is continually repaired, plank by plank, to the point whereupon its return home not a single part that set sail remains, is this the same ship? For many people, the answer is of course, "yes," though that does somewhat rely on the duration of the journey and the replacement rate of the parts (a storm-wrecked ship that was completely rebuilt in one go feels less like the same ship than one that has a plank or part replaced each day on a lengthy voyage). Later, Thomas Hobbes offered a variation that made the challenge even more complicated. What if the discarded parts were retained and then used to create the original ship again. Which of the two would be the ship of Theseus? Variants on this exist too. For example, if a ship does have its parts completely replaced, at what point in that process is it no longer the original? Does one part replacement indicate a sufficient change? Probably not, but what if all but one part, or ten, twenty etc. are replaced? For a general overview of this philosophical problem, see Williams (2021).

The nuance in the question speaks directly to our physical life. Humans are material beings. But our bodies change, piece by piece, continually, essentially renewing themselves every seven years. While the start of life comes with the expectations of growth, even after we mature our cells continually renew, and it is often only when we see a picture of our former selves from years back that we can even recognize the changes in our

DOI: 10.4324/9781003026112-5

physical form. Yes, we typically feel we are the same being, no matter. For most of us, we consider our identity to be more than our physical form, we remain the same person, regardless of the cellular activity and replenishment, much as a ship of Theseus can be seen as more than the planks that make it up but also the experience of sailing it, the journeys it has taken, and the way others view it.

The conundrum is not easily solved but it speaks directly to a layer of user experience that we too tend to take for granted as fixed while it is constantly changing, our physical form. We all are material beings. Our existence, at least for most of us and for the foreseeable future, is tied to our body. We are, as users, physical creatures continually immersed in the world around us, a complicated mix of carbon, water, oxygen, hydrogen, calcium, and phosphorous, manifest in a skeleto-muscular form connected via a massive neural network with specialized organs that enable us to interface with the world and each other. Nutrition and medicine might have helped current generations grow a little taller and maintain our individual presence on the planet a little longer, but there's not a tremendous physical difference between the homo sapiens who painted the caves and those now sending texts via their phones. If asked what a human looks like, most of us would generate a fairly similar representation of our form.

At first glance, the literature in user experience design seemingly pays little attention to the material level of human existence, placing more emphasis on perceptual, cognitive, or social qualities of devices and interactions, but first glances can be deceiving. Most devices we design for humans have a touchpoint, a control or display interface that receives input from a human finger pressing, touching or sliding over it. Our homes are full of switches, levers, dials and buttons for controlling everything from lights and heating to clocks and screens. Our laptops physically embody keyboards, even now, which we press and push to issue words and commands. Our tablets have touchscreens, sometimes with a stylus that mimics the age-old manipulations of quills (and before that, sticks on clay or sand), testimony to the inherent coupling of our bodily form to our material world that we exploit in order to communicate. For all the breathless excitement uttered about the rapid pace of technical change, some aspects of our interactive devices seem remarkably fixed.

Today's laptop is a fraction of the size and exponentially more powerful than the original workstations of the 1950s. In the intervening decades, the scaling down of hardware has given us mobile tools that might seem like science fiction to the operator of an old mainframe computer. The seemingly continual push to shrink form factor is now facing resistance. With the explosive adoption of smart phones this century, smaller is no longer always better as screen size or viewable area competes with pocketability and weight. But striking the right balance is not simple. Apple received a lot of negative feedback, particularly from women, when they released their iPhone X with a 6" screen that many felt was too large for single handed use and too bulky to carry comfortably in a pocket (see e.g., Taylor, 2019). As we continually are reminded, despite population norms, one size rarely fits all.

Preferences aside, users have continually employed physical input to control information technologies, and for all the changes in products, the old QWERTY keyboard layout seems to be hard for us to avoid. Today's mobile technologies typically offer virtual keyboards that might appear and disappear on screen as needed but still employ this layout standardized in the mechanical age, requiring the same basic finger presses to render text and commands. Over time we've seen alternative input forms proposed such as the mouse, the stylus, the chording keyboard, the touch wheel, the touchscreen, the touchpad (you get the idea) that all leverage our physical moves and gestures to initiate actions at the interface. Certainly, we are witnessing more sophisticated voice input and may indeed be on the verge of exploiting brain activity for some commands (see e.g., Wolpaw et al., 2020) but the nature of our physical form means certain parts of our body remain the primary way most users engage with their devices. When one considers the physical shrinking of most computer parts over time, it is not hard to see keyboard and to some extent the attached screens as major design bottlenecks on truly innovative personal devices.

Within UX, the term "ergonomics" is often used to refer to the physical design attributes of a product. This is not actually an accurate usage as the origin of that word lies in the early industrial design practices that aimed to couple humans with systems for the design of efficient and healthy work practices (derived from "ergon", a Greek word for work). While this certainly involves the design of controls and input devices, ergonomists typically cover a far broader set of concerns with the designed environment such as noise and light conditions, information and workspace layout, stress, fatigue and operator safety. Indeed, for many years, the terms "ergonomics" and "human factors" were used interchangeably, or at least internationally (Europeans favored the ergonomics label while American professionals leaned toward the human factors title, although the largest professional association has embraced both and titled itself the Human Factors and Ergonomics Society, which might suggest equal recognition but distinct identities). And just as we understand the term "human factors" to refer to myriad aspects of design that impact humans, traditional ergonomists would say the same of themselves. Nevertheless, meaning, to paraphrase Wittgenstein, is found in use, and by now, the idea of "physical ergonomics" (which we might distinguish from "cognitive ergonomics") is widely employed when discussing those parts of a interface that a user touches, pushes, views, hears and holds when interacting, the "touchpoints" of interaction, if you will. So for the purposes of this chapter, when I speak of ergonomics, I'll be employing it mainly in this more casual usage to deal with input devices and screen displays and the physical nature of technology use.

The Ergonomic User

At the level of physical analysis, social scientists have generated an extraordinary amount of data summarizing the anthropometrics of our physiques. In simple terms, these data sets provide guidelines for a wide range of design choices for objects and spaces, e.g., if we know the distribution of height among a population is normal and has, for example, a median of 70.8" and a standard deviation of 2" then we can plot some of the size requirements for doors or clothes or shelving units or whatever it is that we are trying to construct that needs to take account of human stature. This ensures that we construct buildings that most people can walk through without ducking under doors or can create grocery displays that most people can view and select from comfortably (though we might note that in their efforts to maximize capacity, many supermarkets have shelves that can be too high, or uncomfortably low, for some people, a clear indication that user-centeredness has some ground to make up in that realm). In fact, over many years, ergonomists have measured and plotted the data concerning an incredible array of physical characteristics of people such as their reach, hand strength, range of head movement, calf length, foot size, digit span, shoulder length, elbow height, and more, publishing these in books and tables of standards that allow for quick look up of typical values and ranges (see an example of a summary table on physical height produced by the US Government in Figure 5.1).

Such data points are also frequently mapped for age and nationality so that it's possible, for example, to get measurement data on physical attributes for middle aged Malaysians or for Italian teenagers etc. Because physical characteristics are comparatively easy to capture and are relatively stable (though there are shifts within populations over time as nutrition and

Table 8. Height in inches for children and adolescents aged 2–19 years and number of examined persons, mean, standard error of the mean, and selected percentiles, by sex and age: United States, 2007–2010

Sex and age[1]	Number of examined persons	Mean	Standard error of the mean	Percentile								
				5th	10th	15th	25th	50th	75th	85th	90th	95th
Male								Inches				
2 years	285	36.2	0.15	33.1	33.7	34.2	34.9	36.2	37.4	37.9	38.4	39.2
3 years	202	38.9	0.14	35.9	36.8	37.2	37.8	38.9	40.0	40.9	41.2	41.7
4 years	244	41.8	0.17	38.5	39.4	39.8	40.6	41.7	42.8	43.8	44.4	45.2
5 years	205	44.8	0.22	41.0	42.0	42.2	43.1	44.5	46.0	47.0	47.9	†
6 years	193	47.0	0.18	42.7	44.1	44.4	45.4	47.0	48.5	49.1	49.7	50.5
7 years	215	49.4	0.17	46.1	46.5	46.7	47.4	49.1	50.8	51.9	52.6	53.8
8 years	210	51.8	0.26	48.0	48.6	49.3	50.4	51.7	53.3	54.1	54.6	†
9 years	190	54.3	0.35	48.6	50.2	51.3	52.1	53.8	56.4	57.2	57.7	59.5
10 years	197	56.0	0.25	51.8	52.5	53.3	54.1	56.1	57.9	58.5	59.0	60.2
11 years	211	59.0	0.24	54.7	55.2	56.0	57.1	58.8	60.6	61.8	63.1	64.2
12 years	159	60.9	0.24	56.3	56.9	57.5	58.6	60.4	63.2	64.3	65.3	66.2
13 years	146	64.5	0.27	58.1	59.6	61.1	61.9	64.8	66.5	67.8	68.8	†
14 years	177	66.3	0.37	61.0	62.1	63.0	64.0	66.7	68.6	69.4	69.9	†
15 years	160	68.4	0.35	63.1	64.6	65.7	66.9	68.4	70.1	71.5	72.2	73.9
16 years	175	68.9	0.20	64.3	65.4	66.2	67.3	69.1	70.3	71.7	72.2	73.4
17 years	188	69.3	0.27	64.0	65.1	65.9	67.8	69.3	71.0	72.1	73.0	†
18 years	142	69.4	0.21	64.6	66.5	66.8	67.8	69.6	70.9	72.0	72.6	73.1
19 years	179	70.0	0.32	64.8	66.3	67.0	68.2	70.2	71.6	72.8	73.7	†

Figure 5.1 Summary of height distribution for US Males ages 2–19, by National Center for Health Statistics (Vital Health Stat 11 (252), 2012)

lifestyle choices shift), the published anthropometric data sets offer reliable resource for designers concerned with the physical aspects of their products. For the record, those median height and standard deviation measures mentioned above are not indicative of the US where the median height for males and females is 70" and 64.5", respectively, with the standard deviation being closer to 3" for males, 2.5" for females. Compare this, for example, with the adult population in China where the median height for males and females is 65.8" and 61.3", respectively, with a standard deviation of 2.9" and 2.8". If interested, you can find many websites for simple national comparisons such as https://tall.life/height-percentile-calculator-age-country/

While it is relatively easy to understand the application of anthropometric data to the design of constrained environments like buildings and car interiors or to the layout of workstations and office furniture in free space, the capturing and measurement of physical qualities among populations also covers properties such as grip strength, wrist torque, finger size, etc., and in a world of increasingly mobile technologies, the form factor and layout of suitable controls are dependent on the distribution of physical characteristics across the user population. Such a summary barely scratches the surface however. A quick examination of a classic ergonomics text such as Kroemer and Grandjean (1997) reveals that ergonomists have established data related to muscle group movements, trunk inflexion, seated posture, and range of vision among many other sources of physical variability that are deployed to provide guidance on many aspects of workspace and equipment design. Did you know, for example, that sitting down to work uses only 3% more energy consumption than lying down? Ergonomists know this and can tell you that by standing up during the day for some period you will consume 8%–10% more energy, while stooping down to choose something off a low shelf will expend even greater amounts (perhaps as much as 50%–60% more during that phase). In short, the study and interpretation of ergonomics can provide us with insight into many physical aspects of design that impact user experience.

All modern phones and touchscreens use capacitance, the slight electrical charge from a user's skin where it contacts the screen serves as input. This does not prevent angry users pressing with more force when the dialog jams or a button seems to not work, but the relatively small size of a mobile phone screen and the variability in hand and finger size we find in the population means some careful design choices need to be made when planning how to present options. Interestingly, there is considerable variability in the way people hold phones too, some using both hands, some just one, or using one thumb or one index finger or two, probably varying it as a function of activity (writing text, scrolling or swiping a screen, aiming for a precise target in the upper left or bottom right and so forth) and all this without even mentioning any possible differences based on handedness (it should not be forgotten that approximately 10% of the world is left-handed, an issue that is increasingly seen as one to be addressed for accessibility and inclusivity, see e.g., Huang, 2019).

Curiously, even though we now know a great deal about the physiology of the hand, we are a little less informed on the physical interactions people have with their mobile devices. Part of reason for this gap is the rapid rise of mobile devices (smart phones have gone from 20% market penetration to almost 80% in the US alone from 2008–2020) but the transition from full keyboard input common to devices at the turn of the century to small touch and gesture interfaces has been understudied within the UX community. In terms of basic digital literacy, we've witnessed what must be seen as a radical move to a new form of physical interaction across the globe. To the extent that our modern form of handwriting is primarily thumb or index finger-based, it is not unreasonable to ask what impacts on textual and graphical communication will follow? We can perhaps begin to appreciate this when trying to decipher the emoji and acronym laden forms of text sent by anyone aged under 30 to the rest of us, a form of writing that Wired magazine called the first language born of the digital world (Pardes, 2018), and one tightly coupled to the single finger keypress form of handheld technology.

Attempting to summarize what data we have on physical interactions with handheld smart phones, Hoober (2017) reports that 75% of people tend to use only one thumb to touch the screen and select options. Since more than 50% use both hands to hold their phones, this points to an interaction style that seems to treat one finger as a stylus or input device. Since the thumb has a fixed range of motion, he reports that people are most comfortable touching the middle part of a screen, the "thumb zone" as it is often called, rather than the edges which is interesting since most menu options or selectable commands are placed somewhere other than the screen center. Obviously, this has implications not just for design of displays but also size of targets as the human hand can point more accurately at the center, selections at the edges need to be larger, a variant of Fitts Law (described below) which tells us that time it takes a person to touch a target is essentially a function of distance to the target and the target size.

Surprisingly, Hoober reports no real differences between age or gender in his general physical usage tendencies but one has to wonder if this is simply because we have not studied these variables sufficiently. When I informally observe the most complicated physical device interactions (think of handheld gaming control with multiple buttons, levers, and combinatorial actions) and then try to use these as a novice, I am cognizant of reports from users of the hours of practice required to develop the co-ordination necessary to interact effectively, which my fumbling initial attempts invariably confirm. The learning curve is acceptable in gaming contexts where the challenge to improve is part of the total engagement with the game, but it would be a market-shrinker for any modern consumer device like a smart phone to require such learning from users. Do we really imagine age has no impact here? There is a strong negative correlation between gamers and age (according to a Statista survey in 2021, 58% of gamers are under 34 years of age, only 7% are over 65, though gaming industry insiders sometimes offer alternative numbers to bolster their arguments of growing use among older people). I suspect the complex physical skills required to use many contemporary gaming handsets is a deterrent to older learners whose reaction times and physical co-ordination are generally slower. As always, task and context matter, and it will be interesting to see if today's gamers maintain their interest and usage level as they age. Speculation aside, it is clear that even for routine popular devices where the basic form of interaction is stripped down to single finger pointing and clicking, with an occasional swipe, there are significant design decisions to consider that cannot be simply resolved by looking up a handbook.

Beyond the Handheld

Handheld devices certainly characterize our era (can you remember the last time you were at a concert or public gathering where people did not pull out their phones to record some of the event or text someone?) but we are physical users in myriad ways. Our smartphones produce sound as well as video, so people often sport headphones of various kinds as they move about the world enabling private listening (though sadly, not always private conversations). In combination, a screen, microphone, and earbuds with cellular connectivity can provide people with a portable information environment that is not constrained by physical space. Our information technologies come with us or are augmented in cars where the coupling between the person and the device needs to be carefully considered in physical terms to ensure comfort, performance, and safety. In fact, the rise of mobile technologies that interface with our vehicle environments has only increased our need to understand the physical ergonomics of design, bringing a very traditional area of the human factors discipline into the forefront of contemporary user experience design. Car interiors are constrained, the primary user is seated and belted in, a significant part of their visual field must be left free to observe the road, so interface layout becomes crucial. While it is common for most of us to imagine office workstations when we hear about ergonomics, it is the driving environment, with its increasing connectivity to communications and data on the move which represents some of the most cutting-edge work in the physical design of user experience (see e.g., Ebel et al., 2021).

Increasingly, the design of wearable and portable devices reminds us that even in information space, we are physical creatures, and while we can anticipate ongoing improvements in speech-based interfaces, augmented spectacles, and sensor-enabled wearables, the human body will remain a constant, providing constraints on how we reach, touch, carry, move and ultimately interact with any new forms of information technology. Ensuring a good physical connection is no assurance of usability or acceptance but many designs will fail if they do not take appropriate account of how we are put together, so to speak, as physical creatures when we couple with designed items.

But thinking of the user as a human body in isolation is not the goal. As more information technologies are embedded into the world around us, we can anticipate the emergence of hybrid physical-digital environments, not just the much touted "internet of things" which captures data from our actions or allows integration and updating of services, but truly mixed spaces where our homes and immediate environments around us are digitally enhanced to tailor information experiences in a seamless and dynamic form. Here, the hardware of interaction will move beyond keyboards to built spaces, relying on a network of sensors to process virtual touch, gesture, voice, and movement. It is impossible to conceive of meeting such design challenges without a deep understanding and analysis of how we physically exist and move in such locations. Tactile and tangible interfaces will likely be part of many objects in our homes, cars, built spaces and perhaps our clothes. Some will be passive but it is not difficult to imagine our needing to touch, push, swipe, or physically signal through far more connection points than are presented via our phones or laptop computers. This has long been an interest of UX professionals but we are still not there yet. A Gartner technical report in 2010 (Gartner Research, 2010) suggested such interfaces would become commonplace within a decade but this has proved to be optimistic (as is true of most predictions of technical revolutions) but the goal remains. In this sense, the ergonomic understanding of humans as users, while one of the oldest aspects of the UX discipline, requires fresh attention from researchers and designers.

Obviously, some of this work can leverage our well-established models of human anthropometry, but it is also the case that the emerging information spaces will need to revisit the psychophysiological level of human behavior to better understand how our nature as sensing and perceiving beings, in concert with our physical bodies, allows us to interact seemingly effortlessly with our world. Design history points to mobile technology as a break from workstations, encouraging UX researchers and developers to think again about how we conceive of information tools and their use, but it can be argued that mobile, as we have understood it so far, is but an intervening step on the path to hybrid physical-digital environments that we will all inhabit in the coming years. Our physical form is not subject to near-term change but our occupied spaces undoubtedly are, meaning physical ergonomics will be more important than ever in the design of user experiences.

The Physical Continuum

Of course, ergonomic analysis does not stop at the body, just as calling humans "physical beings" does not limit us only to considerations of form factor, size, fit, and layout when conceiving of user experience. Our bodies might be thought of primarily as muscle and bone but they contain a wonderful, complicated network of neural activity that enables us to affect movement, to reach, touch and manipulate our bodies into active engagement with the world. Our nervous system is physical, almost 45 miles of it is packed into our frames (or more according to some estimates, it's not exactly simple to measure!) transmitting signals at rates greater than 100 m per second. It enables our inner psychological experience, reports the results of our physical actions through feedback and certainly lets us know when something is going wrong or our body is experiencing threat or damage by carrying rapid signals that we perceive as pain. We tend to refer to this level of activity as "psychophysiology" in the scholarly literature, a nod to the continuum of experience that exists where the physical and psychological meet.

The boundaries of where the body and mind connect are contested within theoretical social and medical science but are intuitively obvious to us as self-aware beings. For most of us, our bodies and mind work seamlessly together, allowing us to walk and talk (or perhaps to even chew gum) at the same time, to touch objects that we reach for, avoid immovable objects in our path, tie our laces, bring cups to our lips and so forth. In fact, until we experience an error, or our bodies and the world fail to connect in the way we expect, such as losing our balance or finding ourselves tensed up from poor posture, we rarely notice how closely coupled our physical form is to the world around us and how easily we engage in a continual cycle of interactions with it through the apparently simple exercise of will. However, when we reach for an object and it eludes our touch because we misjudged the distance, or when we drop a ball that is tossed our way, we recognize, at least momentarily, that our bodies and minds need to co-exist in a seamless fashion if we seek a safe and comfortable existence.

Part of the challenge of ergonomic design is to create use environments where we take advantage of out natural psychophysiological processing while limiting the chances of our experiencing discomfort or error. Office workstations have been a sort of paradigm case for ergonomists since the 1970s and this serves as a good example of how the physical and the psychological are largely inseparable for user experience design. The classic statistical tables of population physiology certainly provide guidance on optimal seat heights, desk to floor distance, wrist angle for comfortable keyboarding, and many basic physical parameters of the workspace, including lighting and sound levels, but it's impossible to think of these attributes without invoking more psychological properties also. Workstations have screens so viewing distance and angle, while physical measuresimpact perceptual phenomena, which in turn evoke cognitive processes. Input devices such as the mouse or keyboard are certainly touchpoints, physical objects located in space that users engage with in a tactile manner, but typing is a learned skill for many, mouse movements require a recognition and calibration of physical movements with viewable screen responses, easy once understood but still subject to the perceptual and cognitive processes of users, not just their physical actions. Once again, we are reminded that as humans, our information experience exists at and involves multiple levels.

Seen in this light, it makes little sense to think of ergonomics as purely a concern with physical design, we humans are simply not constructed in the way the time sliced model of social science research has presented us. Rather, we are a multi-layered, living creatures with a bodily form that contains billions of neural connections allowing us to engage with the world through sense organs that respond to light, sound, force, and chemicals. A body without a mind cannot make direct use of any design, so just trying to imagine user experience as a physical process makes little sense. But the corollary of this is also true. Being sentient is insufficient to affect use, in most cases. Even the recent "camera switch" feature built into recent Android phones (see e.g., Panchwagh, 2021) that improves accessibility by enabling users to control basic functions with facial gestures such as raised eyebrows or glances to the side, requires a physical means of engaging with interfaces, in this case facial gestures captured by camera, hence the necessity of addressing physical ergonomics of any interactive product.

I make this point repeatedly to students in my class but it really helps to experience this connection between physical acts and control, and it's easy enough to try this for yourself. Take a large book and place it within reach on a nearby surface, like a table. Your task then is to touch the book by simply reaching out and placing a finger anywhere on it. Of course, you, like most people, can do this quickly. Now let us require a little more precision. Try to touch the book only in a specific place e.g., the last word of the title. Even now, in your mind, you probably can envisage these two "touching" tasks representing slightly different experiences. The precision required in the second task involves a significantly greater degree of co-ordination between your hand and your eyes than the first, and this difference manifests itself not only in what we might term a cognitive demand for attention (it would be far easier to perform the first task, touching an open book, while scanning the room around you than it would the second task, where your eyes must be engaged to hit the target placement) but it also carries a time cost. Invariably the single word target (or if you really want a challenge, pick a target letter within the title) takes noticeably longer time than the whole book target. This is common sense really (though perhaps not as common as we might hope, given some designs that exist) but the scientific study of people has elevated this task to a level of understanding that we even have a mathematical model for the parameters that govern the movement time for most people.

Fitts' Law, so-called as it was proposed by psychologist Paul Fitts in 1954, is expressed mathematically as:

$$T(\textit{time taken to point}) = a + b \; log_z(2 \; D/W).$$

In this formula, D is the distance your finger must travel, W is the width of the target in the direction traveled, with *a* and *b* serving as estimates, if needed, of the time taken to initiate/stop movement, and the difficulty involved. These *a* and *b* values, or coefficients to be technically correct, are usually important only where direct observation in tests shows that they add observably to the task, perhaps if the input device has a built-in lag or the user is challenged to recognize or locate the cursor or mouse before moving it to the target. Similarly, some people use (1+ D/W) rather than (2 D/W) in their derivations but the difference is more theoretical than practically important. In some ways, this is a case study of the transfer of science to design, a precise calculable law of human behaviour with pracrtical implications Most designers understand it, but the precision it elicits is often deemed unnecessary, which can be a mistake. As we know from the science base around this law, the improved speed in hitting the target tails off quickly after a certain point. In other words, just increasing the size of a target might be quite impactful when the original target is small and therefore requires a high degree of precision and conscious processing on the part of the user to touch it, but it will have less impact, and even perhaps negatively affect other aspects of a design, once an optimal target size is exceeded (so you can now tell people that science has shown indisputably that bigger is not always better).

Similarly, the more recently developed Steering Law (Ascot and Zhai, 1997) reflects the speed with which users can steer a pointer along a constrained path as a function of path width (think of those stepped or "walking" menu designs where you selected one option from a drop down menu which then reveals a sub-menu of optionsas shown in Figure 5.2).

Each menu option has a selectable area in which the cursor activates the option's sub-menu and the user "steps" across the options to make a final selection at the lowest level. The width of this selection area is important. The Steering Law suggests the speed with which users can accurately move among menus to choose a final target is related to the path width and distance the cursor must travel. Again, it's apparently obvious that this

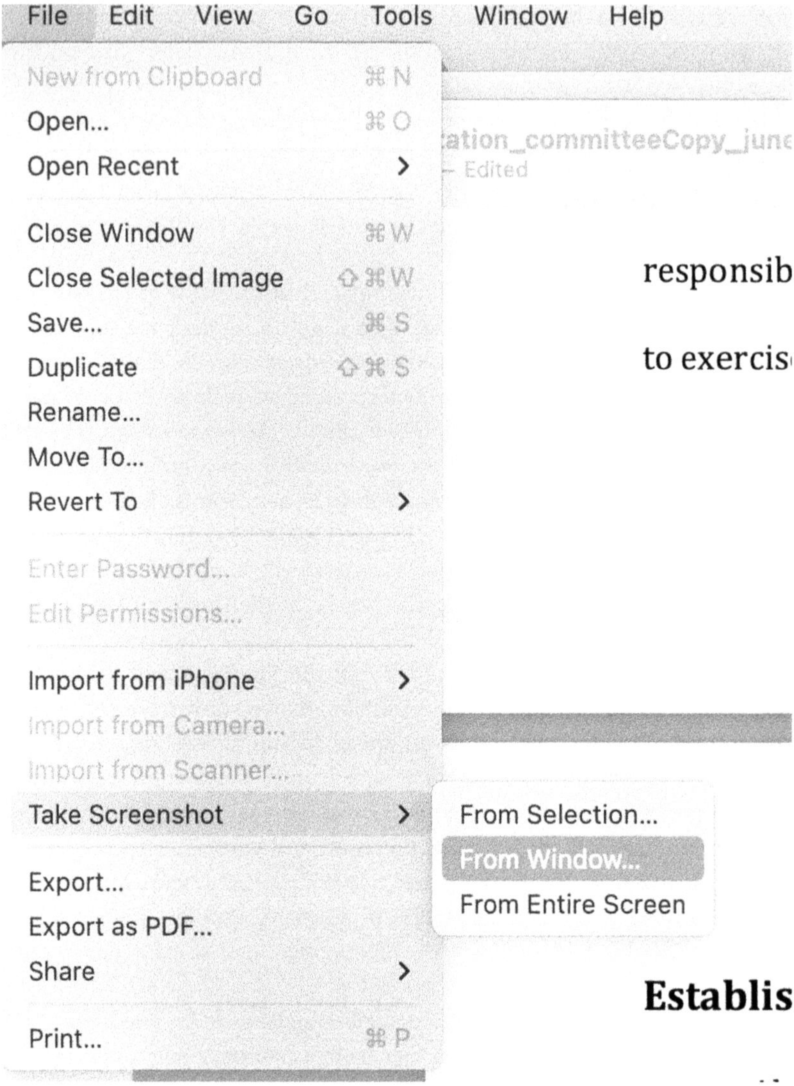

Figure 5.2 Example of stepped or walking menu

width will impact the user's performance. An overly narrow area can make the selection of a menu option difficult for some users who might move the cursor outside of the selection window and thus have to retrace their path, but after increasing the area it to a certain point, greater width disrupts the visual design and can cost users more time in order to move greater distances required for some targets. Yes, it too is common-sense when you think about it, but then empirical findings in interaction design often take on the appearance of common sense after the fact, rarely before when they compete with several other plausible claims about what is important for users. Further still, as with Fitts' Law, there is more than mere common sense on offer, the Steering Law actually enables us to estimate reliably and in advance, the actual impact of menu design choices on user performance.

Such laws provide useful examples of how scientific models can yield tools that move design decisions beyond the application of judgement. As Newell and Card (1985) argued, a set of such models or appropriate laws of interaction would allow for appropriate calculations of the time costs associated with multiple design choices. Imagine the benefits of being able to do this for a set of design alternatives without having to build prototypes to test on real users? The designer could model various scenarios and use the tools to determine which interface would result in the fastest use. This is still a goal for some researchers, but I would note that while we have generated many empirical findings on the user response to various interface configurations, we have identified relatively few such laws that we can apply for most decisions. In fairness to Newell and Card, they no doubt would justifiably counter that they have generated a task analytic approach that will allow for calculational power using widely agreed speed parameters for many human cognitive acts (as we will discuss later) but this whole approach is tied very much to generating estimates of task speed, a useful but not always vital criterion for assessing the quality of the user experience, especially in non-work related information activities. While we are therefore still someway off from a formal science of design as some would like, I believe the more important lesson here is that common sense is rarely a reliable basis for design decisions.

More importantly, the amount of evidence we have accumulated in ergonomics and human factors research also reminds us continually that users are physical beings with perceptual and cognitive capabilities. We are not immune to the material world but operate within it, subject to a range of abilities and constraints that our bodies afford us. Any interface we design cannot escape the situated and embedded nature of our existence in the experiential domain where physical and mental coincide. Yes, our bodies, sized within recognized population parameters, are directly involved in use since we reside in a three-dimensional physical environment, using our hands to move cursors and land on targets, pushing a button to select an item, but to discriminate a target from a background requires perception, to stop and start a movement precisely takes control, and to even understand the norms of targets and their labels involves complex cognitive processes invariably combining linguistic experience and learned responses. Yes, even in Fitts' Law we invariably find the other layers of our minds engaged.

So our physical form, much like the ship of Theseus, is constantly undergoing repair and replacement of parts, and maybe the first fingers you ever swiped on a screen are not the same fingers that hold this book, but they are still recognizably yours. The real parallel however is not the renewal of our form but the sense that the form, as with the ship, is not just the sum of physical parts but the quality of experience a ship, or a body, enables. The ship of Theseus is so called because of the adventures, the journey, the passage of time it has provided to its owner, properties that cannot be reduced to timber and planks. Yet the timber and the planks are essential; no planks, no ship. And so it is with physical aspects of user experience. We will not design user-centered technology without addressing the physical layer, but the body alone cannot determine the full quality of the experiences we wish to support.

References

Ascot, J., and Zhai, S. (1997). Beyond Fitts' Law: Models for trajectory-based HCI tasks. CHI'97: Proceedings of the ACM SIGCHI Conference on Human Factors in Computing Systems, pp. 295–302. New York: ACM Press.

Ebel, P., Orlovska, J., Hünemeyer, S., Wickman, C., Vogelsang, A., and Söderberg, R. (2021). Automotive UX design and data-driven development: Narrowing the gap to support practitioners. *Transportation Research Interdisciplinary Perspectives*, *11*, 100455, 10.1016/j.trip.2021.100455

Gartner Research. Hype Cycle for Emerging Technologies, 2010. Aug. 2, 2010. https://www.gartner.com/en/documents/1414917/hype-cycle-for-emerging-technologies-2010

Hoober, S. (2017, March 6). Design for Fingers, Touch, and People, part 1. Mobile Matters. https://www.uxmatters.com/archives/2017/03/design-for-fingers-touch-and-people-part-1.php

Huang, J. (2019). Discover hidden UX flaws with the opposite handed UX test. *UX Planet*, downloaded 6/21/22. https://uxplanet.org/discover-ux-flaws-with-the-opposite-handed-ux-test-e2543223d4a3

Kroemer, K., and Grandjean, E. (1997). *Fitting the Task to the Human: A Textbook of Occupational Ergonomics*, 5th ed. Bristol PA: Taylor and Francis.

Newell, A., and Card, S. (1985). *The Prospects for Psychological Science in Human-Computer Interaction Human-Computer Interaction*, *1*, 209–242.

Panchwagh, P. (2021). How to control the Android phone your face gestures. *MakeUseOf*, Nov 30th, 2021. https://www.makeuseof.com/how-to-control-android-with-facial-gestures/ downloaded 6/22/22

Pardes, A. (2018). The wired guide to emojis, culture, Feb 1 2018, https://www.wired.com/story/guide-emoji/, downloaded, 6/21/22

Statista (2021). Distribution of video gamers in the United States in 2021, by age group. https://www.statista.com/statistics/189582/age-of-us-video-game-players/

Taylor, K. (2019). Apple's new iPhones have a sexist design flaw. *Insider Magazine*. https://www.businessinsider.com/apples-iphones-are-too-big-for-many-women-including-me-2019-6

Williams, B. (2021, July 8th). The Ship of Theseus Thought Experiment. The Collector. https://www.thecollector.com/the-ship-of-theseus/

Wolpaw, J.R., Millán, J.D.R., and Ramsey, N.F. (2020). Brain-computer interfaces: Definitions and principles. *Handbook of Clinical Neurology*, *168*, 15–23. 10.1016/B978-0-444-63934-9.00002-0. PMID: 32164849.

The Cogito-Tech Layer 6

Users as Cognitive Beings

As we extend our exploration of use beyond the analysis of our physical engagement with technology, we enter an area of research interest that concerns itself with how people perform tasks, how interface variables influence decision making, navigation, error recovery, and goal completion. The research on these topics tends to lean heavily into perceptual and cognitive theories of the human mind and behavior to understand what people are doing and how we can shape their interactive experience to enhance ease of use and satisfaction.

This academic literature on human perception and cognition is not only extensive, it is extremely dense, with a level of detail and measurement that can be baffling to outsiders. Since we are dealing with internal mechanisms that cannot be directly observed, it often seems incredible that we can reliably discriminate mental processes that are of millisecond durations, yet decades of experimental work, blending clever research procedures and increasingly sophisticated measurement techniques, have yielded an impressive and consistent set of findings about the human mind.

Many books have been written on how we think but we should recognize at the outset that the top scholarly works on cognitive psychology read quite differently from the best sellers you might find on Amazon or hear about on a talk show. This is hardly surprising since the readerships are quite different. Psychology as a science is taught formally at university level and a book such as Eysenck and Keane's (2020) *Cognitive Psychology* will contain far more detail, and adopt a more rational tone on claims about humans, while probably selling far fewer copies than, for example, Fields' (2016) *Understanding the Human Mind*. In fact, the existence of so many popular distillations of scientific

DOI: 10.4324/9781003026112-6

psychology into mainstream books for non-technical readers is testimony both the insatiable curiosity people have for examinations of our inner mental workings and the ever-growing body of research we generate on this topic.

Obviously, new findings require us to adjust our theories and models, but outside of the specialist literature, there seems to be a good deal of consensus on how we understand ourselves as cognitive beings. While they are not the same, we do need to acknowledge the basis of mental experience is the human brain. Consisting of some 80 billion neurons (give or take a few billion) and an equal number of non-neural cells, the human brain consists of three basic areas: the cerebrum (to the fore); the brainstem (midbrain); and the cerebellum (the hindbrain). Weighing about 3 lbs and made up a lot of fats and water, the actual physical structure is fascinating but not quite where the action, so to speak, is for design purposes. While science has established particular areas of the brain that are most associated with certain activities (e.g., the parietal lobe, the middle part of the cerebrum is directly involved in the recognition of spatial relationships, while the occipital lobe toward the back is involved in vision), there is deep interconnectedness in the physiology of the brain which means that while the cerebrum seems to control movement, the cerebellum is involved in balance, both of which are important for mobility).

The study of the human mind, for the most part, however, does not rest on a physiological level of analysis. Cognitive psychologists are interested primarily in higher level mental functions such as language, perception, memory and learning. In so doing, they have created a theoretical framing that refers to experiences and activities that are not explained or tied directly to neural or physiological functions. Clearly the two are related and recent developments in imaging technology have offered us glimpses of neural involvement and correlates in mental experience but for the most part, cognition is conceived of using terms, structures and processes that do not directly map to the physiology of the brain.

Fundamentally, psychology posits of view of our mental life as a form of information processing, with our minds serving as both a filter and storer of the sensory stimulation we continually receive from the light, sound, physical, and chemical data that impinge on us in the world. We can capture the essential cognitive view of human psychology using a variant of Ulrich Neisser's (1976) classic representation of the human perceptual and cognitive system being engaged in an ongoing cycle of interaction with the world (see Figure 6.1). One can enter this cycle at any point but it makes intuitive sense to enter the cycle at the top, what Neisser calls the object, or rather the available information that is presented to our senses. The world

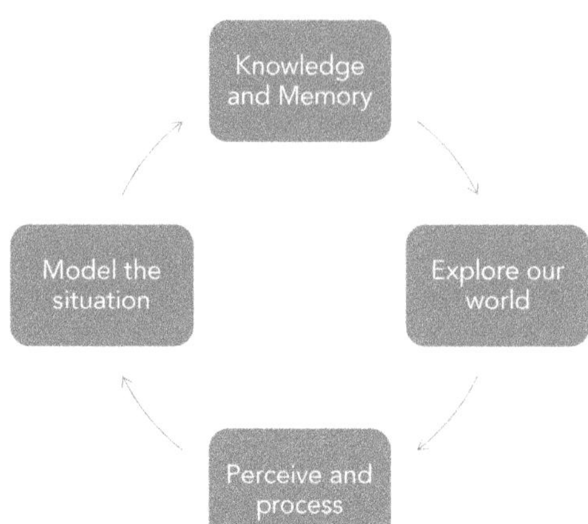

Figure 6.1 Perceptual cycle based on active exploration, sampling, and modeling our world

bombards us with data and we meet this with an interpretive framework, which is termed here "schema" and can be thought of as our current understanding of what is happening in the world around us. This interpretation is, of course, personal and selective, and it governs how we engage with the world and how we understand the data we are receiving. But the process of being in the world, and the point Neisser wishes to highlight is that human psychology is *active*. As our current schema or interpretive framework accommodates incoming data, it can cause us to explore the world around us to sample new data and to continue this cycle of input, processing, and action.

Clearly, this is a very simple representation but it conveys some essential characteristics of human psychology as framed within the scholarly literature and I use it routinely to introduce basic cognitive principles to those who have not been exposed to such work before. We are not creatures that ingest an undiluted signal from the world and file it away. Rather, we are continually engaged in sampling from the available data and interpreting this input stream to guide our actions. Second, we do not perceive the world objectively as is, with only one truth to be deduced from the available data in our environments. Rather, we interpret the world's signals according to our frames of reference, our knowledge structures (or schema, to use the technical term of cognitive science) that enable us to contextualize and connect the incoming data to our existing understanding. If the inputs leave us with questions, we can adjust our perception to increase or reduce attention to particular information as we explore the world around us (a process that might be far less active in routine instances than that verb might suggest).

The elegance of Neisser's representation is that it makes little direct claim about the inner workings of our cognitive system, and certainly has no direct tie to brain physiology, but it conveys a wealth of insight about some fundamental truths. Most importantly, it highlights the role of existing knowledge on how we see the world in any given moment, acknowledging that people have a personal framework, built up over time from their continuing engagement with the world and that real-time conditions shape our responses but not in an entirely predictable way. For example, if I am driving a car, the perceptual cycle conveys the idea that I have knowledge of the act of driving and the rules of the road, both required knowledge structures for this act, that I am applying while I continually update my awareness of where I am, what's around me, and how I can safely proceed. If I am unsure what's behind me, I can explore the world with a glance in my rear-view or side mirrors and update my mental representation of my current surroundings as I drive. Other cars and their movements serve as objects of available information, and my behavior adjusts to the environment through the application of my schema for driving.

The suggestion that we perceive the world through our schema or knowledge structures highlights how individual people might interpret similar data points differently. By cueing the mind to receive certain types of data, two people in the same situation but with different schema might both hear the same utterance but interpret its meaning quite differently. Since hearing is an active process, the sound signal imposing on the ears is decoded and interpreted according to the perceivers' knowledge. Classic studies of schema also show that the expectation of certain kinds of data being present in a context increase the likelihood of you reporting that you saw it, even when not there. In one study, Brewer and Treyens (1981) had participants wait in an office space for a short period in preparation for meeting someone, then being asked to recall later what they remember seeing in the office. Not only did people accurately recall objects one expects to see in an office such as a chair and desk, almost a third claimed to have seen books, even though there were none present in office used in this experiment. Interestingly, only a third of participants correctly reported seeing some unusual objects that actually were present, such as a skull. What this tells us is that data or "available information" from the world is not simply input to the cognitive system and then filtered out, leaving us all with a reduced but otherwise accurate representation of the world, but that non-available information (in this case, books) can also be incorporated into our representation of the current environment purely based on our expectations and activated schema. As such work confirms, our minds can influence what we think we "see" or "hear" in the world around us.

I find it useful to have new designers consider the process of human-computer interaction within this perceptual cycle framework. Here, the object is the interface or information display, the user's cognitive state is represented by the schema, and input devices or controls can enable exploration. Now, as a user manipulates the controls, the information on display alters, which the user perceives and interprets in accordance with their goals. The rapid cycles of interaction underlying any task can clearly be envisaged, and the interconnected nature of our physical form with our cognitive processing enacting changes through the user interface to the information world can begin to be appreciated. Just thinking through the cycle in this way can be insightful and help us to recognize that many users might not interpret the interaction in the way the design team intended, a very useful first step on the road to user-centeredness.

Of course, the processes underlying the perceptual cycle are more complex than is summarized in this model, and researchers within UX have favored many other ways of trying to convey more detail in their descriptions of user actions. Card et al. (1983) proposed the ultimate formal model of human-computer interaction that attempted to capture the fundamental cognitive, perceptual, and psychomotor steps that must be taken by any user to complete a typical task. Employing time estimates derived from the experimental literature on human performance they represented the user as a screen reading, mouse moving, keyboard operator whose world typically consists of routine task sequences built up from base actions, such as entering a keystroke, (estimated to take 0.23 s), moving your hand to the mouse (an act that takes approximately 0.36 s), and so forth. In other words, where Neisser conveys the idea of our being in a world that is made of information we explore and interpret continually, Card et al represented our inner life as a series of routine, often automated tasks which can be analyzed and divided into a series of basic acts, each of which incurs a small time cost to complete.

Far more detailed than Neisser, this model human processor represents even now perhaps the most specific representation of user activity in terms of internal processes, and while it has demonstrated power to predict routine performance times on well-practiced tasks quite well (e.g., saving a file, or selecting items on a menu) its emphasis on metrics and routine, automated, expert performance made it less practical for many design

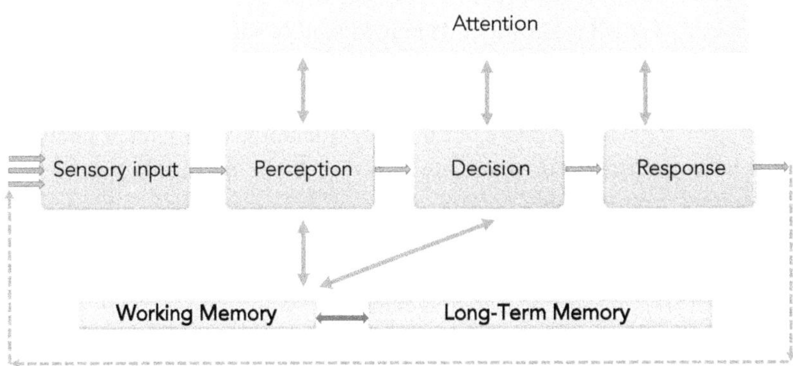

Figure 6.2 Common cognitive architecture of users

challenges. I'll say more about this in a later chapter when we examine the evaluation of usability, but question to hand is how well we can convey an understanding of human psychology to people who are not fully immersed or willing to study formally the literature from cognitive research? In other words, in the true spirit of user-centeredness, how well can psychology serve those who wish to understand enough of its science base to help them solve their own design challenges in UX.

While there are many ways we can try to synthesize what we have learned about ourselves as information processors, I find a variant of the a model proposed by Wickens et al. (2021) to be a an excellent overview of human cognition that we can use to explain the workings of the human mind to those seeking to apply psychology to the design of better user experiences (Figure 6.2).

Now it is important to acknowledge that any model of our own mind's inner workings is just that, a model, an abstraction, a useful fiction if you will. There are many theorists and experimentalists who will argue over the details, some even objecting to the idea of the mind being likened to a computational device that can be outlined in processing stages. Nevertheless, the basic information processing steps summarized in Wickens' model serve, if nothing else, both as a good summary of what we have learned about ourselves from decades of study and as an organized expression of how our mental processes function that designers can use to conceive of the impact certain interface characteristics might have on users.

Considered in general terms, the mind is conceived as a series of structures and associated processes, and it is useful to walk through the activities we imagine are occurring as humans deal with the continual input of data from the world and subsequently respond with decisions or actions. To start, let's try a small experiment. When you get to the end of this sentence, stop what you are doing and sit silently for 30 s, before reading on.

In everyday life, we take for granted there is noise around us. Sometimes it is disruptive and hard to ignore but in many situations, we are often unaware of just how much data our senses are receiving. If you managed to sit silently as suggested, you probably became aware of the sounds that your ears are continually receiving, even if prior to this, you likely had not paid many of them much attention. The average "quiet" room produces about 40 db of background sound, most of which we filter out. You become aware of these when consciously sitting quietly and listening, but in normal life this kind of sonic data is always present but not actually perceived by most of us. Why? The answer lies in our perceptual and cognitive processing. At any one moment of time we are on the receiving end of a rich data stream from the external world, most of which is of little interest to us. Some of this data will be below our threshold level of perception (conveniently scaled as being 0 db but sound perception is related to pitch and frequency, among other variables, so it's not as simple as just considering the decibel level, see e.g., Oxenham, 2018). As the quiet sitting exercise reveals, above threshold level there are continual sounds that generally we pay little attention. Cognitive psychologists believe we have a very short-term sensory store where data, which has the potential for stimulating our system is buffered, but unless we focus on it, the stimulus will fade within 150 ms or so, to be replaced or overwritten by the next sample of data in a continuous flow of input from the world.

It's worth noting that what we are describing as sensory input is not restricted to sound. If you did this little experiment in sitting silently, did you become aware of any other signals impinging on your consciousness? Perhaps you realized you were not sitting comfortably when the sensation of pressure from your legs or back became noticeable. Or maybe you noticed that your elbow was sending a signal that your arm was pressing too heavily on the chair, that your breathing was perhaps too shallow, or that you were thirsty, the light was a little low, the room was too warm, and so forth. All of these data points were already there in the world, available for your consideration, but you had mostly filtered them out while you were focused on reading, listening, or viewing, etc. This is the normal state of our psychological existence: more data is available than we typically can process at any one time. We sample and select from the data impinging on our senses, as Neisser explained. Some of the data is one-off (a temporary noise, a fleeting image and so forth) while some is continual (e.g., ongoing background sounds from the air conditioning or outside traffic).

Extending the Moment: The Role of Working Memory

If we do attend to a stimulus, we effectively register and extend its existence in our minds, at least for as long as we consider it. At this point, it is thought the data is the focus of conscious attention, and enters what we refer to as our working or short-term memory store (since "short-term" is used in reference to the sensory store and memory in a way that sometimes confuses casual readers, I'll use working memory here to refer to this particular processing stage). Now there are some interesting aspects of working memory that are worth considering for design. To get into our working memory, a stimulus must have reached a threshold level of perception and be deemed relevant enough for us to consider further (or impossible to ignore). There are various reasons why this might occur. Most of the time, the stimulus would be sufficiently strong, or unique, to make it stand out from other components of the data stream impinging on us. One can imagine how this would be useful for survival, it is important that we notice dangerous situations and if a loud signal or some noise that suggests threat (e.g., a breaking twig behind us in forest) occurs unexpectedly then it helps that we react. Sometimes the signal reflects a sought after or desired part of the data stream e.g., being in a room full of people and actively trying to find your partner by scanning faces and listening to voices. You tune out (discard) some of the data while searching for the image or sound that will match your target. After the fact, you will have seen many faces and heard many voices that you probably cannot remember (which you might describe as 'not noticing') as you gave them limited consideration in your search for your target.

Working memory is thought of as a limited capacity space that contains our current conscious thoughts. The classical approach to studying this capacity is the digit span test where people listen to a list of random numbers and then try to repeat them back. While there are individual differences, most people remember 5–7 items under these conditions, with a performance bias towards the first and last numbers in the list, a finding that has given rise the popular claim that our memory is limited to 7+/−2 chunks before we are overwhelmed. A couple of important aspects of this, unrelated to the exact number (which cumulative research suggests is more likely toward 5 as a general capacity rather than 7 anyway) are the bias effects for primacy and latency and the concept of chunking.

Since we tend to remember the first items in the list better than some of the later items (primacy), but also remember the very last items better than those in the middle (latency) this bias is taken as support for the idea that our processing is initiated by the new (we allocate attention to the new data and our capacity starts to diminish as we add more signals), and that once our capacity limit is reached, we "free up" space by replacing the last item added. This type of framing fits well with the sense that humans are designed to notice the new (the initial stimuli) which serve to anchor our sense of attention and activate our schema, then to allocate the remaining capacity we have to maintain focus until the activity ends (assuming of course that the activity is meaningful to us and warrants our continual attention). In the digit span test, the first few numbers tend to be easily added as we have ample capacity but once we have added six or seven numbers and the stimuli keep coming, we start to run out of room, so to speak, and thus replace say, the seventh occuring digit with the eighth, which itself might get replaced by the ninth in the list and so on. After 10 digits are presented to us for recall, we show better accuracy for the first few (primacy) and the last (latency) than we do for those in the middle, a phenomenon that seems pretty standard for most people tested.

The second important quality of working memory is our ability to "chunk" or group some data together meaningfully. Incoming signals activate our abilities to group and organize new material based on our experience, memories, and knowledge of previous data occurrences. Over time, we develop a sense of the patterns of stimuli from our world, and these regularities allow us to categorize and associate certain inputs with particular behaviors ior occurences. As we group, we abstract meanings from the data stream and use less of our resources to handle the familiar. For our working memory, this can mean that some data streams do not so quickly overload our working memory as the task of remembering random numbers might. If for example, the incoming numbers formed a meaningful pattern for you, say for example your 10-digit telephone number, you would have few difficulties repeating that stream back without error; no latency or recency bias, no apparent capacity limitation operating here. How is this possible? As you might surmise, your telephone number is not a random stream to you but a meaningful sequence that you have committed over time to long-term memory, and which usually can be called upon as needed. We think of this as a single chunk, triggered by the thought of "my telephone number," and as such it might only take up a small part, perhaps just one slot of your working memory, freeing you to remember quite a few more random digits if tested.

In fact, some recent evidence suggests the 7+/−2 capacity rule might need to be reconsidered as we know that people who train themselves can at least temporarily exceed the normal range of short-term memory, and they seem to do this by imposing patterns wherever possible on the data stream coming at them, or applying mental imagery for extra cues, so that instead of hearing 20 random numbers, they see calendar dates, mathematical patterns, sport statistics, or other personally meaningful connections between the individual digits so that they can better recall the data stream when it stops. Additional cues from the environment also can be exploited by our memory system, so if the items that tend to be missed on recall (those middle digits that were replaced by the later signals) have extra signal strength added (e.g., the spoken list gets noticeably louder or pronounced differently for these items than other numbers) then the recall of these numbers also tends to be improved.

Of course, what makes some data "chunkable" is highly personal and involves the application of our knowledge that we think of as stored in long-term memory. We have an apparently infinite capacity for storing meaningful memories, so while our short-term perceptions are continually changing, the data we consider important generally gets extracted into a form we can remember, that is, it eventually finds its way to long-term memory. This is the source of our schema and frameworks for interpreting what is happening in the world. We use these knowledge stores to help us interpret the incoming data stream, determining what's relevant, how it fits with what we know, and most elegantly, guiding our actions appropriately to handle the constantly changing environmental conditions that would otherwise overload our working memory capacity.

Organizing the World: The Role of Long-Term Memory

The expression "long-term" is a bit of a catch-all, it can refer to material we remember for a few minutes or a lifetime. You need to maintain memory for some tasks for longer than your working memory can handle it if you are to exist in the world but that information might not be worth you remembering tomorrow once a task is completed and can be safely forgotten. Memories of childhood might be very meaningful and stay with a person for their lifetime. Psychologists tend to consider human long-term memory as having practically infinite capacity, but as the old joke goes, we have no problem adding new memories even when we age, it's just recalling them when required that becomes the problem.

Long-term memories are thought of as taking several forms: semantic (knowledge of facts and concepts), episodic (experienced events), procedural (knowing how to do something) and emotional (associated feelings with stimuli or events). For most studies of human learning, which relies on long-term memory, the distinction between knowing "what" and knowing "how" is considered particularly meaningful as it highlights the range of knowledge structures a typical human develops. Learning algebra, for example, involves acquiring a set of declarative rules about logic, numbers and relationships. These can be expressed verbally (which is not the same as saying they are expressed clearly, as generations of students can attest). Learning to ride a bicycle is a form of procedural knowledge that resides in long-term memory, but you probably did not learn to do that by reading a book or having someone describe how to do it (though parents often try to do precisely this).

In grasping the essentials of human psychology, the main point of this framework is that we can usefully envisage humans as processing information in two directions: stimuli coming at us from the world, and interpretive frameworks for handling the stream being applied from within us. The meeting of these two processes can be thought of as creating our mental model of the current situation, or focus of attention. At any one time, we all have mental sense of our own cognition, what we are thinking about, trying to do, what we are seeing and feeling, and this sense is dynamic, continually updating as new inputs and new thoughts emerge from the interplay of our incoming data and activated knowledge structures. We can certainly appreciate this when we think about humans interacting with computers. Two users, each with different life experiences and training, will view the interface through the lens of their own understanding, each possessing a mental model of how the technology works and what is required to achieve a task. The design challenge can be thought of as trying to create a useful mental model for most users by carefully choosing terms, action sequences, and feedback signals that will exploit people's existing knowledge to render the process of use smooth and easy for people to understand.

It is clear we are not all-sensing beings, rather we filter the world through our senses, both by the natural limits of our range of awareness and the choices we make, consciously and otherwise, to focus and give attention to only a sample of the stimuli around us. We can appreciate this when recognizing how we adjust to a constant low-level noise in the background, often filtering such signals out of our awareness until such time as they cease, e.g., realizing the air conditioning was on only when it reaches an off-cycle. Low level, steady-state stimuli are eventually ignored as humans seem wired to perceive change, not constants. Again, the survival value of this characteristic seems obvious.

A core attribute of our perception and cognition then seems to be how we allocate our attention. We speak of something "capturing" our attention, and when this happens, we understand that this data or signal is in our working memory. Here it can remain part of our consciousness for longer than its initial occurrence as we start to characterize it, label it or consider it in terms of our current knowledge of the world. This activity is what we consider attention-intensive and represents one of the characteristic qualities of our cognitive architecture. Attention, the specific ability to actively process and focus on particular stimuli, is a powerful component of our conscious mental life, but it is a limited resource. A good deal of research has tried to estimate the capacity humans have to keep information in focus, and there is general acceptance that our ability to process new signals and data is subject to constraints and capacity limitations that are easily observed.

Even the language we use to describe attention speaks to this quality. Not only is attention "captured" but we "pay" attention, "selectively" attend, or ask others to "give" us their attention. It is a resource that costs, can be captured, divided and given or taken. Such language reflects our own awareness that attention is a precious resource, and without it, information from the world can fade from our sensory stores and be lost. Attention capture can also be irritating to us when it distracts and takes us off task, such as someone touching us to get our attention while we are trying to do something, or a pop-up window containing advertising information overwrites part of the screen when we open a webpage. Such incidents disrupt our flow and force us to place attention elsewhere, often to our irritation.

In practical terms, we often treat attention and the contents of working memory as equivalent, so while you are listening to someone speak or you are reading a book (like now!), your attention is mostly on the last few words that you heard or read. As you continue listening or reading, those words are replaced by new ones as you attend to the incoming meaning of the data. This continual overriding of older information by new data would be disruptive and limiting if our mental world stopped there. However, the meeting of incoming data with our activated long-term memory offers us the framework for extended processing that enables learning.

Language is an obvious example of our evolved mental capabilities. As we learn a language, either as an infant or as an adult trying to master a new one, there is an effortful process of parsing the auditory stimuli into words we can understand. We hear someone speak a word and we translate that sound into meaning. As we master this skill (that is, we repeatedly hear the sound and tie its occurrence to something) we slowly move from the conscious deliberation on the sound signal to the extraction of meaning in real-time. Our long-term memory helps us interpret the perceptions of sound and we can engage actively in considering the message and deciding how to respond. In fact, holding a conversation involves each step of the cognitive architecture outlined in Fig 6.2. We must hear the sound of someone speaking as discernible and distinct from other stimuli, understand it, create a form of active representation in working memory of what is being said and decide how we are going to respond when the appropriate moment comes. Our responses involve our own long-term knowledge of the subject under discussion as well as the short-term memory of something specific the speaker uttered. Our response must be handled similarly by the other participant in the conversation so the process repeats, two people employing and exploiting their knowledge structures, perceptual systems, attentional resources, and decision/response processes to engage in communicative exchange, each with an activated mental model of the situation and their role in it that enables turn-taking and meaningful interaction. And all this occurs within a culturally influenced set of norms for politeness or appropriate forms of exchange.

Cognition Over Time: The Power of Automation

In design terms, the architecture of cognition can be a useful window into what might be happening during use. As we look, for example, at the screen of our phones, we are extracting cues of interest from a frames visual array of data. If the task is to make a call, for example, we need to locate the appropriate icon from among alternatives on the home page (or scroll to the appropriate page if the icon is not on the opening screen). Just this seemingly simple act involves our entire cognitive architecture. Attention goes to the visual stimuli, we apply knowledge of icons to recognize the one we need (a combination of perception, memory, and decision processes, all of which consumes more attention) before responding with a movement of our hand to allow a finger or thumb to activate the target icon with a press or touch. At that point, the screen likely changes, introducing a new visual array that appears connected to the action we just took, and the process largely repeats itself as we scan for relevant name or option for making the call, iteratively engaging perceptual, decision and response processes while utilizing knowledge from long-term memory, and monitoring our progress through the task steps to ensure successful completion. We perform such acts so routinely and repeatedly, almost every waking moment in some form or other, that for the most part we are simply not conscious of doing so or of the learning and practice such skills are built upon.

Over the course of our life, we see many of the same stimuli repeatedly, and in certain contexts, this repetition lays down representations in our memory that we can retain for the long-term. Better yet, as we see, the creation of memory not only builds up our knowledge of the world, it provides us with ways of handling further incoming data more efficiently, saving on attentional resources. Instead of having to register sensory inputs as new information every time they are above threshold and perceived, we learn to recognize the familiar in ways that save us the effort of considering every detail. Co-occurring aspects of a data set tend to be identified and used for connecting parts of the stream together. We connect names to faces, colors to objects, shapes to functions, physical actions to results, people to emotions, over and over again, sometimes in powerful combinatorial ways so that we build a set of expectations about the world impinging on our senses over time that helps us manage the continual changes in stimuli around us.

In terms of attention, our extraction of patterns in the incoming stream creates a form of template that we can use to interpret the inputs, as we fit it to an expected set of relationships and co-occurrences that we have learned are typical or normal in a particular environment. When we know someone, the sound of their voice alone is sufficient to trigger the recognition of them, and that recognition might bring to mind (our conscious attention) many memories, particularly time-relevant ones such as "we have a meeting at 10 am" or "I am supposed to remind her of something." That associated memory is built up from previous data streams, some from years ago, some from minutes earlier, but they typically are effortlessly brought from long-term to working memory once triggered by the auditory or visual stimulus. Having this ability to rely on memory to help interpret the world around us as it bombards us with endless data makes it possible for us to engage in extended, focused, and complex interactions with the world even though our mental resources are distinctly finite.

A key quality of this psychological processing is our innate ability to automate many types of responses. I'm not talking of simple reflex arcs, the type of immediate response one makes to touching a very hot surface which we believe is more neurological than cognitive (if we have to add in even milliseconds of extra processing time for our minds to register the intense heat on our skin before deciding on our reaction we would suffer more damage), but the type of automatic processing you are engaging in as you read this sentence. You were not born with reading ability, you needed to learn it, from the recognition of letters and words to the association of words and sounds, rules of grammar and sentence construction and more.

Reading is a complex and skilled act that takes most humans years to gain proficiency (and an unfortunate few never do) and which involves the full engagement of our cognitive capabilities. Yet even as we attended to the process actively in learning, through repetition over years we end up performing it effortlessly, at least until our comprehension is disrupted by novel words or grammatical errors.

This shift in processing style, from what has been termed controlled to automatic, underlies many responses we make to the world around us. In learning new skills, we must attend to new data, fit it with our existing knowledge structures, monitor our responses, and repeat this cycle, often intensively and extensively, until our processing no longer occupies our full attention. As we scan the world around us, most objects and people we see are familiar enough that we do not have to make an effort to interpret them. We immediately recognize people, even if we have never encountered these exact individuals before, and in so doing might pick up on numerous cues such as gender, age, height, nearness etc. Unless something original or novel strikes us, we likely pay little conscious attention to anyone and keep moving. But while moving, we do negotiate space, adjust our movements to those of others, attend to signals on crosswalks. In short, we manifest a continual engagement of automatic and controlled cognitive processes as we interact with the world.

What would it be like if we lacked this capability? It's almost impossible to know but we all likely started out with a good deal of sensory overload. In the words of William James, considered by many to be the founding father of American psychology, babies experience the world initially as "one great blooming, buzzing confusion" (James, 1890), echoing the popular philosophical argument that we are all born blank slates who have to learn about the world. Evidence suggests we might not be as blank as imagined, with a set of innate skills and abilities coming with our brain on arrival, but the point is a generally insightful one. What we experience as conscious living beings is a product of learning and making sense of our environments over time. To acquire this awareness without infinite attentional capacity necessitates a form of pattern recognition and knowledge acquisition that is active and can be rapidly applied.

The path from controlled to automatic processing is familiar to most people who learn a musical instrument, at least to the point of being able to play a tune at its intended speed. Fingerings have to be learned, scales practiced, all very controlled acts which lay down the building blocks of skilled performance. With appropriate repetition, the acts of playing scales and ultimately music, become less conscious and more a smooth, automatic process as the player's fingers move accurately and appropriately across the keyboard or the fretboard. What once seemed almost beyond one's ability to do can become a routine act with sufficient practice, reinforcement, and commitment. The initial steps of learning any instrument are quite difficult, string pressing or finger stretching causes discomfort, repeated practice can be slow and not very inspiring to hear (we all wince at the thought of the first sounds anyone tries to make on a violin), and the discipline required to move from continual effortful acts to the skilled fluent playing often discourages people from pursuing this path. But leaving aside the differences in innate talent or imagined musical ability among people, everyone who develops automated skills started with more effortful controlled acts.

Of course, learning is more than just automating our responses to stimuli, there is a host of skills that most of us never master but can perform competently enough to get by using our limited knowledge, conscious real-time processing and decision making, and sometimes additional resources such as books, guides and YouTube videos. Further, there are some types of acts that humans do not ever automate, such as complex judgments where we must consider a range of data in order to determine an appropriate answer or where the cost of an error might be high. Deciding where to invest your money, how to manage your project team, or even which car to buy are not automated but involve a series of choices, hopefully appropriate ones, that might involve research, experience, and judgment. Creative acts, such as design, invention, composing, or cooking are similarly controlled acts, each of which might have automated sub-components, but which require a level of thoughtful, deliberate cognition, which commands our attention, to perform well.

To become automated, the perceptual and cognitive steps involved must be repetitive, relying on the same types of processing which we learn to identify and, importantly, to chunk or group together so that a rapid stimulus can trigger a combined response. In this way, even quite complex activities which initially tax our attentional and processing capacity, can, with sufficient practice, become routine. Driving a car, particularly involving a stick shift and clutch, involves a seemingly overwhelming set of stimuli that need to be recognized and responded to with both cognitive and physical actions, which themselves are temporally contingent for success (it's important to press the clutch with one's foot at the right time to allow a smooth gear change with the hand while recognizing the outside visual field is also continually updating your sense of the road conditions). What is amazing about the human mind is that we are able to become so practiced in this type of processing that in time, driving hardly consumes our full attention and we find we have capacity to handle even more stimuli on other tasks while completing it. In fact, the design of many cars now typically involves a variety of monitoring systems to make sure the driver does give attention if the car speeds up or approaches too close to a vehicle in front, veers off lane or if the driver forgets to take the key fob upon exist. Clearly, it is important to understand the limits of our attention but it is also vital that we design technologies to channel our attention on critical matters, especially as cars now come with many other sources of distraction such as large screens and complicated dashboards.

Of course, we don't remember everything we attend to, and even in the case of digit recall tests, if we delay asking people to repeat the stimulus, their accuracy drops quickly. If we know this going to happen, we can try to keep the signal active by saying it ourselves, rehearsing the response we will give, usually encoding it verbally, until we have to deliver it. But as you might now realize, doing so is itself attention-consuming, and if we try to do this while simultaneously performing another task, there will be errors. Typically, if we don't rehearse, the short-term memory of the data stream we received will decay within 15 s or so, which is why if someone says something to you and you are not paying attention, you might remember that they spoke but not what they actually said after a while. Experimental psychologists usually test people by asking them to remember a stream of digits, then to perform some other act, such as counting out loud backwards from 100 in 3's for 30 s or so, before then being asked to repeat the original data stream (a classic early study of this can be found in Peterson and Peterson, 1959). If you think such tests sound like a form of punishment, you might be right, but they clearly show the limitations of our working memory.

Thankfully, as we go through life, we are not typically subject to the cunning manipulations of experimental investigators, and our cognitive system works remarkably well. Quick, effortless processing of routine stimuli becomes normal while our controlled processing deals with more complex activities as needed, absorbing our attention and enabling deliberate or intentional responses. In more popular writings people now refer to these attributes of our cognition as two systems, *system 1* for the automatic, involuntary responses we make, and *system 2* for the conscious, intentional level but this suggests that we might have two cognitive systems which can confuse the issue if we try to demarcate the boundaries formally (see e.g., Kahneman, 2011). For most of us, these processes are interwoven and natural.

In user experience terms, we most notice these different processes when we make mistakes, or when a habitual response learned on one version of a system proves no longer appropriate in a new version. We might find ourselves pressing the wrong key sequence, inputting the wrong password, or choosing the wrong menu item based on long-standing interactions that have largely become automated and then need to be re-learned for the new interface. However, designers need to also understand that automatic user behaviors are plentiful before they ever experience an interface. Our reading skills are heavily automated, most users have learned to type, our eyes are drawn to movement, and we group information by layout and order (the classic Gestalt principles reflect the typical way we 'see' patterns and relationships) If a design violates too many conventions, relies on unfamiliar terms, or offers inappropriate feedback to user input, then it is likely to trigger conscious and negative responses from many users as it breaks the flow of interaction that is most comfortable for us.

This is not to say that all interaction should be designed for automaticity, that very much needs to be seen in terms of the tasks being supported. For routine activities such as logging in, saving files, or typing number and letter sequences, then leveraging the automated skills of users makes for effective design (even if these skills might reflect habits from a earlier technology like the QWERTY keyboard layout). However, where the consequences of a mistake are high, such as closing a file before saving changes, or deleting important data, or submitting a formal record or financial transfer request, it is better to capture the user's attention so as to ensure that a controlled response is required before such action is taken. Here, a so-called forcing function, the use of an extra step such as an "are you sure?" prompt that must be answered serves to break up the habitual task flow and require users to give their attention to a decision before pressing a final button.

For the last 40 years there have been innumerable books produced to summarize what we know about human psychology and how it might help us design better experiences. These range from detailed listing of formal guidelines based on the psychological science (such as my favorite, Gardiner and Christie's (1987) *Applying Cognitive Psychology to User Interface Design* which might seem old but then the human mind has not changed much since) to the popular contemporary summary of cognition and how to apply it to evaluating interactions generally (of which Jeff Johnson's (2014) *Designing with the Mind in Mind* is an excellent example). I have no need to reproduce here such good summaries, the more important point is that we do understand a lot about people as psychological creatures and by at least grasping the essentials of how we think, how our perceptual and cognitive processes seem to handle the world, even in general terms, we can derive useful guidance. Attempts to apply books of guidelines without a good sense of the underlying structure and processes of human cognition are almost certainly going to result in less-than-optimal results.

Limitations of the Perceptual and Cognitive View of Users

While our internal processing of data from the world is fascinating and at least reasonably well explained by contemporary psychological theories, you might feel still that something is missing. We certainly have limited attentional resources which we allocate according to task and contextual demands, our working memory can be easily filled, and we fit incoming data to our current model of how the world around us is unfolding, but this hardly explains everything about us as humans. Where in this view do we recognize our interests or feelings? Where does emotion fit in this story? And in terms of information use, what else must we understand about people if we want to design experiences for them that they enjoy, seek out, feel enriched by or share with others?

Affective psychology tends to complement the purely cognitive approach by raising questions such as those to help us think about humans as emotional and feeling organisms. This is not a new idea, psychology has wrestled with human emotional experience for over a century since the earliest view of emotion as a direct response to physiological activities induced by stimuli (the James-Lange theory from the 1880s) and since then a range of theories that place more or less emphasis on either physiology or cognition has been proposed. There is no dominant theory in today's psychological literature because there seems to be a very complicated set of factors that are associated with human emotional responses. Sometimes we do experience strong emotion in response to physiological events, other times we must appraise a situation and our interpretation can induce an emotional response. What does seem to be agreed is that emotional aspects of our experience do not fit simply into the standard information-processing framework and consequently, for me at least, this points to another limitation of the time-sliced approach to studying humans. Emotions certainly are associated with memories and experiences, as well as chemical processes in our bodies, but do not lend themselves as easily to measurement in experiments, hence they have been given limited treatment within the study of cognition.

We do know, with certainty, that humans have an emotional side, and while no theory fully explains our responses, it does seem as if our hypothalamus, limbic system, and prefrontal lobes of the cerebral cortex play an active part. Evolutionary theorists suggest there are survival benefits from an emotional response as it can trigger us to avoid harmful situations where we may otherwise have incomplete information, and that providing emotional signals to others can foster communication between individuals and groups. Research does indeed support the idea that primary emotional expressions are universal, that is, no matter where we are from, we can accurately read the face of another human that is displaying anger, disgust, fear or happiness and surprise, though different groups have their own norms for how publicly such emotions should be expressed.

I am not convinced we should treat affect as distinct from cognition, I prefer the general framework outlined in this chapter be adjusted appropriately to incorporate affect more directly into consideration of our memory processes and attention. This seems unlikely with current theories however. That emotion often seems to follow a different temporal sequence than signal perception suggests a further need for a more vertical slicing of human activity than social science has typically followed. For now however, as we tour these slices, we find that emotion and affect have been considered but usually at the social and cultural levels, which are the next steps on our journey.

References

Brewer, W.F., and Treyens, J.C. (1981). Role of schemata in memory for places. *Cognitive Psychology*, *13*(2), 207–230. 10.1016/0010-0285(81)90008-6

Card, S., Newell, A., and Moran, T. (1983). *The Psychology of Human Computer Interaction*. Hillsdale New Jersey: Lawrence Erlbaum Associates.

Eysenck, M., and Keane, M. (2020). *Cognitive Psychology*, 8th ed. London: Psychology Press.

Fields, A. (2016). *Human Psychology 101: Understanding the Human Mind and What Makes People Tick*. CreateSpace: Online.

Gartner Research. Hype Cycle for Emerging Technologies, 2010. Aug. 2, 2010. https://www.gartner.com/en/documents/1414917/hype-cycle-for-emerging-technologies-2010

Gardiner, M., and Christie, B. (1987). *Applying Cognitive Psychology to User Interface Design*. Chichester UK: Wiley.

James, W. (1890). *Principles of Psychology*. New York: Henry Holt and Co.

Johnson, J. (2014). *Designing with the Mind in Mind. Simple Guide to Understanding User Interface Design Guidelines*, 2nd ed. New York: Morgan Kaufmann.

Kahneman, D. (2011). *Thinking Fast and Slow*. New York: Farrar, Strauss, and Giroux.

Neisser, U. (1976). *Cognition and Reality: Principles and Implications of Cognitive Psychology*. San Francisco: W.H. Freeman and Co.

Oxenham, A.J. (2018). How we hear: The perception and neural coding of sound. *Annual Review of Psychology*, 69(1), 27–50.

Peterson, L.R., and Peterson, M.J. (1959). Short-term retention of individual verbal items. *Journal of Experimental Psychology*, 58(3), 193–198.

Wickens, C., Helton, W., Hollands, J., and Banbury, S. (2021). *Engineering Psychology and Human Performance*, 5th ed. New York: Routledge.

The Socio-Tech Layer 7

Users as Social Beings

In November 2020, Linda Barnes and her husband drove their new Porsche Taycan 4S, a luxury electric vehicle (EV), on a trip to Bournemouth in England, a journey of some 130 miles from their home in Kent. The car has a range of 250 miles between charges and in their part of the UK, stations are plentiful. Getting to Bournemouth was fine but what should have been an equally easy and comfortable two-hour trip home turned into a nightmare over nine hours as the couple struggled to find the power needed for their vehicle. As reported in the Guardian newspaper, the Barnes had to visit six different stations before they could sufficiently charge their Porsche's batteries to drive home safely. At every stop they found non-functional chargers, backed up lanes of other EV drivers waiting their turn to plug in, or out of date versions of a charger that would not deliver the power they needed for their vehicle. Acknowledging their tremendous sense of relief when they finally managed to get their car charged, Linda was quoted as saying: "We ran through the entire gamut of emotions in those nine hours – resignation, range anxiety, annoyance and disbelief that this was happening – and finally elation when we realised we'd get home." (The Guardian, *Why did it take 9 hours to go 130 miles in our new electric Porsche?*, November 28th, 2020).

The Barnes experience highlights a vital but frequently overlooked part of using a new technology, the need for a supporting infrastructure. A car is usually purchased and used, at least in the owner's mind, as a standalone item, and the choice of model is typically tied to multiple influences ranging from personal finances to travel needs, wrapped up, of course, in the interplay of desire, image and impression management on the part of the owner/driver.

DOI: 10.4324/9781003026112-7

But use of a car comes with an assumption of supporting facilities that enable it to function as intended, including the provision of roads, gas stations, traffic signals, and repair services. When choosing which car to purchase or lease, such forms of supporting infrastructure are often taken for granted, assumed to be part of the everyday world, until that is, like the Barnes, gaps appear in the supporting eco-system. When a breakdown in the infrastructure underlying use occurs, all the unstated aspects of use that prove necessary for successful exploitation of a technology start to reveal themselves, more through their absence than their presence.

While cars form a specific application of UX design, most of the professional attention we give them concerns dashboard controls, light and sound environments, and appropriate information channeling across changing task demands. However, there is a much broader context of use in driving that must be considered part of the user experience, and it forces us to attend to the concerns of drivers that are not directly impacted the imagined single user model that dominates so much of our research on interaction. In the case of the Barnes desire to drive to Bournemouth, we see that an electric car cannot function without regular recharging, a process that is reliant, if the driver wishes to travel any distance from home, on an external infrastructure of stations where drivers can stop and plug in their vehicles before proceeding. These stations themselves need to provide interfaces that are usable and reliable across differing engine implementations, with associated payment networks. These must exist within a range that meets the currently limited driving distance available with electric cars (a station that is beyond your battery's reserve is essentially non-existent to you) and charging stations must be findable using invariably, cell phones. As the Barnes realized to their cost, a break in this infrastructure at any level (findability, availability, compatibility, etc.) can render even the most elegant or desirable vehicle useless, with the commensurate personal discomfort that results. The Barnes made it home, but not without a series of emotional responses that most designers would wish to avoid in promoting a positive user experience.

In our attempts to understand people as users of information technology, such concerns make apparent that need to consider variables beyond the immediate touchpoint of interaction as is typical when considering the usability of a control interface. We also need to address how people behave with technologies in contexts where there are other people also using the same, or a connected technology that forms a distributed network of interactions which affect individual and collective outcomes and performance. Social scientists have recognized since the earliest studies of industrial performance and worker selection that the behavior of a group or community of people was not simply reducible to individual factors and that the only means of understanding certain phenomena such as shared language use and behavioral constraints was to consider the group as the fundamental unit, not the person. Kurt Lewin, writing in the 1940s, is generally considered to have coined the term "group dynamics" to refer to the drivers of action and behavior in a social collective, and since then, social psychologists and sociologists have emphasized analysis of human activities at the group or community level as key to understanding why people behave as they do in social environments (see e.g., Lewin, 1943).

At a fundamental level, this example cautions us to think of usage contexts as more than a series of tasks we must support. While we could plausibly map out all parts of the Barnes' EV journey and treat the distinct parts as a task set (e.g., driving the car, locating a charging station, connecting a charger, etc.), all of which are design challenges, we quickly see that there is more to successful use of this technology than the concerns of an individual driver. The lack of standards for charging stations, the distribution and provision of stations within geographic areas, the push for this technology to be adopted for environmental reasons and so forth extend our design envelope out from the point of contact between a user and an interface to encircle a much larger context involving more than other drivers.

But we don't even have to think about the challenges of EVs to recognize the importance of infrastructure, it underlies our cellular networks at home and work, the successful purchase and delivery of items when using the Amazon app, and even the water supply that comes out of the faucet when we turn a tap. In short, it is difficult to think of a meaningful outcome for a user experience with technology that does not rely on an infrastructure of support that involves others. We tend not to consider this too directly when focused on the user at physical or cognitive layers, but it is apparent once we begin to go up (or down, depending on your viewpoint) the vertical slice that user experience plays out significantly at a social level too. And while the important question of infrastructure provision forces our attention in this direction, there is much more to users as social beings than this.

Thinking of Use as a Social Process

This emphasis on moving beyond the individual to understand our interactions with information technology in a group or collective context has its roots in the formal emergence of social psychology and sociology. At the turn of the 20th-century social scientists began to look more closely at the relationship between individuals and society and in so doing began to identify structures operating at a collective or group level that seemed to impact individual behavior and beliefs. Paraphrasing Thomas and Thomas (1928), theorists argued that if people believed the situations they experienced were real, then we needed to study these closely, and that meant focusing on interaction with and among other people across real life situations. A more sociological or social psychological focus on people resulted in important levels of analysis that incorporated social relations, interaction among groups, the ordering of society and how our beliefs, attitudes and personalities reflect our social settings. This situational level of study builds on the more individualistic level of typical perceptual and cognitive analyses yet retains a concern with the person by addressing personality, attitude, and belief, considering these important attributes of psychological experience that are shaped by social forces.

In moving to this higher-level of analysis we can sense that the divisions that might appear firm in the time-sliced model of social science are, in reality, blurred and less precise than one might infer. The formal cognitive approach, built on a theoretical architecture of information processes and structures such as working memory, does not cover everything we would wish to study about people. However, this cogntiive architecture does not cease to operate or lose relevance once our concerns move from knowledge or task performance to longer-term experiences, or to affective, that is emotional or attitudinal, responses to the world around us. We do possess qualities that seem well-explained in the cognitive framework, but we also have other qualities that we need to acknowledge influence how we act and behave, and the more social level of analysis has shed some very useful light on key aspects of our psychology that matter enormously in designing better technologies.

So called socio-technical thinking, the recognition that people and technologies form a system that is best understood at a level higher than the user interface, has been particularly influential in the field of human-computer interaction. While the term "socio-technical" is often used rather generically to refer to any perspective that acknowledges the group or social context, it has a quite specific history that can help us appreciate the similarities and differences between the levels of analysis we have considered so far and in so doing help us appreciate why a time-based framing of social science has inevitable faults.

We can trace socio-technical thinking directly back to research by Eric Trist and colleagues at the Tavistock Institute in London during the 1950s and early 1960s who investigated the changing mining industry of post-WWII Great Britain. At that time, coal was the primary source of the nation's energy and a vital resource for industry and power production. While mine owners had developed a functional process of coal extraction that relied heavily on human labor organized on classic scientific management principles of top-down control, the government wanted to ensure predictable and cheap supply of this vital resource for the reconstruction effort of a war-weary nation Hope lay in greater application of mechanization in mines to improve efficiencies but despite these efforts, productivity was dropping amid high worker absenteeism and disquiet at salary inequities resulting from the use of new machinery. To understand the problem better, Trist and colleagues had the opportunity to study, with full co-operation of the mine and workers, the ways in which new working practices were evolving. What they observed proved an eye-opener for them and changed our understanding of how users and technologies could be viewed (Trist (1981) offers an excellent summary overview of the development of socio-technical systems theory).

Specifically, Trist and colleagues spent time observing work practices at the Haighmoor colliery in West Yorkshire, the heart of the coal mining industry in the UK where innovation seemed to be thriving. Here, with participation of the miners, trade unions, and management, a new form of work practice had evolved, involving autonomous groups who set their goals, shared and interchanged tasks to make good use of the new technology, and generally regulated themselves without heavy supervision. As a result, productivity here was high and absenteeism low, in contrast to the results reported in other mines. These observations led Trist to the insight that rather than focusing on the productivity and activities of the individual worker, or on the capability of new technology to increase yield on its own as was typical of old-style work design or scientific management, a focus on the work group as the basic unit, coupled with the capability of this unit to regulate individual and collective behavior involving technology, might shed light on what worked and did not work well. Their framing gave rise to the general idea that people and technologies in every work context formed a socio-technical system, a combination of users and technologies, that should be optimized for collective functioning through shared goals and agreed regulations.

The socio-technical theorists posited a new kind of organizational form that resisted what they called the "technological imperative," the view of users as an extension of the machines, expendable or replaceable like any other spare part, trained to perform a narrow range of tasks in a prescribed manner, and discouraged from taking risk or tailoring their practices for themselves. In its place they proposed work environments where technology and people could form jointly optimized sub-systems that workers could regulate and develop collaboratively to meet individual and organizational goals. In so doing, this approach challenged much of what we considered normal in technology-mediated work environments and raised questions of the naïve technocratic view which held that improvements in technology would lead to greater productivity. Though originating in the traditional work environment of coal mining, socio-technical thinking began to be recognized as relevant to any process of change management in organizations. As the computer revolution began to impact traditional office work in the 1970s, the theory came to be recognized as relevant to a far boarder range of industries.

While the connection between the Barnes experience of powering their Porsche and the shortwall miners of Haighmoor might seem distant, they both speak to the importance of our treating technologies as part of a broader system of implementation and use. Key to the socio-technical framing is the raising of the unit level analysis from the individual user at the interface to what became known as "the work system," the complete set of activities and technologies that form a functional whole. The terminology, as usual for social science, might be less than clear but for our purposes, we can just think of the socio-technical system as the components and processes required for meaningful activities to occur. For Trist and colleagues, this was originally the organizing of a mining team around mechanical devices, arguing that we would never understand the impact of a new machine on a mine by only studying its operator, it was necessary to broaden our view to incorporate the other miners directly impacted by the technology, and their context of work. In the case of the Barnes, a car and driver does not form the functional unit or work system, it is rather the cars and drivers, making use of environmentally distributed power stations, charging interfaces and various navigation and payment tools to ensure a successful outcome, in this case a safe return journey.

For the routine technologies we all employ in our daily lives, there is invariably an underlying infrastructure that makes itself visible to us when it breaks. Your cell phone or Wi-Fi router requires telecommunications networks, just as your shower requires water, to operate fully. But within any underlying infrastructure are people, "stakeholders" in the terminology of socio-technical systems, who are invested in, responsible for, and directly supplying, managing or using components of the system that enable each of us to accomplish what we hope for with our technology. This can be difficult to map out directly as lines of responsibility and impact are often vague or invisible in routine use. When you make a call on your smart phone, your task, as such, seems quite direct, the selection of a recipient, the connection through appropriate send and receive tools (in this case the phone) and a conversational participant on the other end. As a user-centered designer it might seem simple enough to envisage this as a matter of enabling usable smart phone features for placing and targeting a call, signaling it to other party, and then getting out of the way. However, the design challenge of providing telecommunications that enable global connection is clearly far more complicated than this.

Invariably, we are all living in an interwoven series of socio-technical systems that form the populated environments of 21st century work and leisure. Deloitte, the US consulting firm, reported in 2020 that the average US household possessed 11 connected information devices, but this grew to 25 per household over the course of the COVID-19 pandemic which produced a surge in device ownership and use as many people were required to work or pursue education from home (Deloitte, 2022). From cellphones to smart TVs, most of these devices contain screens, and we are all spending more time in front of them. Recent estimates put average daily time online, from work to entertainment, at over 8 hours a day (*The Scotsman*, April 23rd, 2021) with social media alone accounting for 147 minutes of this (Statista, 2022). Tempting as it might be to imagine the pandemic of the 2020s pushed a recalcitrant public toward greater screen time, the reality is we have been on this path for years as more and more of our activities became mediated by digital tools. The Deloitte survey also indicated a strong intent among respondents to purchase even more devices once 5G became widely available. Couple this with the reliance on digital tools for many jobs, from offering access to ensuring control over distributed workers, mediation and connectivity are inevitable contingencies in the design of information which must be considered appropriately. All our world is a set of socio-technical systems.

The Socio-Technical Approach to User-Centered Design

So how are we to think about user-centeredness in the context of socio-technical systems? In his classic book organizational change via information, Ken Eason (1988) listed 10 propositions of socio-technical systems that need to be considered when trying to ensure the successful adoption of new tools, summarized in Table 7.1.

Table 7.1 Eason's Ten Propositions (Eason, 1988)

1. Exploitation of resources depends on ability and willingness of users
2. IT must serve organizational goals
3. Introduction to be planned as process of change
4. All relevant stakeholders to be involved
5. IT only works where it solves problems or exploits opportunities to serve goals
6. Tasks must be seen by users as worthwhile
7. Technology must be usable
8. Exploiting IT requires organizational and individual learning
9. Exploitation is evolutionary
10. Should complement existing design processes and change procedures

Eason's emphasis clearly is on the organizational setting, with a focus on exploiting opportunities, serving the group's goals, and involving users in the process, but even if we recognize that many contemporary socio-technical systems are domestic or involve non-formal groupings of users, these basic propositions still seem applicable. Note the view of users in these propositions. There is little emphasis on any of the levels covered so far, no mention of cognition or physical ergonomics, but there is the argument that users must see the interaction as worthwhile, and they must be willing to engage. These are clearly vital parts of the challenge for design but they speak to qualities of the user that do not fit easily within the time-sliced framework of social science as usually adopted in UX. The Barnes, in their new electric car, seemed to engage IT that did not meet their goals, nor was it well planned so as exploit travel opportunities for them. And certainly, they found aspects of the technology to be quite unusable when pushed. What the socio-technical imperative asks of us is a design process that involves people in design decisions, recognizing that there are both direct and indirect users of any technology who have an interest, a stake (as socio-technical theory puts it), in its optimization, and that the design process embraces the deployment step sufficiently seriously so as to engage people in an extended process of adoption rather than assuming design ends when a product is manufactured, tested, and shipped.

The emergence of a socio-technical perspective has driven distinctive thinking about design, particularly in two areas that matter for user-centric thinking. The first, and perhaps most noticeable area, is socio-technical thinking's advocacy of what is often termed the "participatory" design movement, the idea that user involvement in the process needs to involve more than test participation, a chance to try out and give quick reactions to prototypes, or being observed while performing some activity that the design team wishes to understand better. Valuable as such activities can be, they do not always provide an opportunity for real participation as much as provide a source of data that the designers extract and analyze, decontextualized from actual use. The participatory goal is much more nuanced, it seeks an appreciation of the richness of user experience in situ, helping the design team to more fully understand how the interactions unfold and are interpreted by users. Further, it wants to take these interpretations explicitly as a means of interrogating the very design choices that are being made as part of the process. It recognizes that any current interaction contains many constraints that might not be observed or even articulated in a user test or observation and that people have a wealth of insights about their own work and activities that could be valuable guides to how any new processes might improve or offer alternatives.

True participation must also allow for all stakeholders to have influence the resulting designs choices that are made. Eason's proposition of involvement by relevant parties applies to all, and if we take user-centeredness seriously, then actual users, at some level, should be involved in deciding how the technology is designed, developed, and deployed. Of course, in free market settings, we might allow for consumer choice to serve a similar function, but this would likely be insufficient in terms of the socio-technical ideal since market choices are limited to those products that already have been built and the economics of the consumer base. Within large organizations however, where we might have greater ability to examine multiple stakeholders and gain their inputs, what evidence we do have seems to suggest that true participatory design remains more an aspiration than a reality, a desire for involvement from advocates that rarely survives contact with the real world of organizational politics.

Baxter and Sommerville (2011), in their overview of socio-technical approaches to systems design note several problems in implementing these ideas in practice. In particular, drawing on Land's (2000) recognition of value conflicts in design, they suggest that the design team's concerns with empowerment of users and the more humanistic values of satisfaction and quality of experience are often at odds with the organization's managers who are more focused on delivering on business performance. This is not the simple good-guy versus bad-guy argument that pits two competing forces against each other in a simple narrative but a more subtle distinction that draws attention to the reality of decision making. Socio-technical thinking places high value on the improving the organization's performance by ensuring quality of life for those engaged in the work, while managers tend to view quality of life as a by-product of company success. Both perspectives seek a similar outcome but they also suggest quite different ways of ensuring it. As Baxter and Sommerville note, adoption of socio technical methods is rarely straightforward.

The second way in which socio-technical thinking has influenced user-centered design is in its conception of the user as a psychological being. As argued throughout this book, there is a strong reliance in user-centered design on the social scientific framing of users as information processers with a consistent cognitive architecture enabling perceptual, memory and decision-making activities. This model of the user has served as the basis for much of what we consider when determining the quality of an interface or in designing for particular user experiences. Socio-technical theory draws our attention to other concerns however, especially to unconscious drivers of human behavior that can influence our reasoning about technology and work processes. In particular, socio-technical theorists try to understand the conditions under which people will chose to change their current activities or practices in order to facilitate the deployment of new tools. In classic socio-technical terms, all new designs necessitate change, this is considered unavoidable, but for the change to occur in the direction that is intended or desired, the key stakeholders in a team must be willing to embrace and accept these changes. Users, in this framing, are less like the independent rational information processors of cognitive science, the type presented in usability studies, and more like members of a constituency of interest, with personal needs for influence and control on collective outcomes.

Specifically, the socio-technical user is generally seen as well-intentioned, that is, willing to serve the goals of the community or group but with particular dynamic forces operating within their minds: a desire to develop their own skills or mastery, to have autonomy in key aspects of their lives, and a preference for co-operation over conflict in relationship to others. This view of users draws more on a psychodynamic than cognitive tradition within social science, suggesting we are all creatures of needs and motivations more than rational actors. This view leads us to the consideration of quite different questions about tasks, technologies, and their design. Trist (1981) identifies a range of intrinsic and extrinsic factors that he argues impact how users see their work which includes such variables as a desire for recognition, learning, discretion and variety (on the intrinsic side) and security, fairness and safety (on the extrinsic side) which offers us a very different view of how we might think about design beyond a touchpoint or interaction.

Thinking of users in socio-technical rather than cognitive terms is noticeably different when it comes to understanding their decision to use information technology. Whereas the classic HCI or UX approach emphasizes such design values as "ease of use" or "usability" as the goal, and evaluates success in terms of proportion or rate of task completion by users, the socio-technical framing seems is more concerned with understanding if a user will accept a new design or if they will consider the changes it introduces as disruptive or empowering. To this end, socio-technical theory posits really two key drivers in people that determine if they will engage in new practices, adopt changes or for our purposes, use new information technologies: perceived level of control, and enhancement. It's worth examining these drivers more closely as they reveal both the differences and ultimately, the shared understanding across these alternative treatments of people as users.

The Desire for Control

It is a natural human desire to be able to exert some control over one's environment, to have influence over the events occurring in one's life, and to determine courses of action that make sense for oneself. While acknowledging that many variables in life are not directly under our control, we nevertheless try to shape our own experiences and, given free choice, prefer to make decisions for ourselves than have them made for us by others. Often, we are forced to trade off some control when we engage in collective or organized activities, such as work, but we do so more or less willingly, depending on other factors such as rewards, salary, status, obligations, and so forth, according to our individual needs and preferences. The socio-technical perspective asks us to recognize this as a condition of human existence, a prevailing tendency in all of us to move the locus of control in our lives towards ourselves and away from others, wherever possible. In any one situation of use, this control dynamic underlies our actions.

The Desire for Enhancement

Socio-technical theorists also consider an important driver to be the level of enhancement people experience as outcomes of their activities and life choices. The argument is made that all of us seek and take pleasure in developing our abilities and competencies. From solving puzzles to acquiring an education, we are positively disposed to developing our skills and competencies to some extent. In making career choices or pursuing hobbies, humans seem more satisfied when they perceive an enhancement in themselves, and this tendency, which some might argue is a drive (though most theorists tend to avoid such a term) also shapes how we respond to work and changes in our life environments. But enhancement is related to more than work or hobbies, the purchases we make, at some level, relate to enhancing our existence and self-image too. Obviously, control and enhancement are connected, we tend to gain more of the former as we develop more of the latter, while the latter can help deliver us more of the former, though of course there are a host of mediating variables at work in this relationship.

This conception of the user's mind is quite applicable to questions of information technology design and deployment and has been applied directly in efforts to understand acceptance and resistance among groups to new technologies. For example, if we consider users as motivated by desires for increased perception of control and for enhancement of their skills, then it is logical that when new technologies are introduced, with the inevitable disruption these cause to existing structures and practices, then people will react to the new context in ways that are not attributable simply to the interface design. Socio-technical theorists posit, for example, if a workplace is changed by a new information system, this potentially disrupts the perceived levels of control among key stakeholders, and such a disruption must be planned and designed for carefully if organizational acceptance is to occur.

In studies of organizational deployment of new information technology, the control and enhancement issues often prove to be recognized too late. Eason (1988) documents cases when an otherwise well-planned tool for improving group efficiency were received negatively by key user groups who felt control over work practices shifted too far away from them and toward outside agents or groups. Similarly, when new technologies are seen by some users as introducing pacing, monitoring, and mandatory procedures, even when users receive training in the new practices, there can be a perception that not only is control over working conditions being altered but the technology is deskilling rather than enhancing the operator's personal status which will inevitably lead to resistance rather than acceptance of the new design. But it's not just job characteristics that have impact here. Even the perception of unreliability in the new technology can negatively impact enhancement and the user's perceived level of control. For socio-technical thinkers, the control and enhancement impacts should form part of the earliest requirements gathering in the design process and the deisgn should proceed to deliver benefits that will align with these basic motivational drivers of people.

Much work in socio-technical systems design has studied how to leverage the positive aspects of perceived control and enhancement while reducing the negative consequences through design, work group structure, management processes, and organization-wide training programs. It's probably fair to say that the practices involved here are very complicated, and well-controlled studies of participatory design using socio-technical principles are difficult to set up and reproduce. Certainly, we might say the results are mixed (see e.g., Baxter and Sommerville, 2011). Participatory groups are not without their own power dynamics and merely allowing representation of all stakeholders is no guarantee of enabling it. However, if nothing else, socio-technical thinking has moved our understanding of technology adoption beyond more simplistic, single variable explanations of technical failure or resistance. It is rarely the case that an innovation in technology fails simply because of some characteristic of the intended user population (such as their personality or cognitive style) or a feature of the technology (a single poor interface feature for example). People are adaptable and while they do bring their personalities to interactions and the usability of a designed feature set really does matter, we often chose to use or resist a new design based on more than these characteristics. Socio-technical thinking encourages us to consider the dynamics of adoption and long-term use as a balance of personal dispositions and contextual processes, aligned with a shared goal.

Though its origins are in work design, socio-technical theory is not limited to framing work contexts. In a post-pandemic world where many information practices are altered, and not tied, as before, to shared physical spaces, it is an open question if socio-technical theory might offer even greater insight in this new environment. Distributed people and practices, almost entirely mediated by digital technologies, create an organizational form that has been theorized about but rarely realized. Interestingly, one consequence of this is the blurring of lines between professional and personal life is the ability to apply socio-technical perspectives to non-work life and the adoption and use of new information technology that serves our personal, social, and cultural lives. In this light, it would seem appropriate to consider the role of motivators such as control and enhancement in our consideration of all users, regardless of usage environment.

Adoption of New Technology as a Social Process

Allowing for the shaping influence of social forces, including the presence of others with varying degrees of authority, is key to one theory of innovation adoptions proposed by Everett Rogers (2003). His model, which has been developed and refined since its original formulation in the 1960s, has been applied across numerous domains, from its original examination of why agricultural techniques might be resisted to contemporary research on consumer electronics purchases. Perhaps unsurprisingly, in trying to explain how people decide what to use, Rogers' thinking has been popular with manufactures in their efforts to understand their markets and to determine how their designs might compare to competitive products. However, at its core, Rogers' Innovation Diffusion Theory is a model of behavior change, an attempt to explain why, given a range of options, people might adopt some ideas or products while resisting or rejecting others. What makes it particularly interesting for our consideration of information technology is the model's holistic construction of the process, embracing as it does qualities of the innovation or product, characteristics of the people or users involved, observed over time and through a social system within which decisions and actions occur.

Rogers examined the diffusion of ideas and products over many years and developed a framework that he and his colleagues argued consistently reflects the underlying drivers or dynamics of user choice. The theory posits five stages in any adoption process: awareness, persuasion, decision, implementation, and continuation. In simple terms, an idea or new product has to be communicated through a social network in order to be recognized by participants who then make a decision to adopt or not, over time. Unpacking this, the theory suggests that within this common framework, any adoption is ultimately determined by the qualities of the idea or design itself, and certain characteristics of the participants which in combination influence the rate and spread of any adoption. In our world, ideas and innovations occur frequently, but many never reach widespread adoption because awareness of them is limited. New ideas or designs must compete for the attention of potential customers or users, hence the importance of advertising or advocates in raising awareness. Awareness is necessary but it is hardly sufficient for any successful innovation, further acts of persuasion and decision necessarily precede diffusion over time.

The attraction of Rogers' model rests heavily, I believe, on its dual attribution of successful innovation to seemingly explicit characteristics of both the design or innovation and the actual adopters or users. In this sense, it offers a balanced framing of the interplay between created products or ideas and the discretionary users or adopters of same. The theory presents five characteristics of the innovation and five types of adopter or user, as outlined below.

The Five Characteristics of Successful Designs

Relative Advantage

For an innovation to gain an audience, it is argued that it must offer some clear benefits over existing practices or products. Simply reinventing what is currently available, or worse, trying to generate a receptive audience for an innovation that offers only the same or fewer advantages than existing options is obviously problematic. So, in simple terms, success follows ideas and innovations that improve our lot in life, our satisfaction, efficiency, or general well-being. However, plausible as it seems, this is not quite as simple as it sounds. The determination of advantage might refer equally to functionality or to cost, for example, and some people might trade one for another, choosing a design that is objectively less capable than a current artifact, but which comes at a more affordable price. In this case, cost rather than performance, is the relative advantage that sways some participants more than anything else.

Compatibility

Given the existence of established practices among participants, the recognition that the current state of the world reflects a history of choices previously made for ideas and products, the reception of any innovation is influenced by how well it fits, or the degree of disruption it entails, in our current environment. Rogers particularly considered compatibility in terms of values and needs of the participants, a form of high-level orientation a group has involving their lifestyle, sense of what's important in their lives, and their routine behaviors in and understanding of their world. Innovations that are not compatible with these will lead to disruption, and for any innovation to succeed in that context requires it be positively viewed on other dimensions (e.g., offer strong relative advantage over current options). We might envisage compatibility to be a classic user-centered concern of designing appropriately for a given context.

Ease of Use

Rogers recognized that if an innovation was complicated to understand, to learn or to use, it would face obstacles in adoption. This is obviously well-established within the UX design world where considerable effort is made to ensure usability, and while the principle seems the same here, the complexity aspect of an innovation also incorporates the idea of understanding what the innovation might offer participants. Tied to the awareness-raising aspect of the diffusion process, there is an element in this variable of ensuring the potential of any innovation must be visible and comprehensible to potential adopters so that ease of use is recognized quickly. In this we can also see a direct connection to the socio-technical idea of technology being judged in terms of its perceived enhancement potential.

Trialability

Innovations, by their nature, change people's practices so it is to be expected that their adoption involves appropriate consideration by participants. Where there is an opportunity for people to engage in trials or test runs of new ideas and products, it should, all things being equal, increase the potential for adoption. For some goods or services, the ability to offer free samples or adverti- supported limited versions of software is directly related to this idea but obviously more complex or expensive innovations face a greater challenge. Where innovations offer lower trialability, then it is important for the innovator or earliest adopters to be able to report compelling evidence for the value it offers or the enhancements it provides. The rise of influencers on social media is testimony to the importance of shaping expectations when direct trials are not possible for many.

Observability of Outcome

The fifth characteristic, and somewhat related to trialability, is the ability to assess value or positive outcomes from adopting an innovation. Rogers considers adoption as a temporally extended process, acknowledging the fact that any diffusion is likely adopted at different rates by different people, and for some, the experiences of other, early adopters shape their views of the outcomes they can anticipate from embracing the innovation themselves. It is important that claims made for the outcomes can be observed if participants are to see value in an innovation.

As you might infer from the description of these characteristics, there is some imprecision or overlap in the definitions which a cynic might argue offers the theory a fair amount of elasticity in use. Trialability, for example, implies observability of some outcomes else there is no real trial. The question might be asked, in a large complex organization, for example, who is the observer of a trial and is it important that the outcomes of multiple observer groups should align? Relative advantage might be found in performance, in ease of use, in preference, or in cost terms, for example, and this can differ for the same innovation among various participants. If a design is more difficult to use at first but is more affordable to acquire, does it or does it not offer relative advantage over a competitor? Critics have not been shy in pointing these weaknesses out over the years, suggesting possible confounds among the characteristics and certainly arguing, as might be expected, that all key variables in the theory should be better defined.

There have also been proposed additional characteristics. Given the socio-technical framing underlying this kind of research there has been strong suggestion by some that an innovation, which offered people a degree of discretion in its use, might be considered a positive characteristic, though of course this raises the counter-idea that mandatory use at least has the advantage of ensuring some degree of adoption, even if it violates a core socio-technical principle. Moore and Benbesat (1991) suggested that the degree to which an innovation's adoption might enhance a participant's status in their social system was important, a view that echoes some of the socio-technical theory that diffusion reflects, going so far as proposing an "image" characteristic in addition to the existing five in Rogers' theory. These criticisms aside, the basic five characteristis of the original theory have survived, largely unchanged over multiple editions of Rogers' book.

The Five Types of Adopting Users

As with the characteristics of innovations, Rogers theory posits five general types of adopters, that is, five types of 'user' for any technology, each with particular traits or dispositions: innovators, early adopters, early majority, late majority, and laggards. Rather interestingly, Rogers proposed these are normally distributed within a population as outlined in Figure 7.1.

Innovators, as the name suggests, are the small proportion of the population who are risk-taskers, new idea generators or people who want to be

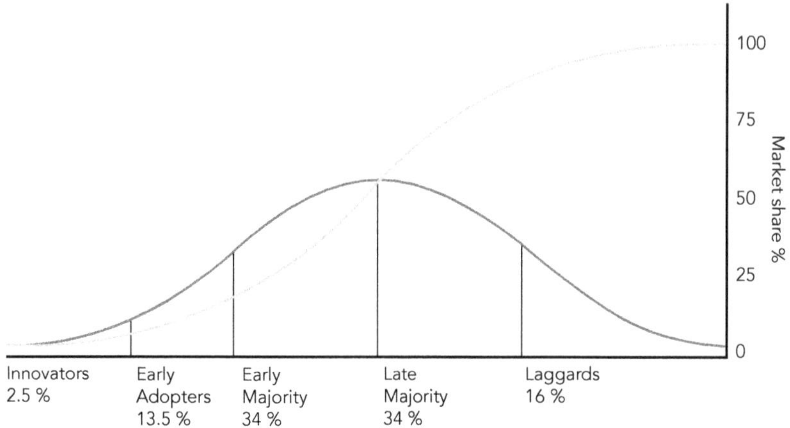

Figure 7.1 Proportion of adopter types according to Rogers' theory of Innovation Diffusion (image courtesy of Wikimedia Commons https://commons.wikimedia.org/wiki/File:Diffusion_of_ideas.svg)

the first to try out inventions or new creations. As the name suggests, these are often the people who generate the ideas or new products. Rogers argues also that such people often are well-resourced, financially and intellectually, with a wider than normal network of like-minded people.

Similar in many ways, early adopters are more locally oriented than the cosmopolitan innovator. Lacking something of the reputation for rash or risky behavior associated with innovators, the early adopter is still perceived as an opinion-leader, well-regarded and integrated into their communities. The early adopter types are often a reliable source of information for other people and their choices on products and services are thought to be influential on the adoption patterns of others.

For Rogers, most people fall into the early or late majority categories. The two types are similar, distinguished mainly by their disposition toward change. Both groups tend to deliberate on the change process for longer than early adopters but the early majority who seem to be connected to and more influenced by early adopters while those deemed to be in the late majority are perhaps more skeptical of change. As before, economic issues may play a role here with late majority types often moving toward adoption when economic and social pressure enables or pushes them.

The wonderfully labeled "laggards" form the tail end of the distribution when it comes to adoption. This group contains few opinion leaders, apparently, and covers people who seem to be quite intolerant of uncertainty, and who base decisions on the past or traditional ways of thinking. Rogers argues that laggards tend to interact with each other and are somewhat suspicious of innovators and new ideas. Indeed, a classic characterization of laggards is that they tend to adopt at the last moment, and sometimes only when the innovation might already be passé.

As these categories suggest, there is a mix of economic, personality, and educational factors underlying one's position, and it's fair to say that over the years numerous research studies have sought to refine the categories or produce simple distinguishers among them e.g., laggards are considered more price conscious than early adopters, innovators are generally younger than late adopters etc. which reflect an attempt to firm up the distinctions in ways that perhaps run counter to Rogers' original thinking. Since diffusion is necessarily a drawn-out process, and innovations occur across a wide range of activities, it is not simply the case that we can imagine members of one adoption category to be homogenous with respect to age or personality type. There are young laggards who resist an innovation for economic or personality reasons, perhaps reflecting their social group's distaste for certain commercial developments. Similarly, there are older early adopters for some innovations, particularly in health technologies or lifestyle products. In fact, what seems most true of adopter categories is that any one individual might be a member of different ones, depending on the type of innovation being considered. This is an example of how the domain of innovation alters the positioning of a potential adopter in the diffusion curve.

What's perhaps a little too convenient here is the portrayal of the distribution of adopters forming a perfect bell curve, with the majority falling neatly within proportions suggesting early and late majority being a symmetrical 34% each, laggards forming 16% and the remaining 16% being broken into 13.5% early adopters and 2.5% innovators. As a convenient approximation this is probably acceptable if one can resist the supposed precision in these proportions. It is not inevitable that in any social system one will find roughly one in eight people to be laggards or one in three to be more enthusiastic but not fast adopters as would be predicted if this distribution curve was interpreted precisely. I prefer to ignore the numbers and recognize that true innovators and early adopters are a relatively smaller proportion of the population, as are true laggards, with the vast majority of people being an adopter of innovations at some point.

The real strength of the Innovation Diffusion theory, to my eyes, is its encouragement to think relatively broadly about the dynamics of user behavior in the context of adoption. For new information devices and appliances, Rogers asks us to recognize that one size rarely fits all. Certainly, usability is important, but so is the chance to learn from others' use. Few of us can afford to make adoption decisions without considering costs, but we also might be less concerned with costs than we might be with disrupting our current practices, or we might want to adopt because we believe all new technologies are better than older versions, or that having the latest model is cool and reflects well on our status in the world. Rogers asks us to consider innovations in their dynamic and situational contexts, within the social systems in which we participate, and to acknowlede that reasons for adopting can reflect personality as much as utility or cost.

That said, there are some real limitations to this framework. The theory is often invoked to make the case that adoption is particularly influenced by key people who have status and standing within a social system, so we should target these people, design for them, and hope that they will in turn lead other people to adopt. One might be forgiven for imagining this is the basis of all YouTube product marketing in the digital age. Similarly, general advice often deduced from the theory by marketers suggests that it is a futile effort to sell the idea or innovation to laggards directly since they cannot be sped up and will only come along reluctantly once other adopter categories are exhausted. These are plausibly true occurrences in specific instances but one should be wary of generalizing such claims across all domains. Some people, perhaps, might be discouraged by hard promotions from influencers, justifiably concerned that perhaps some degree of shilling or promotional encouragement lies behind the advocacy. There is certainly evidence that in our new information age the increased possible connections available to people might allow for interesting new tests of the theory. Girardi and Chiragouris (2018) for example have examined patterns of communication reported by consumers over decades, leading them to suggest that early adopters now have greater connectivity and seem to engage in more comparisons using search tools to determine their own adoptions. These authors suggest this is marks a shift in typical early adopter behavior and that we are seeing greater impulsivity among them perhaps pointing to a blurring of the boundary between them and innovators. Their analysis is interesting in that consumers report not only a growing tendency to make impulse purchases but an increase in waiting for the reports of other consumers before deciding, which seems somewhat contradictory but might suggest that the greater connectivity of our digiral world allows for rapid decisions informed by a larger network of other consumers. Since Rogers was adamant that the channels of communication were vital to the diffusion process, he likely would not be surprised by the impact of the internet on the dynamics of adoption.

But even as diffusion theory suggests where change agents might best spend their efforts, one can challenge some of the implications of the theory when taking a broader socio-technical view of change management. The latter theory is highly sensitive to all stakeholders, and some, such as Eason, suggest the best way of encouraging the adoption of a new information technology within an organization is to directly aim training and incentives at the users Rogers deems laggards, in contradiction to the advice of most diffusion theorists when discussing this user group. Naturally, in all aspects of social science, the processes involved in shaping our behavior and acts are rarely simple or singular, again reminding us that while we might have strong arguments and even data to support one interpretation, but when it comes to humans it is best to accept there will always be exceptions.

Though its limitations are perhaps understood by social scientists, the theory has itself been widely diffused into industry and adopted by marketing teams across multiple domains, from medicine to manufacturing, and clothing to computing. Like all popularized theories, the nuances are often ignored or forgotten in favor of a simplified telling that is easy to grasp and even easier to share. Hence it is common to hear marketing reports that speak broadly about people as being an early adopter or one of the late majority as if this was fixed and definitive for everyone. But we cannot fault the theory for the oversimplified application others make of it. It is common in UX that many complicated theories or models of human performance or behavior gets reduced to "principles" or "guidelines" that are spoken of as if they were immutable laws ("people can only remember 7+/−2 things" or "interfaces should be simple to use from the first moment"). The essence of good UX is understanding the context for any interpretation or application of a theory. To that end, we can see that the diffusion theory or socio-technical theory first require us to understand what situation we are trying to affect, and only then to think more specifically in terms of the characteristics of the innovation or the stakeholders that we can find there. If nothing else, we must acknowledge that while each of us might be in the early or late majority in one context, there are plausibly many other contexts wherein we might be laggards or early adopters, the label is rarely the full story.

So What?

Leaving aside the predictive power of socio-technical thinking or diffusion theory, what is most important to recognize in such theories is their conception of the individual that underlies this more social perspective on users. Not only do both theories acknowledge the importance of context, including the presence and action of others on our own thinking and reasoning, but both emphasize qualities of the individual as a social being that are distinct from social science models at other time-slices. Certainly, socio-technical and innovation diffiusion approaches emphasize the extended duration of decisions to adopt and use or even adjust to and make sense of new technologies but in so doing these approaches offer a quite different view of human thinking than is found at the cognitive level.

Within the social level of being we find concern with people's beliefs, motivations, attitudes, and emotions that are mediated through social and group dynamics to determine outcomes. Socio-technical thinking considers people to be generally well-meaning, seeking co-operation rather than conflict in their social interactions but unconsciously motivated by enhancement of self within a situation and the avoidance of undue control by others. Diffusion theory allows for rational consideration of benefits from adoption but also presents a view of the individual as situated socially, concerned with self-image, mostly viewing change as necessary but preferring it under certain conditions and using comparisons with others as a major basis for decision-making. Personality forms a key part of diffusion theory's conception of individuals, again emphasizing affect over cognition in seeking to frame an understanding of the user.

This shifting emphasis on cognition and affect can be confusing for those untrained in social science who are trying to make sense of the myriad theories, models, and findings about people and technology. Rogers and Eason are both explicit in mentioning ease of use as important, acknowledging a value in design that is predominantly studied through a cognitive lens, yet both diffusion and socio-technical approaches emphasize the fundamental influence of people's social network, work group, or organizational culture in shaping responses. In as much as we get a picture of the internal workings of the human mind in these approaches, users are understood to be driven more by unconscious than purely rational responses, valuing control, enhancement, positive self-image, and status relative to the group. The questions asked by social level theorists tend to use different terms and constructs than those of cognitive level theorists, but we should not lose sight of the fact that either way, we are still examining and attempting to explain human behavior as it relates to user-centered design. Having an unconscious desire for enhancement or control does not mean an individual does not also have a working memory or limited attentional resources. We manifest all of these qualities across our lived experience, a further example of why we should avoid simply treating our understanding of people at a single layer. A person can be concerned with usability and with enhancement, reliant on their own long-term memories and the underlying infrastructure of the environment in which they use a device. We exist at more than one level. And yet there is another layer above the social treatment of people that is also important for us to acknowledge and incorporate into our understanding of users, that of culture. Let us turn to this now.

References

Baxter, G., and Sommerville, I. (2011). Socio-technical systems: From design methods to systems engineering. *Interacting with Computers*, *23*(1), 4–17. 10.1016/j.intcom.2010.07.003

Deloitte (2022). Build it and they will embrace it. https://www2.deloitte.com/content/dam/insights/us/articles/6457_Mobile-trends-survey/DI_Build-it-and-they-will-embrace-it.pdf

Eason, K. (1988). *Information Technology and Organizational Change*. London: Taylor and Francis.

Girardi, P., and Chiagouris, L. (2018). The digital marketplace: Early adopters have changed. *Journal of Marketing Development and Competitiveness*, *12*(1), 84–95.

Land, F. (2000). Evaluation in a socio-technical context. In R. Baskerville, J. Stage, and J. DeGross (eds.), *Organisational and Social Perspectives on Information Technology* (pp. 115–126). Dordrecht, The Netherlands: Kluwer Academic Publishers.

Lewin, K. (1943). Defining the "Field at a Given Time." *Psychological Review*, *50*, 292–310.

Moore, G.C., and Benbasat, I. (1991). Development of an instrument to measure the perceptions of adopting an information technology innovation. *Information Systems Research*, *2*(3), 192–222.

Rogers, E. (2003). *Diffusion of Innovations*, 5th ed. New York: Free Press.

Statista (2022). Daily social media usage worldwide. https://www.statista.com/statistics/433871/daily-social-media-usage-worldwide/

Thomas, W., and Thomas, D. (1928). *The Child in America: Behavior Problems and Programs*. New York: Knopf.

Trist, E. (1981). *The Evolution of Socio-Technical Systems: A Conceptual Framework and an Action Research Program*. Toronto: Ontario Min. of Labour.

The Culturo-Tech Layer 8

Anthropologist Geert Hofstede tells a simple but insightful story of looking at the world from the perspective of three different maps, each centered differently. The first, with Europe in the middle, has the meridian line running through Greenwich in London offering our first delineation of east and west. The second, with the Pacific Ocean as the midpoint places North America to the right, Asia just off-center and Britain and Ireland far left in the apparent outer regions of the west. Finally, the third map is built around New Zealand, but now with the north/south axis inverted, literally turning our world upside down, at least from some perspectives. Since our world is a globe, each map is accurate but, according to Hofstede, depending on where you were born and first became aware of the geography of near and far, you probably have a particular comfort level with maps that place your country of origin closer to the center than not; one world, but three very different perspectives.

How many Americans are raised with the image of North and South America as the center, and the rest of the world spread out east and west from there? And how normal does it seem to British folks that the dividing line between east and west runs through their capital city where they can literally straddle it while having their photo taken, one foot in the east, the other in the west, at the Greenwich Observatory? In a simple way, the maps reveal something about this elusive and yet grounding nature of order, place, belonging and shared identity that underlies the concept of culture. Beyond group membership or social network, our way of seeing the world, how it is organized, how the parts connect and where we fit most comfortably within it tends to go unnoticed until alternative views are presented. Only then do we perhaps start to question how we orient to the world and realize that other peoples might justifiably not see the world in the same way. This

DOI: 10.4324/9781003026112-8

unconscious sense of order manifests itself even in our speech about ourselves and others. Europeans refer to Asia as "the Far East" precisely because of a world view built off Euro-centric representations of where the center lies. To most inhabitants of Asia, they are at the center, and it is the US that is to the east!

Place and centrality, which nations are core and which are periphery in our model of the world, provide an interesting window into collective identity and the way we view ourselves and others, but culture is not reducible to location. With 8 billion people on the planet, we are distributed rather unevenly over 195 countries, give or take a contested boundary or two. Belief systems, religious orientation, cuisine, language, legal regulations, family size, sense of belonging, humor, norms, customs, and multiple other qualities of collective life that we recognize as being inside or outside of "our" world seem to matter to people and form yet another layer of existence that we experience but sometimes fail to recognize in everyday life until changes occur, when we travel or move to a location where different qualities seem to be dominant. It is this layer that social scientists refer to as culture and all of us living on this planet are cultural beings.

There are so many ways we can slice and dice apparently meaningful differences among societies around the globe that the catch-all of label of culture presents us with a similar problem to that faced by Justice Potter when determining what constituted pornography, we recognize it when we see it but are somewhat challenged when asked to define it. But social science would hardly live up to its name if it did not at least attempt formal definition and among the many that have been provided, the following, from the Center for Advanced Research on Language Acquisition at the University of Minnesota strikes me as quite useful. It defines culture as the "shared patterns of behaviors and interactions, cognitive constructs and understanding that are learned by socialization. Thus, it can be seen as the growth of a group identity fostered by social patterns unique to the group." (https://carla.umn.edu/culture/definitions.html).

There are two key aspects to this definition that fit well for our purpose. First, it provides a focus on people, particularly groups of people, and not on regions or nationalities. Culture might be a collective force, a set of social patterns, but it is still experienced by people, which means it also has impact at the individual level. Second, it speaks directly to the idea of shared understanding of the world developed through a lengthy process, the long-term learning that children and young adults go through which shapes their values and awareness of the world around them. Socialization is enculturation, quite literally, the imposition and fostering of a shared perspective, acknowledging that we are, all of us, products of group processes that form our cognitive representation of, and sense of place in, the world. Here, in classic social science terms, we view culture as the longest time-slice of human experience to study and ask questions that tap into thinking patterns, beliefs and attitudes that are often decades in the making.

But What About the Digital World?

The importance of culture in facilitating group integration, providing shared understanding of how to behave and what to expect of others can obviously help communities manage and maintain order. The duration of cultural processes also reflects an ability and desire to pass knowledge on, for new members of a community to gain from the experiences of previous generations. In evolutionary terms, we might infer many advantages to groups that learn, communicate, and find ways of signaling to each other what is acceptable behavior. It is not unreasonable to ask however, if the role of culture is shifting in a networked world.

Since over 40% of the world's citizens still lack basic access to the internet, we might well recognize another major division of core and periphery that has less to do with regional than virtual location. Right now, on this planet, you can be divided coarsely into one of two cultures, the information "haves" and the "have-nots." In any month during 2022, more than 10 billion visits by the "info-haves" are made to YouTube or Google websites. If we round the numbers to assume a total user population of some five billion people, then on average, every "information-have" is visiting these websites twice a month. Of course, such numbers are imprecise, some people never visit Google or YouTube in a month while others access it daily. Some governments limit their citizens access to these sites, distorting the distribution further. However, the broad implication is hard to counter: the potential for the "information haves" to gain access to the same ideas and data, regardless of geographic location, has never been as great. Where media and information channels were once national, regional, or local, they are increasingly global, and a citizen in the US can read the news from other countries, view the available housing stock in another city, or check the price of goods or the weather in a different continent, virtually and instantly from their smart phone. For the "haves" and "have-nots," its one world but with two very different perspectives.

In such an environment, there is a growing belief that regional and international boundaries are far more porous than before, that the emergence of global citizens over nationalities will come to be the norm, all of us members of a shared information world. Such a world would seem to require a quite different kind of atlas than any representing geography. Louise Drulhe, a French artist has tried to find ways of representing this with in her "Critical Atlas of the Internet," (https://louisedrulhe.fr/internet-atlas/) a series of visual representations that speak of the internet being both a global infrastructure and a shared space, a place where everything is close and far at the same time. As she argues, the internet is the only common space shared worldwide, where distance is meaningless when everything is potentially only a click away. Little wonder then, people ask if cultural diversity is shrinking as globalization is accelerated by information technologies (to give just one example, UNESCO recently reported that more than 600 languages have become extinct due to globalization, and more will surely follow, see Mosley and Alexandre (2010)).

The challenge for user-centered designers is trying to understand which cultural differences might be determinants of user preferences or responses to digital technologies. Given the rather catch-all nature of the concept, where almost any general attitudinal, linguistic or interpretive variation can be attributed to culture, it can be difficult to capture the concept operationally or meaningfully for design purposes. Given the definition above, where culture is conceived as shared behaviors and constructs, learned through socialization, the challenge is to identify a set of variables that both seem to reflect these differences and are appropriately measurable or observable. In the following section, we consider the main theoretical contributions from social science that seem to offer at least some applicability for design.

Symbols and Sagas – The Stories We Tell About Ourselves

Those disposed to studying culture have long argued that a group's culture is reflected in its own telling of its history, its literature, stories, myths, and belief systems. The earliest stories of life on the planet, our creation, a tribal event in the past, a tragedy or disaster that befell our ancestors, such events are woven into tales and repeated, then passed on to educate new or young members of our group. As ever, information is at the root of human connectivity. Added to our species fondness for telling is the showing; displays of arts, crafts, symbols, and artefacts typically represent what we consider indicative of our people, our group, our place in the world. All human societies seem to possess their own tales and their own symbols, beliefs and crafts, so it is no wonder that anthropologists seeking to understand a culture examine these closely in their search for insights on a group's collective identity and practices.

Hoftsede et al. (2010) summarize these common manifestations of culture in four words: symbols, heroes, rituals and values, which they group in their "onion" model of culture, each particular manifestation forming a layer, from surface to core, that reflects its strength or durability. According to these scholars, symbols are the outermost layer, reflecting the phrases, images, gestures, clothing or otherwise somewhat superficial aspects of behavior and interactions that are recognized mainly by people within the group and which can easily be observed from outside. Symbols are subject to change over time, perhaps at the whim of fashion and can be easily replaced, but some symbols within a culture might endure through collective agreement (e.g., the national or regional flag). Every culture has multiple symbols, usually well understood by members, which signal identity, history and a sense of collective distinction.

Similarly, within any culture's history and sense of identity, there are key figures, living or dead, who represent the embodiment of what is considered "good," "notable" or as an exemplar of some desirable attribute. Classically we find these in the sagas and myths of a people, the narrative of a hero's achievements over great odds, or wisdom in the face of a challenge. Most cultures have figures that represent leadership, bravery, or defiance in the face of enemies. These names form part of the culture's history lessons passed down through education. But, as anthropologists are quick to note, some heroes in our society are more transient than permanent: popstars or athletes, for example, might be considered heroic in the short-term, only to be soon forgotten when a new fad, fashion or sporting hero renders them yesterday's news. The role of media in shaping the perception of such stars as "heroes" is a topical form of interest in contemporary cultural studies.

The third layer in Hofstede et al.'s onion model is rituals, the expected performative acts we see expressed within a group. Such acts are rarely essential to completing a task or reaching a collective goal, but they can be deemed important enough to be enacted routinely through expectation and social desirability. Formally, we witness these in ceremonial acts or religious practices involving rites, but they may also occur in routine interactions such as the norms for interpersonal address when meeting or greeting others, the expression of manners, and behavioral exchange. Group cohesion is often the unstated but essential part of the rituals observed in business and political interactions.

The core of this model is the layer of values, which refers to the preferences a group tends to have, over time, for ordering the world into a given state, with associated principles for how others should be treated and interacted with in a meaningful manner. Hofstede et al draw a firm distinction between values and the other layers, which they deem a form of practice. Practices can usually be observed as they manifest themselves through behaviors or objects though the full meaning of some practices is often only apparent to members of a culture. Values are not practices, a distinction that Hofstede and others are firm to maintain. Rather, they are deeply held preferences manifest in a series of dispositions that can be described in positive or negative terms such as "good and evil," "right and wrong" or "dangerous or safe." Values also reflect the groups recognition of aesthetics ("beautiful or ugly") and normalcy ("permitted or forbidden" and "rational or irrational"). Because of this dispositional form, expressible on a high or low axis, values offer a key to measuring the deepest expressions of a culture.

Through the use of symbols, the recognition of heroes, the practice of rituals, and the internalization of values, it is argued that humans, and particularly groups of humans, slowly acquire and pass on collective dispositions toward the world which become shared among members of a community. Research suggests that values tend to be formed over the first 12 or so years of life and remain relatively stable thereafter, though as adults we might continue to change and adopt new practices (symbols, heroes etc.). Early learning of cultural identity is somewhat unconscious, all part of the slow process of socialization. As adults, our cultural identities can be more consciously considered.

The empirical basis for this symbol-heroes-rituals-values framing is somewhat unclear, but it offers a plausible summary of many impressions we have of culture. However, the operationalization of values as an axis on which cultures might differ fits very well with extant social science efforts to define and measure. Anthropologists and sociologists such as Parsons and Shils (1951) proposed similar axes such as "gratification v. restraint" or "universalism v. particularism" to highlight gross distinctions between groups or communities. The challenge is that observing any such distinctions leaves considerable room for interpretation, and with that comes the possibility of bias and worse, as when distinctions between cultures or nations are latched onto by others, and cast in moral terms, with one end of any dimension deemed "superior" or "better" than the other.

Where social science has tried to distinguish itself from simplistic distinctions, it does so primarily on the assumption, argued early on by anthropologist Margaret Mead, that all groups and societies, regardless of wealth or geography, essentially face similar problems in dealing with their environment. Accordingly, the articulation of culture might be tied to observing how a group or community respond to their challenges, with differences among cultures partly attributable to external forces and the manner in which the collective chooses to resolve problems. A landmark study by Inkeles and Levinson (1954) on what was, from our contemporary lens, perhaps unfortunately called "national character," suggested that every society, regardless of other differences, is required to adress a set of issues concerning authority, gender, the relationship between the individual and the group, and the resolution of conflict. Writing some forty years later, Inkeles stated that their aim was to understand the extent to which "the patterned conditions of life in a particular society, give rise to certain specific patterns in the personalities of its members" (Inkeles, 1997, p. 1). This has proven to be a major research challenge that social scientists have struggled to address (is personality really the key here?) but it is the representation and analysis of those recurring challenges and responses within groups which has given other scholars a path forward in trying to understand and measure the elusive concept of culture.

Almost 20 years after Inkeles and Levinson's pioneering work, Hofstede was offered access to a large data set generated by IBM through a series of surveys the company had conducted across its global organization. As a multinational company, IBM had attempted to capture the attitudes and values of its workers around the world to multiple personal and social issues, with a view to helping the company's managers better understand their employees. For a global corporation, with a shared set of organizational goals, it was felt that such a better understanding of any regional differences would help managers interact more appropriately and effectively with employees resulting in improved business functions. As Hofstede observed, this data set was a social scientist's dream as it contained the responses of more than 100,000 employees in over 50 countries. Analyzing the data led Hofstede to conclude that social challenges of the kind Inkeles and Levinson had first suggested as constructive of group identity were also emergent at the national level.

Hofstede outlined four basic themes in what he termed "dimensions of culture," variables that could be measured and applied to describe and to determine similarities and differences between communities or groups. He named them power distance, collectivism/individualism, femininity/masculinity, and uncertainty avoidance. In subsequent work, he added two more, long-term/short-term orientation, and indulgence/restraint to provide a set of six that has become almost standard in the research literature on global cultures. Let's look at these in more detail.

Power Distance

Societies or communities tend to vary in the distribution of authority among their members and the spread between the most and least powerful citizens is deemed the power distance. Accordingly, in societies where authority is invested in a particular sub-group or role, and subordinates are expected to behave in compliance with the rules and expectations of such figures, inequality, or distance in power would be considered high. In contrast, a society where members are committed to finding a legitimate basis for investing authority in others, (e.g., through elections), and subordinates are expected to be consulted in decision-making, power distance would be deemed low. Hofstede et al provided numerous data points as indices of how power distances might be observed in a culture. For example, the respective roles of teachers or parents in a culture reflect differences on this dimension. Where power distance is low, education is considered more student-centered, and parents are thought of as caregivers and nurturers rather than instructors of children. In high power distance societies, the teacher or parent is invested with greater authority, and children are expected to obey their orders. The higher the power distance in a society, the more we find power residing in a ruling class, an elite sub-group whose legitimacy is accepted as given rather than established through negotiation or elections.

Individualism/Collectivism

The relationship of the individual to the group has long interested social scientists and offers another variable that is readily invoked in discussions of national culture and of course, political systems. Countries or groups that score more toward the collectivism end of this dimension place emphasis on communal relationships and group harmony. In such communities, families and clans form an important network for protection, and loyalty to the sub-unit is highly valued by members. Societies ranking toward the individualism end of this dimension are seen to value personal attributes over collective concerns, personal privacy is valued highly, and citizens are encouraged to accept personal responsibility for their own well-being. Individualistic work cultures consider task completion as a more important work goal than maintaining positive group attitudes or relationships, quite the opposite of collective cultures. Interestingly, some research suggests that this cultural difference can be indexed or observed directly by counting the frequency of the term "I" in a culture's language and writing, since speaking of oneself and one's own needs or opinions is thought to be significantly more common in individualistic than collectivist societies (Kashima and Kashima, 2003).

Femininity/Masculinity

The gender dimension reflects terminology that is typical of anthropological concerns with social structures which have focused on the differentiation between males and females across societies. We might reasonably question this binary framing, but Hofstede's use of the labels is nuanced and considers both roles and dispositions within a group toward matters such as work-family balance and attitudes toward others. A culture that is deemed strongly masculine tends to express admiration for strong individuals and reveal less sympathy or support for members of the group who are struggling or in difficulties. Cultures on the masculine end of the spectraspectrum also place a strong emphasis on the importance of work for social status, and place high value on salary-level and advancement for status within the group. Feminine-leaning societies view family life as more important than work, and place greater value on healthy working relationships and job security than on salary. In more literal indices of the dimension, it is argued that the gender make-up of political leadership, or size of family unit (more children per family in masculine cultures) are quantifiable reflections of cultural disposition on this dimension. In their 2010 outline, Hofstede et al. (2010) also use the "modesty-assertive" labels as synonyms for femininity-masculinity, which captures some other facets of the values covered under this dimension.

Uncertainty Avoidance

Tolerance of ambiguity and the acceptance of uncertainty in life underlie the fourth of Hofstede's original dimensions. The dimension runs on a weak-strong scale, with those cultures scoring highly on the strong end of uncertainty avoidance considered to be more rigid in terms of rules and regulations that must be followed and to show greater intolerance of deviance within the community. Toward the weak end of this dimension, societies deemed to have low uncertainty avoidance demonstrate greater tolerance for ambiguity, greater faith in the self-directedness of members, and more acceptance of the belief that not knowing all the answers to life's challenges is normal. Hofstede et al also suggest that cultures on the strong uncertainty avoidance end of the dimension manifest greater degrees of stress and emotionality among members than weak avoidance cultures.

Orientation: Long-Term Versus Short-Term

The importance within a society of planning for the future gives rise to the orientation dimension added by Hoftsede et al in the 1980s, with endpoints of long-term and short term. As the name implies, this dimension distinguishes between cultures that have a strong sense of history and which acknowledge the importance of tradition as opposed to those that accept and encourage change and that value future events as more important than past ones. Cultures with a long-term orientation tend to place high value on commitment to a shared purpose, individual perseverance, and thrift, while respecting the stratification of society across members. In contrast, short-term orientation cultures are characterized more by consumption and spending of resources, a determination to address and solve problems quickly, and a view that success or failure is based more on luck than effort. A further example of avoiding oversimplification on this axis, Hofstede argues that short-term oriented cultures are prone to fundamentalist thinking over the more pragmatic attitudes manifest in long-term oriented cultures.

Indulgence Versus Restraint

There has long been an interest among social scientists in understanding the sense of well-being within a community and how it manifests itself in members' behavior. Hofstede and colleagues recognized this in their final dimension, which expresses a cultural distinction based on indulgence at one end of the spectrum and restraint at the other. An indulgent society encourages ready gratification of desires and needs, particularly when it comes to gaining personal happiness, freedom of speech is encouraged, and leisure activities are considered important. At the other end, a culture scoring higher on restraint reflects a belief among members that easy gratification of personal needs is not healthy for the group, and members should accept regulations of behavior through collective norms. Restraint-oriented groups also place higher priority on law and order, and this is quantifiable through measures such as levels of police per capita, or birthrates among the educated (high restraint societies show lower birth rates than indulgent cultures among this demographic).

At first glance, these dimensions might seem overly broad, insufficiently distinct from each other, and perhaps even employing unflattering stereotypes that one culture might apply to another, but one needs to read beneath the labels to recognize the qualities of each dimension as operationalized. While it might be something of a cliché to speak of America as the land of "rugged individualism," and "indulgence," the characterization offered through these Hofestedian dimensions speaks more to the question of how societies see the relationship between an individual and the group. It's not simply a case that one culture offers individual rights and the other demands collective submission, though these can certainly be extreme points on the axis under some political regimes, it is more the case of how the interests of the group are to be enacted, and what responsibilities are placed on an individual. For example, an apparently "collective" society, with strong sense of the ties between members, might enact business customs differently, or place importance in particular areas of child education, the role of family, lifestyle choices, and might even speak differently about themselves in conversation.

Similarly, indulgence, as operationalized by Hofstede, is not just a measure of the members tendency to spend rather than save, or to enjoy leisure over labor, but it speaks to the sense of happiness people in a culture report, or the degree of control they report having over their own lives. In fact, if one reads Hofstede et al. (2010) in full, one can find an incredible range of data points about cultures that counter an over-simplified interpretation of any single dimension. Through their own work and the research of many other scholars in the last decades, Hofdstede et al. (2010) can insightfully correlate a host of behavioral, attitudinal, and demographic data with their dimensions. For example, they report there are lower rates of heart disease in indulgent cultures than found in those manifesting greater restraint. They note that media advertising in high uncertainty avoidance cultures tends to rely on expert voicings to market products to consumers compared to the greater use of humor in low uncertainty avoidance cultures. Surprisingly perhaps, they also show that spending on health care from private and public funds is lower in collectivist than individualistic cultures.

What is most impressive about the huge data sets this framework has generated over time is the ability these now provide for comparisons of many countries on these dimensions. Thus, one can visit the Hofestede-Insights.com website and use a free comparison tool to generate a histogram of scores on each dimension for each country in their database, as shown below (Figure 8.1).

Here we see a comparison between China, Germany, India, and the US. For each factor, scores are given by nation. Each dimension is scored from 0 to 100 to mark the two end points, and a quick visual scan affords an easy representation of the similarities and differences among countries on each dimension. So, for example, both China and India score higher on power distance than the US and Germany, suggesting significantly larger differences in influence and authority among citizens of India and China compared to the United States and Germany. Similarly, on the individualism dimension, we can see if the United States has significantly greater tendency towards individualism than China which unsurprisingly leans more towards collectivism. Other large differences are observed in the long-term orientation dimension, with China and India reporting a greater disposition towards long-term orientation in their culture then the United States, with Germany somewhere in the middle.

Interestingly, for all the differences we observe in these comparisons, all four countries in this example seem to score similarly on the masculinity dimension. For variability on this dimension, we need to look to

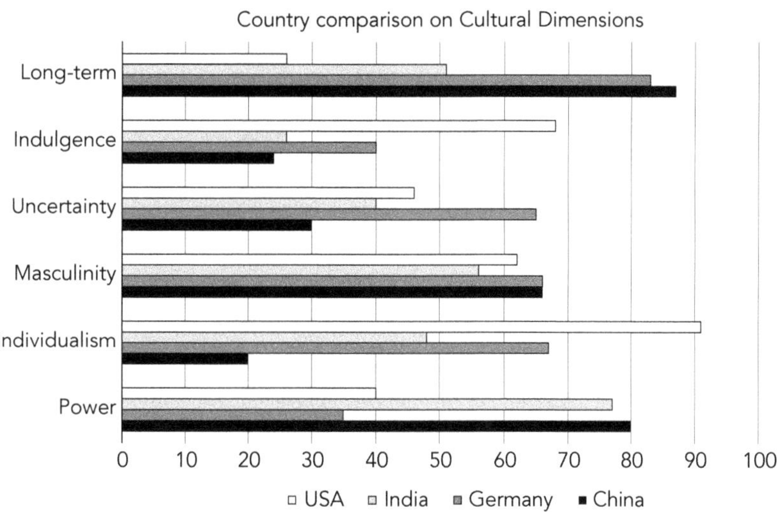

Figure 8.1 Comparison of four countries on Hofstede's six dimensions of culture. See comparison tool at https://www.hofstede-insights.com)

other countries. The Hofstede data shows nations such as Chile, score much lower on the masculinity scale (score of 28 compared to the mid-60s rates of Germany and China). In fact, Japan (masculinity score of 92) and Sweden (masculinity score of 5) are the most differentiated on this dimension which speaks to the some aspects of the competitiveness of Japanese culture and the emphasis on quality of life in the Swedish context. Obviously, this type of range indicates the importance of considering a culture in multi-dimensional terms rather than on a single scale.

While the decades of data collection and comparison have given the Hofstede model of culture a dominant position in research on this layer of experience, it has been criticized for over-reach and the reduction of culture, at least in its calculation and reporting form, to nationhood. Clearly, culture and nation are not equivalent. Nationalities are political constructions as much as regional or geographical referents, and one does not change a culture simply by labeling parts of it differently each time a border map gets redrawn. The variability of size (in terms of population and terrain) of nation states makes such a reduction even less useful. India, with a population of more than 1.2 billion people and occupying almost 2.4% of the world's area across 28 states and 8 union areas, is a hugely diverse country that makes any interpretation of culture based on a single score or set of scores rather difficult. Compare this with countries like Belgium, about 0.01% of the size of India, with only 11 million citizens and one might imagine that nation is insufficiently precise to capture culture as understood by its members, though even here, there are well-identified distinctions within its citizenry. One only has need look at Britain, one culture according to the Hofstede index, but speak to the people of Wales or Scotland about the very real cultural differences they perceive between themselves and the English and you may wonder if 'British' is the most meaninfgul unit of analysis.

Hofstede and colleagues have certainly blurred the nation and culture distinction across their writings, and frequently refer to the dimensions as indices of "national culture." In practice, most researchers have come to accept this as a workable, if not ideal, solution. Notwithstanding that concern, the comparisons are often quite interesting, both confirming some of our expectations (the US really is more individualistic than collective and yes, the culture seems to lean toward indulgence over restraint), but also inviting us to question assumptions or view cultural qualities anew (the US is closer to India or China in uncertainty avoidance than it is to Germany). Perhaps international and cross-cultural relations would be improved if we all re-considered our assumptions in the light of such data.

But beyond the criticism of reduction to nationality, there remain concerns that the operationalization of culture in this manner offers very little predictive power at the individual level, e.g., knowing I am a citizen of South Korea would not really give you much confidence in estimating my personal disposition toward power, gender, or indulgence, etc. This, however, is hardly damning, any cultural analysis invariably is challenged in being reduced to the level of the individual. None of us is just a member of a culture, we are individual physical and psychological organisms, as repeatedly argued in this book, and we should not expect one level of analysis, in this case culture, to satisfactorily explain our full human experience any more than we would hope for complete understanding to result from the physical or perceptual layers of analysis. Another common criticism made of this model stems from the original data set Hofstede used to generate the dimensions being too limited, but this ignores the fact that by now Hofstede and his colleagues have extended their original work far beyond the large IBM sample he started with on the 1970s. In fact, large re-analyses and comparisons using other substantial data sets such as the World Values Survey tend to lend more support than not to the Hofstede model (see Hofstede et al., 2010 for a detailed treatment of this issue).

In the end, while it is important to understand the limitations of culture so imagined, Hofstede's dimensions do offer a way of operationalizing this complex construct and providing a useful index for comparison. As a result, the model has been widely employed, much like Rogers' model of diffusion has itself been adopted, by researchers in many other disciplines, particularly in business, market research and education. Designers are becoming increasingly aware that user populations around the globe vary in ways that might be important for us to understand so the argument goes if we can tie use preferences to cultural awareness and identification, we might advance user-centered design in important ways.

So What Does Culture Mean for User Centeredness?

Several recent reviews of work on culture and user interface design have attempted to map the six dimensions to particular aspects of interaction (see e.g., Kyriakoullis and Zaphiris, 2016). Such work represents an attempt to identify patterns of user response that seem distinct across user groups drawn from different cultures (operationalized, as expected, by nationality). Typical of such work, for example is a study by Haddad et al. (2014) who compared two interface designs for a self-test health site (one rich in content to help users, one with only minimal information to guide selections on a menu of options). Comparing older users from a mix of Canadian, US, German and British participants) with east Asians (predominantly Chinese with one Japanese participant), these researchers report clear differences between these two groups which might be mapped to culture. Specifically, the East Asian users showed a preference for, and manifested less anxiety with, the richer, more content-rich interface, which Haddad et al suggest reflected their cultural disposition to avoid or lessen uncertainty. By extension, the more spartan alternative was thought to increase the sense of ambiguity or uncertainty among East Asian users.

While we might be slow to draw firm conclusions from such studies, it is clear that the operationalization of culture provided by Hofstede offers a tempting variable for experimental investigation. The rise of the global web has brought increased research attention to national preferences for web design where the Hofstede framework is commonly applied. So, we have learned that users from low power distance cultures tend to correct or edit wiki entries more than users from high power distance cultures (Pfeil et al., 2006), and that this same dimension also distinguishes user groups in terms of willingness to comment on or review items on consumer product websites (Lai et al., 2013). This culturally informed approach to user behavior has now given rise to a laundry list of design recommendations on the use of images on websites to ensure compliance with such cultural norms for dress, expression, relationships and so forth (see Viera, 2017, or Malachi, 2017). So while we might indeed be on a path to global citizenry in the long term, these early decades of the information revolution seem to tell us that cultural differences are still very real and matter significantly for users.

It will always prove difficult to tie specific interface design qualities to culture since there are far too many sources of variability among people and preferences, but gross distinctions might still prove informative if they can be applied through a process of user-centered design. As always, it is important to treat lists of design guidelines as suggestions, not rules, but I would suggest however a further application of cultural analysis that might be important methodologically. For as long as we rely on gaining input from representative users, it might be important to understand that freely expressing opinions, particularly critical ones, to a designer or UX researcher is likely to be a culturally sensitive activity. Building trust and confidence among respondents or finding ways of enabling their honest input without inducing discomfort would seem to be a very important skill for a UX designer involved in international or cross-cultural research. Without cultural awareness, one might otherwise incorrectly interpret a lack of critical input as a sign that a proposed design was acceptable, failing to understand that the users you are speaking with do not feel empowered to raise criticisms.

While the mapping from cultural dimension to user response in this type of work is unlikely to yield formal or explicit rules for design that apply without caveats, examining culture for insights in design might lessen the chances of gross errors occurring (see e.g., Dolce and Gabbana had to withdraw an advert from the Chinese market after it caused offence, NPR, 2018). As Kyriakoullis and Zaphiris (2016) note, the study of culture invariably reminds us that a diversity of tastes, preferences, interpretations and expectations reflect the differences among peoples around the world. Being sensitive to this in our design processes, even if we are not yet fully able to map cultural dimensions neatly to an interface rule, is all part of our commitment to user-centeredness on a global level.

References

Haddad, S., McGrenere, J., and Jacova, C. (2014). Interface design for older adults with varying cultural attitudes toward uncertainty. In Proceedings of the SIGCHI Conference on Human Factors in Computing Systems CHI. 10.1145/2556288.2557124

Hofstede, G., Hofstede, G.J., and Minkov, M. (2010). *Cultures and Organizations: Software of the Mind*. New York: McGraw Hill.

Inkeles, A. (1997). *National Character: A Psycho-Social Perspective*. New Brunswick: Transaction.

Inkeles, A., and Levinson, D. (1954). National character: The study of modal personality and social systems. In G. Lindzey (ed.), *Handbook of Social Psychology* (pp. 975–1020). Cambridge MA: Addison-Wesley.

Kashima, E., and Kashima, Y. (2003). Individualism, GNP, climate and pronoun drop: Is individualism determined by affluence and climate, or does language use play a role? *Journal of Cross-Cultural Psychology*, *34*(1), 125–134.

Kyriakoullis, L., and Zaphiris, P. (2016). Culture and HCI: A review of recent cultural studies in HCI and social networks. *Universal Access in the Information Society*, *15*, 629–642. 10.1007/s10209-015-0445-9

Lai, J., He, P., Chou, H.-M., and Zhou, L. (2013). Impact of national culture on online consumer review behavior. *Global Journal of Business Research*, *7*(1), 109–115.

Malachi, S. (2017, June 1st). Cross-cultural interface design. *Medium*. https://medium.muz.li/malachidigest-828e37f45117

Mosley, C., and Alexandre, N. (2010). *Atlas of the World's Languages in Danger*, 3rd ed. Paris: UNESCO.

NPR. (2018). Dolce & Gabbana Ad (With Chopsticks) Provokes Public Outrage in China, December 1, 2018. https://www.npr.org/sections/goatsandsoda/2018/12/01/671891818/dolce-gabbana-ad-with-chopsticks-provokes-public-outrage-in-china

Parsons, T., and Shils, E.A. (Eds.). (1951). *Toward A General Theory of Action*. Cambridge, MA: Harvard University Press. 10.4159/harvard.9780674863507

Pfeil, U., Zaphiris, P., and Ang, C.S. (2006). Cultural differences in collaborative authoring of Wikipedia. *Journal of Computer-Meditated Communication*, *12*(1), 88–113. 10.1111/j.1083-6101.2006.00316.x

Viera, J. (2017). The complete guide to cross-cultural design, UX Design. https://www.toptal.com/designers/ux/guide-to-cross-cultural-design

9 Usability as a Design Value

In my kitchen is a five ring Jenn Air gas stove. The gas burners are aligned about a rectangle with one in each corner, as might be expected, and the fifth sitting in the middle, where an imaginary X might be formed by two diagonals. To the right are the five individual burner controls which operate on a push and turn basis. These are aligned vertically, each one controlling a single burner. This layout follows a form that is very common but which might serve as a poster child for poor design. The top control on the right-hand column is for the top-left burner, the bottom control, the one most within-reach of the operator (usually me) activates the lower right burner, and you can probably guess the rest from this. The trouble is, every time I use the stove, I find myself still having to look and mentally map the connection between control and ring. On many occasions I place a pot on one ring but ignite another. Even the middle control, which I really do immediately associate with the center ring, requires a momentary check before use.

Obviously using a linear control layout to affect outcomes on a rectangular burner arrangement made sense to a design team who surely considered the form factor, size, aesthetics and price in determining the final product. However, for a user, there is an apparent challenge, a mismatch between action and outcome that makes the choice of burner control more cognitively cumbersome that it might otherwise be. This mapping challenge is, in design terms, obvious, yet it is curious that over 30 years after Don Norman highlighted a practically identical example in his classic work *The Psychology of Everyday Things* we still find such poor interface layouts in many kitchens. Even more concerning, when I checked Norman's original text, I note that he wrote then that "we have known for 40 years how bad such an arrangement is" (Norman, 1988, p. 78). Clearly, user-centered design has not made as much progress as we might imagine in the last 70 years.

DOI: 10.4324/9781003026112-9

Everyday most of us pick up and use multiple designed objects to affect changes in our environment or to complete basic activities. From smart phones to coffee machines, thermostats to laptops, remote controls to faucets, our daily living involves a continual series of engagements with designed artifacts, and this is before we leave our homes. If we drive, we interact with a machine that is designed according to ergonomic, perceptual, and psychological principles to convey us about the world according to socially enacted rules of behavior. For work we are typically connected via networks of devices that require us to type, touch, input passwords, launch programs, and share files in a series of engagements that convert our thoughts, speech, and actions to digital signals that are transferred and represented to others. Recent data suggest that in the US, 66% of phone owners check their phones 160 times in a day; that is almost once every 9 minutes over 24 hours. Even allowing for minimal sleep this would suggest during waking hours, people are checking their mobile devices every 6 min (though we can't be sure of this reduction since almost 65% of people report that they sleep with their phones beside them and check them if they awake during the night).

We can certainly draw implications from this about the pervasiveness of technology in our lives, and should remember that every one of these interactions is a designed experience, one we take for granted until something goes awry. When it does, our resilience and flexibility as intelligent beings often allow us to repair the interaction by retracing steps or adopting an alternative strategy, perhaps to mild annoyance. Sometimes however, the problem is more serious, proving costly in time (at best) or health (at worst), and it is at these moments that we recognize that some designs are more effortful and prone to error in use than others. We refer to this quality of use to in user-centered design as a product's "usability."

Although usability has a common-sense meaning that we all grasp intuitively, in UX design, the term is a little more contested. How we define usabilitydetermines both what we design to deliver it, and what we evaluate to determine if we have achieved it. In simple terms, usability does indeed mean "ease of use" or how well a product enables its users to operate it as intended, but as we have seen over the preceding chapters, our ideas about what constitutes a user are not uniform, so just claiming we all agree what "ease of use" means should never be accepted at face value. At the very least, we need to agree upon its definition. The first use of the word "usability" also predates user-centered design methods by some time, as I recall the late Brian Shackel often quoting Thomas de Quincey's line "It is not the utility but the use-ability of a thing that is in question", (de Quincey, 1842) a quote that other writers have since turned up (e.g., Lenarcic, 2006), suggesting that even in the nineteenth century people understood that not only was ease of use important, but that there was a meaningful distinction to be drawn between the usefulness of a tool, its utility, and the experience of operating it.

But while we might argue that establishing utility is comparatively straightforward (a tool can or cannot fit a task well, though even this is not always a simple determination since a hammer might make a good door-stop in some situations), the property of usability speaks directly to the contextual nature of exploiting this underlying utility. A tool is only as useful as its operator or user can wield it. The sharpest axe might cut the cleanest, but only if the person swinging it can do so under control and without undue effort. A powerful computer that relies on human inputs will be rendered functionally useless if nobody can operate it. To this end, user-centered design expends a lot of effort trying to determine if the user experience can be improved to allow people to exploit the available functionality. So, while we can employ common sense terms such as "usable" and "useful" to speak generally of the qualities we desire in our designs, the real question is how would we determine usability in our technologies?

The traditional response to this question has been to propose that we test designs with potential users in order to observe if people experience difficulties or make mistakes in use. And even now, representative user testing remains the gold-standard for claims about usability. The trouble with this approach, as you might imagine, is cost, both in terms of time and resources. Even if we were to absorb the expense of continual testing, this process still leaves us with the challenge of determining what we mean by usability for our particular design, and how we will know if we are delivering it sufficiently or not. Recognizing the challenges, user-centered theorists have proposed contextualizing usability through an operational definition to help all stakeholders come to a shared understanding of what a design is trying to achieve.

The operational emphasis is crucial. Rather than defining usability in semantic terms as "ease of use" or "user-friendliness," terms used from the early 1970s to describe the aim of user-centered design, there has been a push within the field to speak directly of measurable or observable qualities of human-computer interactions that could serve as an index of desirable user experience. The origins of this approach lie with Brian Shackel who first proposed such a definition early in the 1980s, stating usability could be seen as any technology's "capability *(in human functional terms)* to be used easily and effectively by the specified range of users, given specified training and support, to fulfill the specified range of tasks within the specified range of environmental scenarios" (Shackel, 1991, p. 24).

At first glance, you might ask if Shackel is not really defining the term as much as pointing to human responses, and you would be right. Shackel explicitly pushed the approach of understanding usability not as a fixed property inherent in the technology but as an emergent construct only manifest through use. This view represented a shift from the dominant (and still unfortunately prevalent) view that a product's usability lay in the interface features it offered such as menu-options, screen resolution, input button layout and so forth. A plethora of experimental findings points to the optimal or preferred aspects of such features, and innumerable handbooks on design present these as guidelines which it was once hoped would provide a rigorous basis for producing usable interfaces. While that science base is useful, and will continue to grow, it is often built of comparative performance (feature A scores better than feature B etc.) which renders generalization difficult. Shackel argued that in practical terms, designers needed a way of understanding and designing usability that was immediately actionable. Further, as technology continues to evolve, the science base on interface qualities or features will always and inevitably be playing catch-up with new developments, unlikely ever to provide a sufficient basis for assuring usability.

This pivot to operationalizing usability pushed a new approach within the user-centered design movement. Rather than make claims for usability based on a consideration of a design's features or appearance, it was argued that we should study the ways in which a proposed design gets used. And to do this, we should not just consider *any* user as a useful indicator but agree in advance who the target users are, for what specific tasks they might use this technology, and where they might engage with it. This operational approach acknowledged that any design could be deemed both usable or not, depending on who was using it, for what purpose, and where. In a world where the term 'user' covers more and more people (in the 1970s there was a quaint belief that only two types of users existed, the specialist and the casual), the idea of usability being a fixed property that applied to everyone makes little sense. Under the operational approach a spreadsheet application that is usable for a frequent task performer in their work office will likely not reflect what an occasional user with little previous experience and working at home considers optimal.

Standardizing Usability

Over the next few decades, not only did the operational approach come to dominate, it became enshrined in international standards, a formal recognition by industry that user-centered design was important. The International Standards Organization (ISO), a global body that has evolved benchmarks or agreed best practices for a host of industry and government practices was created over 50 years ago to set norms for weights and measures for international trade ("a pint's a pound the world around" might roll off the tongue nicely as a truism but it's false, as any beer drinker who has ordered a pint in both the UK and the US can attest) and the needs for standards has grown considerably over the intervening years. In the world of trade and commerce, there are now standards for everything from road safety to medical packaging, and companies wishing to engage in the global marketplace are expected to demonstrate compliance with the ISO standards applicable to their products or services. Most of the products and services we use in daily life follow such standards but unless you pay close attention, you likely take these for granted. In the context of user-centered design, having usability included as an international standard marked a formal recognition in the software industry that user experience was important.

ISO 9241–11, *Guidance on Usability Specification and Measures (1998)* was clearly influenced by Shackel's original operationalization, and it defined usability formally as "the extent to which a product can be used by specified users to achieve specified goals with effectiveness, efficiency and satisfaction in a specified context of use."

Considering the stove top example from the start of this chapter you may argue that the impact of a usability standard in the area of user interface design clearly remains slight, but this is to overlook the achievement of the user-centered design community in gaining formal standards recognition after decades of effort. Much as we all might take pleasure from punishing companies that produce unusable products, we're not there yet. However, the operational definition this standard embodies has advanced a form of usability evaluation that is heavily biased toward task performance measures that have intuitive appeal and can show us where products are going wrong. Specifically, usability is examined through estimates of the effectiveness and efficiency of users employing a product to complete tasks, and a further estimate of how satisfied they felt after trying to do so. These three key indices are typically operationalized as follows:

- Effectiveness: the accuracy and completeness with which users achieve specified goals
- Efficiency: the resources expended in relation to the effectiveness level achieved
- Satisfaction: the comfort and acceptability of use

At first glance, these indices seem relatively straightforward to operationalize and for interactions that are relatively simple and repetitive, effectiveness and efficiency can usually be reduced to completion rate e.g., user can complete X tasks in Y seconds. As a design evolves, this rate can be benchmarked to see if the old and new versions differ. However, on more complex tasks, where users might have a degree of choice in how they complete them or where "completion" is not a simple binary condition (done or not) but is a matter of judgment, e.g., composing a document, exploring budget options, browsing an article etc., then operationalizing effectiveness requires the evaluator to consider some form of grading or scaling task completion in a manner that reflects meaningful differences in outcome.

Efficiency, while typically reduced to time, also has some potential wrinkles in interpretation. If we find that a product requires us to remember certain input sequences or to react to a prompt using a particular keypress combination, this interaction might place a greater load on the user that does not show up in time data but is be experienced as a form of mental effort that absorbs attention. Similarly, a design that requires users to input more commands than an alternative may not reveal itself as extra time on task but will, again, provide a different interactive experience than a design with fewer required steps to achieve the same goal state. Total task time may not reflect these differences but from a usability perspective we certainly would consider these two interactions to differ in terms of efficiency. Again, the operationalization of each measure lies with the evaluator who must determine how they understand the context and what meaningful index they will take for efficiency in their usability rating.

The invocation of satisfaction in the operational definition is important. While we might assume satisfaction positively correlates with effectiveness and efficiency, that is, people will likely be more satisfied with any design they can use effectively and efficiently, and less satisfied with a design they cannot, it turns out this relationship is not quite as linear as we might imagine. Humans being complicated, multi-level creatures, our levels of satisfaction with any product or service are certainly influenced by how successful we are in using them, but in many instances, we are less than completely satisfied even if we can complete a task relatively effectively or efficiently. The converse is also true, even when we engage less than optimally with some devices, we may report sufficient satisfaction with it. In short, our affective or emotional response is not entirely determined by behavioral outcomes.

The complexity of these co-relationships between the three key indices of usability has been reported for many years (see e.g., Frokjaer et al., 2000) though one might be forgiven for thinking otherwise since so many usability evaluations tend to capture only partial data or consider satisfaction or effectiveness scores alone to be sufficient. Such interpretations are flawed. Lindgaard and Dudek (2002), for example, report that estimates of satisfaction from people who just browse a website do not correlate well with ratings from users who complete a set of tasks. Thankfully, it does not seem as if the relationship across indices is random, people generally do seem to report greater satisfaction where they are more effective rather than less, but the caveat "usually" must be added here. One might be reassured by Sauro and Lewis' (2009) examination of over 300 individual cases from 13 studies which reveealed that completion rates, task times, errors, and perceived usability did correlate in the expected directions. That said, Sauro (2016) argues that the most common satisfaction rating tool (the near universal SUS inventory developed by Brooke, 1996) shows only a modest positive correlation with task performance. In short, the recommendation is to capture estimates of all three indices before making any claim for usability in your context.

While it is easy to be distracted by the relationships, the most important contribution of the operational definition is that it not only enables but it requires the evaluation team to negotiate what aspects of interaction matter for the user experience they are trying to provide. One can envisage a phone app aimed at thc public might place greater emphasis on satisfaction than a machine interface aimed at specialist workers in industry, where effectiveness or efficiency might be considered more important. Again, there are no rules here, each scenario can be envisaged in various ways. The team dealing with the consumer app might believe that the path to user satisfaction comes from immediate effectiveness, while the industrial machine designers might feel that long-term satisfaction is best assured through training and successful deployment across the organization. Ideally, both design teams would establish their usability targets through a process involving the determination of users' needs, knowledge and experience, their typical tasks, as well as the environments in which the design is intended to be used. In short, the operational approach can be logically tied to or informed by the outputs of classic user-centered methods.

The challenge then remains agreeing upon what constitutes reasonable targets for effectiveness, efficiency, and satisfaction. This might involve studying users as well as conducting comparative analyses of competitor products or services. If we know, for example, that the current version of a design scores low on user satisfaction, we can then set a target of increasing scores on this criterion. Or if we sense that a competitor product seems to score well on effectiveness but less so on efficiency, we might determine that our alternative must at least match the competitor's effectiveness while proving 20% more efficient. There is no set formula here, the criterion levels are always context-dependent, and part of good user-centered design is to establish and agree target levels that make sense for all stakeholders involved.

From Defining to Evaluating

Whether we accept an operational definition or prefer to treat usability a a general catch-all for the user reactions to a design, there remains the question of how to evaluate the user experience of a design. Ask most practitioners what they mean by conducting a "usability test" and they typically describe a process involving a sample of users performing some predetermined tasks on a design while evaluators capture such data as time to completion, errors made, user ratings of the interface and so forth. This can be quite an illuminating experience for most designers as they witness first hand the possible mismatch between theirs' and the users' models of interaction. However, observing users is not the only evaluation method that can be employed, and in today's world, it might not even be the most common one.

I have previously characterized usability evaluation practices into three broad classes of method that can be observed across the interaction design fields: user-based, expert-based and model-based methods (see Dillon, 2001). While these vary mainly on the *source* of usability data (where we obtain our scores or ratings, e.g., from users or from a usability expert), we can also draw a distinction between the *purpose* of the evaluation i.e., do we conduct a test to help direct an ongoing design process or to determine if a near-completed design meets benchmark requirements, a dichotomy that is often referred to as formative versus summative evaluation. These two distinctions (*source* of data and *purpose* of evaluation) form two axes around which me might plot the space of evaluation methods, available to us. When planning a usability evaluation, we might employ a user-based, summative method, for example, or run an expert-based, formative test; we might prefer a model based, summative evaluation or a user-based, formative test. These methods vary in terms of the insights they can provide, and consequently, we inevitably filter our evaluation outcomes through the methodological choices we make. What this means is that even when a design team decides a usability evaluation is needed, we still must commit to a particular method that makes the best use of the opportunities, needs, and resources available. This choice usually revolves around where we are in product development (e.g., at the early stages when we are conceiving of the interface options, or nearer the final version where we want to confirm we are close to meeting our goals)) as well as the resources (financial, temporal, and personnel) that are available for conducting an evaluation. In the following section we will consider each of these classes of method to highlight the strenghts and the limitations of evaluating usability to determine user experience.

User-based Evaluation Methods

In a formal user-based test, participants are asked to complete a set of tasks with the new design, during which their success at completing the tasks, the type and frequency of any errors they make, and their speed of performance may be noted. After the tasks are completed, users are typically asked to provide comments or ratings on what they liked and disliked about the interaction, either through a survey or an interview, sometimes both. In so doing, the user provides data points on each of the key criteria of the operational definition, their effectiveness, efficiency, and satisfaction. The goal of such an evaluation is to gain as realistic an estimate as possible of how a typical user will react to the new design when using it under expected conditions.

Other data points might also be collected from users. In certain situations, concurrent think-aloud protocols might be solicited to shed light on the users' thought processes while interacting with the tool so that issues of intent and comprehension can be addressed. With this method, users are asked to speak their thoughts aloud, in real time, essentially verbalizing the contents of their working memory. Such data can be very useful as simply observing people's actions (what they touch, press or select from screen) only tells us what they are doing, not what they are thinking and feeling. We want to know, for example, if users appear effective but are guessing rather than confidently making navigation choices, or if they are noticing or ignoring relevant feedback during the interaction. Having people utter their thoughts in a somewhat unfiltered, real-time manner can prove very illuminating. A variation on this technique involves asking participants to watch a recording of their interaction on video while the evaluator asks them to describe in more detail what they were thinking at various key points in the interaction. This is referred to as a retrospective verbal protocol. While it might be less intrusive than asking users to think out loud concurrently, it also has the potential to be misleading if the user cannot really remember their thoughts or tries to rationalize their mistakes. Again, every data-collection method comes with advantages and disadvantages that an experienced evaluator must learn to recognize in order to identify the most appropriate ones for a particular test.

In the 1980s and 1990s, as the software industry began to wrestle with usability as an important design value, many companies created dedicated test facilities, termed usability labs, to conduct evaluations. Usually consisting of a dedicated space, set up, for example, as a typical office, and designed to allow users to engage with a device while being observed, often unobtrusively via one-way dividing windows or through a combination of cameras and screen capturing software, labs still find regular use today. However, with the increased availability of portable screen recording technologies, it is now possible to create a similar type of test environment in the user's natural environment, even remotely, with the tester and the participants never actually being in the same physical space. Highly accurate eye-tracking tools capture where a user looks, how they move through text and graphics, what parts of a display they fixate on and what they overlook, all important sources of data to help us understand how users respond to the design under evaluation (for a good introduction to the use of eye-tracking methods in usability evaluation see Gwizdka et al., 2019).

Not all user-based testing involves such formally structured evaluations. Depending on what we want to know, we might engage ask users to informally interact with the system or prototype in order to gain agreement on what works and what seems problematic with the design, perhaps using this to trigger discussion of what might be a better or more appealing interface. Less like a test scenario than a conversation, such participative approaches can be useful for exploring interface options in the early stages of design, helping guide the design team's understanding of what users might want and need. There are innumerable web and published resources on usability test methods that can serve as pointers for those seeking to explore this space (Rubin and Chisnell, 2008 is a good place to start), the important issue here is that whatever method is employed, it involves representative users providing the data. It is no exaggeration to say that any test involving real people is likely to throw up some surprises along the way, and if not, it might be a sign that the evaluators are not asking the right questions or are not open to hearing what the intended users are really saying.

In an ideal world user testing with a large sample of the intended user population would occur routinely, offering the designers a chance to calibrate their design intentions with genuine responses from intended users. However, due to resource limitations, particularly time and money, user-based tests are often limited to a small sample or left until the later stages of the design process when the product is deemed ready to be tested on real people. As a result, there is considerable interest among HCI professionals in determining how to gain the most information from the smallest sample of users. While popular myths exist about being able to determine a majority of problems with five users, Lewis (1994) has shown that the sample size requirement is practically dependent on the type of errors one seeks to identify and their relative probability of occurrence. Whereas three users might identify most of the obvious problems in a new application that has plenty of room for improvement, substantially more users will be required to tease out the remaining problems in a mature or revised product that supports multiple tasks. This is important to consider when planning any user test as a problem that is not common but proves to be a showstopper when it does occur, can easily be missed with small sample studies, leading to serious consequences when the product is released.

One of Gould and Lewis' (1985) principles of user-centered design, that user testing should occur early and often, is perhaps the most violated in practice. Time and again, UX professionals are given the opportunity to test only near completed designs, when many significant design decisions have already been made and the cost of radically changing the interface can be prohibitive. As mentioned in chapter three, the history of user-centered design is a story of trying continually to get user inputs and data into the earliest stages of the process so as to reduce the chances of only finding serious flaws later. However, while there are many ways of involving real users early, there seems to be a residual belief among many in product development that user feedback is only meaningful when a near complete version of a design is ready. Consequently, a second type of evaluation method, one that allows experts to provide judgments of likely usabilityearly in the process, has become popular.

Expert-based Methods

When users are not available, or where time and cost constraints require a quick assessment of an interface design, UX professionals are often asked to provide an evaluation themselves. Sometimes this might require the UX professional to react to or offer an informed opinion, other times the UX member of a team is asked to estimate more formally how well a design works "from the users' perspective." Over the years, UX professionals and researchers have developed various structured approaches for performing such evaluations which we refer to as expert-based methods. Such expert-based evaluations involve an HCI or UX professional examining the design for an agreed use scenario and articulating how a typical user might respond or identifying what problems might exist in the design In this method, real users are not involved, the basis for the evaluation lies in the judgment of the evaluator (the UX expert) who tries to put themselfin the mind of a typical user, so to speak, and to estimate the reactions users will likely have while performing one or more appropriate tasks.

There is considerable interest in this form of evaluation since it can yield feedback faster and cheaper than most user-based methods. But it is important to note that any expert-based evaluation method needs to be more than just an expression of opinion, it should ideally be tied to principles of good design and a deep knowledge of user issues, an ideal, as we shall see, that is rarely met. Numerous expert-based evaluation methods have been proposed but the two most commonly employed in industry (and hence are most frequently taught) are the Heuristic Evaluation (Nielsen, 1994), and Cognitive Walkthrough (Wharton et al., 1994) methods. Both are worth considering when trying to understand how usability is conceived in design.

The Heuristic Evaluation (HE) method provides a simple list of design guidelines which the evaluator uses to examine the interface, screen by screen, while following a typical path through a given task (see Figure 9.1). The aim is to identify any screens where the guidelines might be violated and to check that screen transitions, the task flow, is coherent. The evaluator reports violations of any guideline as a likely user problem and ranks problem severity from minor to major, identifying where re-design efforts might best be focused.

These heuristics were originally generated in the late 1980s/early 1990s, and despite the changes in interface styles since then, have remained largely unaltered, testimony, Nielsen argues, to their representation of the consistent qualities of interaction that people value. Thus, it is argued, with some justification I might add, that users in the 2020s still place value on flexibility, error-prevention, control, and aesthetics etc. As has been argued throughout this book, technologies may change but human needs are largely fixed.

Conducting a heuristic evaluation is straightforward but the reliability and validity of the results vary considerably depending on the expertise of the evaluator, as we might expect. While it is simple enough to learn the

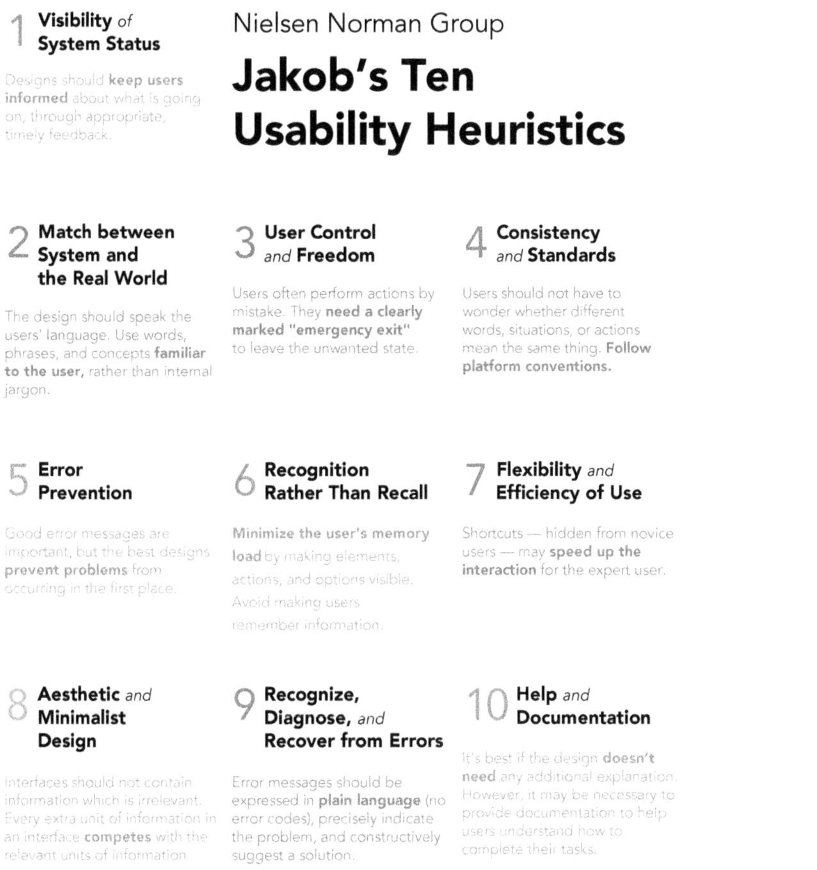

Nielsen Norman Group

Jakob's Ten Usability Heuristics

1 **Visibility** *of* **System Status**

Designs should **keep users informed** about what is going on, through appropriate, timely feedback.

2 **Match between System and the Real World**

The design should speak the users' language. Use words, phrases, and concepts **familiar to the user,** rather than internal jargon.

3 **User Control** *and* **Freedom**

Users often perform actions by mistake. They **need a clearly marked "emergency exit"** to leave the unwanted state.

4 **Consistency** *and* **Standards**

Users should not have to wonder whether different words, situations, or actions mean the same thing. **Follow platform conventions.**

5 **Error Prevention**

Good error messages are important, but the best designs **prevent problems** from occurring in the first place.

6 **Recognition Rather Than Recall**

Minimize the user's memory load by making elements, actions, and options visible. Avoid making users remember information.

7 **Flexibility** *and* **Efficiency of Use**

Shortcuts — hidden from novice users — may **speed up the interaction** for the expert user.

8 **Aesthetic** *and* **Minimalist Design**

Interfaces should not contain information which is irrelevant. Every extra unit of information in an interface **competes** with the relevant units of information.

9 **Recognize, Diagnose,** *and* **Recover from Errors**

Error messages should be expressed in **plain language** (no error codes), precisely indicate the problem, and constructively suggest a solution.

10 **Help** *and* **Documentation**

It's best if the design **doesn't need** any additional explanation. However, it may be necessary to provide documentation to help users understand how to complete their tasks.

Figure 9.1 Nielsen's heuristics for evaluating usability of an interface (downloadable copy freely available at https://media.nngroup.com/media/articles/attachments/Heuristic_Summary1_A4_compressed.pdf)

method, interpreting the guidelines and both recognizing when a violation occurs and how seriously it will impact the experience of users can prove more complicated. Nielsen reported that a typical evaluator would find approximately 35% of existing usability problems using this method and thus recommended the use of 3–5 evaluators rather than one, in particular emphasizing the importance of evaluators having "dual" expertise in both UX and the task domain. When these conditions are met, proponents claim around 75% of the usability problems are found but this success rate has frequently been called into question. There are many reported studies where the agreement rate among experts using this method was found to be very low, sometimes less than 10% (see e.g., White et al., 2011).

Of course, experts might each determine a problem exists but disagree on its cause. This is often less important than recognizing that a problem is real, but the determinant of cause, in this case, which heuristic is being violated, will influence any recommendations on redesign. Important as that might be, the real question we might ask of expert methods such as this is how well the experts predict actual problems that users experience with an interface. If experts fail to find problems that actual users run into, or experts report problems that users never actually experience, the value of such evaluations can justifiably be questioned. Again, the results here are less than reassuring. Khajouei et al. (2018) for example, had three experts conduct a heuristic evaluation of a medical information system and found not only widespread disagreements among the experts but a weak correlation between the problems experts collectively reported and actual user experiences with the system, a generally poor predictive relationship that is common to multiple studies. What this tells us is that we should not consider user-based and heuristic evaluations to be interchangeable with each other. The difficulty with this is convincing teams who believe either heuristic evaluation is a substitute for user testing (in which case it is very likely some important usability issues twill be overlooked) or that it can be employed reliably independent of evaluator expertise (which runs counter to all the evidence showing evaluator experience is crucial). Despite these known shortcomings, the heuristic evaluation approach remains extremely popular among UX professionals, perhaps reflecting an overconfidence among professionals who imagine they are better able to judge user reactions than the data suggest.

An alternative expert-based method, the Cognitive Walkthrough (CW), offers a variant that shifts the focus from heuristics or interface design guidelines toward a more claim-based justification of how well a design works for users. Assuming that the UX professional has an understanding of the underlying psychology of human-computer interaction, the evaluator first determines the exact sequence of correct task performance, that is, the steps a user *must* take to complete a relevant task and then estimates, again on a screen-by-screen basis, the likely success or failure of the user in completing this sequence accurately. As with heuristic evaluation, the expert is required to estimate the likely reaction of users and to explain why certain interface attributes may cause users difficulties. Unlike the heuristic method, the expert does not employ design principles, at least not formally.

Instead, faced with each step in the task, the evaluator must address four questions:

- Will the user try to achieve the desired result?
- Will the user notice what is the right action?
- Will the user relate the right action to their goal?
- Will the user see the progress being made?

The goal in the cognitive walkthrough is for the evaluator to "tell a credible story" about the likely user behavior at each task step, using the four questions as prompts to generate a simple Yes/No answer with an accompanying explanation. For example, if the user's task is to print a document, the evaluator would map out the task in terms of the screen- by-screen actions that must be completed to successfully do so, then proceed to address the four questions at each task step. So, for example, if the proposed design requires the user first to select a printer from those available, the evaluator would ask if the user will attempt this correctly from the initial screen. Maybe a user would think the logical first step is to select a document rather than a printer; in which case the evaluator would flag a possible usability issue with that screen and task step. Each question gets asked in turn for each step of the task sequence, resulting in a story about the user 's experience at that step in the task.

The questions encourage the evaluator to articulate how they imagine a user interpreting the situation. To this end, evaluators are attempting to "get into the mind" of the user and assess how the interface appears to a user engaged in that task and environment Wherever a possible mismatch occurs between the user's intent or understanding and the design's presentation of options and responses, the evaluator records it in their "story." One subtle but important requirement in this method is that even if a problem is observed and recorded, once the screen changes, the evaluator must assume the user has now arrived successfully at this next step and is viewing the new screen in that light. Thus, for each new step in the task sequence, the question prompts start afresh. This is to ensure that each step is evaluated as a standalone part of the interaction. At the end of the task, the "success" and "failure" stories can be ranked to make decisions on possible design changes.

HE and CW are similar though not identical. A benefit I find with CW is the requirement on evaluators to explain why they believe a failure occurred, rather than just flagging a guideline or heuristic violation. The degree to which they can justify their interpretation is made explicit in their "story" and the design team then has a basis for discussing if the problem warrants attention and redesign. Of course, like every method, the experience of the evaluator matters enormously. Hertzum and Jacobson (1999) showed that variability among first time evaluators using CW was significant, and given the method's emphasis on explaining user behavior from a cognitive viewpoint, it is often recommended that evaluators are trained in appropriate psychological theory to make the best use of this method.

Having taught both evaluation methods to many UX professionals, I find that the heuristic approach is quite simple to grasp and, perhaps because of this, is popular with new students. However, the walkthrough technique generally ends up being preferred over time as people gain professional experience. CW concentrates on the difficulties users may experience in learning to use a design, but it can also be applied to evaluations where we anticipate users being experienced, in which case the "stories" that are used to explain success or failure rely on expectations of users with detailed knowledge of the interface. In practice, one does not need to choose between these methods, combining the use of guidelines or heuristics (Nielsen's or others) to provide context and justification for the success or failure stories in CW is both possible and common. That said, the faith we can place in the usability problems reported through the use of these methods is heavily determined by the quality of the expert.

Model-based Methods

A third type of evaluation method for estimating usability employs the formal models derived from psychological theory, drawing heavily on the knowledge base of science that focuses on the narrow bound of cognition, described by Newell and Card as dealing with the 1/10th to 1 sec duration of human activities. Model-based methods rely on a detailed task analysis that provides a fine-grained breakdown of the basic physical, perceptual and cognitive activities involved in using a device, enabling a precise calculation of the time required by a typical user to achieve a goal. (there are more complicated modeling approaches but in mainstream UX evaluation the time-based estimate of expert task completion is dominant).

With model-based methods, the evaluator neither observes real users in action or relies on design principles but applies an analytical model to the task sequence and calculates an estimate of efficiency. The most common model-based approach is the GOMS method of Card et al. (1983), a form of cognitive

Table 9.1 Basic Task Elements for a Model-based Evaluation

LABEL	ACTION	TIME ESTIMATE (SECONDS)
Tk	Enter a keystroke	0.23
Th	Move hands to device	0.36
Tp	Time to point	1.5
Tm	Retrieve from memory	1.2
Tr	Time for computer to respond	1.2
S	Time to swipe touchscreen	0.70

model that casts user behavior into a sequence of fundamental task units (such as moving a cursor to given screen location or typing a well-practiced key sequence) each with associated time estimates for completion derived from decades of experimental findings of human performance. A simple listing of basic actions and time estimates is provided in Table 9.1.

When evaluating a design, the model is applied to an error-free task sequence that a practiced or skilled user would perform. In this way, any interface design can be analyzed to give an estimate of the users' time to complete a task, with the assumption that a faster completion time is better or indicative of a more usable design. Intended to be used at the earliest stages of design, the model-based approach allows a design team to generate competing candidate interfaces and to quickly estimate the efficiency benefits of one over the other, all other things being equal. So, if we consider two layouts for a mobile application interface, this method could support our breaking the task sequence down into basic units (user pointing to screen, selecting a target, pushing a button etc.) and then applying the model's estimates to calculate total time for completing a task with each layout. The appeal of this evaluation approach is that once trained in its application, the evaluator can produce reliable estimates of one parameter of user performance (efficiency) without the cost of running user trials or trying to imagine how a user might respond.

The model-based approach has shown itself to be robust over repeated applications (see e.g., Gray et al., 1993), though it is limited to predicting time taken for error-free completion of tasks involving little or no decision making. The exact value of the estimates can be argued over, and indeed, as much interaction since the original model has moved from desktop to mobile interfaces, new basic acts with associated time estimates (such as the "swipe" act in the table above) have extended the model to touches (see Rice and Lartigue, 2014) but the principle of the model human processor is constant, i.e., decompose the task into its constituent actions and calculate the time involved in the serial completion of these acts.

Of course, this model has its limitations. We cannot use it to estimate how long users will spend on tasks that are not highly practiced, or that require considerable decision making, or planning, activities invoking more controlled than automatic processes. Similarly, where tasks involve parallel processing, it is easy to overestimate times by assuming simple serial processing of the task actions. However, as an applied model of cognition for a constrained range of routine and well-practiced tasks, as much of our interactive behavior seems to be, such a technique can be useful.

Extensions of the model to cover learning of new interactions have also been proposed. Based on a production system analysis, (describing the behavior a user must learn to complete a task in terms of a series IF-THEN rules of interactive sequences, e.g., IF file is "new" THEN select menu option "New File," etc.) Cognitive Complexity Theory enables calculation of the estimated time it would take a user to learn a new procedure. According to current findings, each new If-THEN rule production will take a human approximately 25 seconds to learn (see Bovair et al., 1990). Armed with such knowledge, designers could estimate, for example, the costs involved in changing existing procedures or violating consistency of interaction with new designs. This is obviously a gross estimate and many UX professionals consider such modeling to be too narrow to be practical for many design evaluations but one imagines the training needed to use modeling well is also a deterrent, which raises different questions about how well we educate new UX professioanls which i will address in another chapter.

Comparing the Basic Evaluation Approaches

The relative advantages and disadvantages of each broad method are summarized in Table 9.2. Since usability evaluators are trying to estimate the extent to which real users can employ an application effectively, efficiently and satisfactorily, properly executed user-based methods are always going to provide the best estimate. However, the usability evaluator does not always have the necessary resources to perform such evaluations and therefore other methods must be used. There are good reasons for thinking that the best approach to evaluating usability across a design process is to combine methods e.g., using the expert-based approach to identify problems and inform the developemnt of a user-based test. Obviously, where

Table 9.2 Summarizing the Strengths and Weaknesses of Evaluation Methods

	STRENGTHS	WEAKNESSES
USER BASED	Most realistic estimate of usability Can give clear record of important problems	Can be time consuming Costly for large sample of users Requires prototype to occur
EXPERT BASED	Cheap Fast	Expert-variability unduly affects outcome May overestimate true number of problems
MODEL BASED	Provides rigorous estimate of a usability criterion Can be performed on interface specification	Measures limited aspects of usability Applicable mainly to routine tasks

usability evaluation occurs throughout the design process, the deployment of various methods at different stages is both useful and likely to lead to improved usability in the final product. The challenge however seems to be less about selecting one or other method but being confident that those conducting the evaluation are suitably skilled.

The Limitations of Usability as a Design Value

By agreeing and setting a design target for intended user experience, there is much to be gained from operationally defining usability and this approach has come to dominate practice. However, construing usability in this manner has several shortcomings. First, operational definitions do not lend themselves easily to generalization. We may well learn what design solution meets particular usability criteria for one context but, change the users, alter the task or vary the environment and advocates of the operational approach will argue that you require a new definition. Building a body of knowledge or theory from such data is not easy, which makes for a rather piecemeal set of findings across the discipline on what makes any design usable, which ultimately, we would like to know.

Beyond definition, there is the inconsistency of evaluation. If the success rates of heuristic evaluation are such that we require 3–4 expert evaluators to pool their results for confidence in the findings, we might wonder if we should just ask 3–4 users instead and not bother with HE. This of course also raises the obvious question of what constitutes "expertise" in usability evaluation if there is so little agreement among its practitioners? But it's not just expert methods that are problematic, the very running of user tests comes with built-in potential for distortions. As Lindgaard and Dudek (2002) found, just telling people they were about to participate in a usability test changed the responses they gave when exploring a new design. While we need to gather user input to help keep us on the right track, the pursuit of usability as a primary value has not entirely solved the challenge of designing suitable technologies.

Within the scholarly literature on UX there have been many criticisms of the usability construct. Noam Tractinsky (2018 and 2020) sees the emphasis on usability as a dead end in for UX or HCI research,arguing the construct is too loosely defined to serve more than an umbrella function. He suggests user-centered designers have neither sufficiently formalized the meaning of usability nor generated a significant body of research findings that helps us prescribe it in our designs. We can talk of usability engineering as a set of methods for improving the design by gaining user input to the process but, Tractinsky suggests, either the theoretical strength of the construct (and by extension, the discipline of UX) is weak, or we are unable yet to determine the most important facets of user experience to measure.

Such criticisms echo the type of division we observed earlier between design and science. The former presents knowledge in practice, a set of principles and methods aimed at delivering an artefact, product or service that meets the needs or expectations of its users (among other goals). The latter is, at least in its stereotypical form, intended to abstract and articulate a set of theories and methods that predict and explain the phenomena being studied. In this sense, usability serves a purpose as a design value we can contextualize and evaluate (the design side) but it might well be lacking the theoretical quality of a construct that we can unambiguously measure with any degree of precision. Lewis (2018) counters that ongoing factor analysis of data from industrial usability studies suggests there might well be an underlying construct of usability that manifests itself both behaviorally and subjectively (mapping well with the operational approach) suggesting that claims of usability being dead end might be a little premature.

Rather than arguing about the precision of the construct, one could argue that it is precisely the lack of formalism in user experience design that warrants the application of such an operational definition, and that without one, the goals of any design process would remain diffuse, limited to vague goals such as 'make an improved version' or 'design an interface people like'

By using the effectiveness, efficiency and satisfaction variables to agree targets tied to context, we can at least advance shared goals in a targeted manner. It is in this spirit that I consider the operational interpretation of usability to be useful, though not elegant.

So Where Does This Leave Usability as a Value.?

While criticisms of the lack of precision or reliability of usability evaluations are not easily dismissed, it is important to recognize that the quality of using an interactive device, as experienced by real people, is key to understanding successful design. Usability has intuitive appeal, and with the operational approach, it can be flexibly tailored as a design target for many contexts. But the concept is very much tied to the idea of a user as an individual task performer, and with this comes a strong emphasis on the more rational aspects of interaction: effectiveness and efficiency, even while satisfaction is considered an important third criterion.

While I do not anticipate any major shift occurring in the way we treat usability as a testable quality, I do believe there will be growing recognition that usability, on its own, is a necessary but not sufficient value we need to deliver in user-centered designs. Since most people have experienced a poorly designed device, everyone can recognize the problems of poor usability. But making something usable, at least in the sense of it being effective, efficient, or satisfying to use, is unlikely to lead to great leaps forward in design or to ensure that a design meets the full needs of real people. As multi-leveled beings, users are not simply seeking efficiency in task completion when engaging with technology, we hope for safety, privacy, pleasure and enhancement In UX, the question then is if people can use a design, will they? No amount of usability testing will answer that question but it is probably the most crucial concern for designers, and we address this directly in the next chapter.

References

Bovair, S., Kieras, D., and Polson, P. (1990). The acquisition and performance of text-editing skill: A cognitive complexity analysis. *Human-Computer Interaction*, *5*(1), 1–48. 10.1207/s15327051hci0501_1

Brooke, J. (1996). SUS: a quick and dirty usability scale. In P. Jordan, B. Thomas, B. A. Weerdmeester, and I. McClelland (eds.), *Usability Evaluation in Industry* (pp. 189–194). London: Taylor and Francis.

Card, S., Newell, A., and Moran, T. (1983). *The Psychology of Human Computer Interaction*. Hillsdale New Jersey: Lawrence Erlbaum Associates.

de Quincey, T. (1842). Ricardo made easy; or, What is the radical difference between Ricardo and Adam Smith? With an occasional notice of Ricardo's oversights. *Blackwoods Magazine*. Part III.

Dillon, A. (2001). The evaluation of software usability. In W. Karwowski (ed.), *Encyclopedia of Human Factors and Ergonomics* (pp. 231–237). London: Taylor and Francis.

Frokjaer, T. (2000). Measuring usability: Are effectiveness, efficiency, and satisfaction really correlated? In CHI '00: Proceedings of the SIGCHI conference on Human Factors in Computing Systems, April 2000, pp. 345–352. 10.1145/332040.332455

Gould, J.D., and Lewis, C. (1985). Designing for usability: Key principles and what designers think. *Communications of the ACM, 28*(3), 300–311.

Gray, W., John, B., and Atwood, M. (1993). Project Ernestine: Validating a GOMS analysis for predicting and explaining real world task performance. *Human-Computer Interaction, 8*(2), 237–309.

Gwizdka, J., Zhang, Y., and Dillon, A. (2019). Using the eye-tracking method to study consumer online health information search behaviour. *Aslib Journal of Information Management, 71*(6), 739–754. 10.1108/AJIM-02-2019-0050

Hertzum, M., and Jacobsen, N. (1999). The evaluator effect during first-time use of the cognitive walkthrough technique. In H.-J. Bullinger and J. Ziegler (eds.), Human-Computer Interaction: Ergonomics and User Interfaces. *Proceedings of HCI International '99* (Munich, August 22–26, 1999), vol. I, pp. 1063–1067. London: Lawrence Erlbaum Associates.

ISO-9241 Part 11. (1998). Ergonomics of human-system interaction — Part 11: Usability: Definitions and concepts. https://www.iso.org/obp/ui/#iso:std:iso:9241:-11:ed-2:v1:en. Accessed Nov 28th 2022.

Joo, S. (2010). How are usability elements - efficiency, effectiveness, and satisfaction - correlated with each other in the context of digital libraries? In ASIS&T '10: Proceedings of the 73rd ASIS&T Annual Meeting on Navigating Streams in an Information Ecosystem, vol. 47, October 2010, Art. no. 105, pp. 1–2.

Khajouei, R., Ameri, A., and Jahani, Y. (2018 Sep). Evaluating the agreement of users with usability problems identified by heuristic evaluation. *International Journal of Medical Informatics, 117*, 13–18. 10.1016/j.ijmedinf.2018.05.012. Epub 2018 May 28. PMID: 30032960.

Lenarcic, J. (2006). The anti-usability manifesto. In Proceedings of the 2006 Australasian Computer-Human Interaction Conference, OZCHI 2006, Sydney, Australia, November 20–24, 2006, pp. 337–339. 10.1145/1228175.1228238

Lewis, J. (1994). Sample sizes for usability studies: Additional considerations. *Human Factors, 36*(2), 368–378. 10.1177/001872089403600215

Lewis, J. (2018). Is the report of the death of the construct of usability an exaggeration? *Journal of Usability Studies, 14*(1), 1–7.

Lindgaard, G., and Dudek, C. (2002). User satisfaction, aesthetics and usability: Beyond reductionism. In J., Hammond, T., Gross, and J., Wessen (eds.), Usability: Gaining a Competitive Edge IFlP World Computer Congress, pp. 231–246.

Nielsen, J. (1994). Heuristic evaluation. In J. Nielsen and R. Mack (eds.), *Usability Inspection Methods* (pp. 25–64). New York: Wiley and Sons. Heuristic poster downloadable at https://media.nngroup.com/media/articles/attachments/Heuristic_Summary1-compressed.pdf

Norman, D. (1988). *The Psychology of Everyday Things*. New York: Basic Books.

Rice, A., and Lartigue, J. (2014). Touch-level model (TLM) evolving KLM-GOMS for touchscreen and mobile devices Proceedings of the 2014 ACM Southeast regional conference. Art. no. 53, pp. 1–6. 10.1145/2638404.2638532

Rubin, J., and Chisnell, G. (2008). *Handbook of Usability Testing: How to Plan, Design, and Conduct Effective Tests*, 2nd ed. Hoboken, NJ: Wiley.

Sauro, J. (2016). The challenges and opportunities of measuring the user experience. *Journal of Usability Studies*, *12*(1), 107.

Sauro, J., and Lewis, J.R. (2009). Correlations among prototypical usability metrics: Evidence for the construct of usability. In *Proceedings of CHI 2009* (pp. 1609–1618). Boston, MA: Association for Computing Machinery.

Shackel, B. (1991). Usability – Context, framework, definition, design and evaluation. In B. Shackel and S.J. Richardson (Eds.), *Human Factors for Informatics Usability* (pp. 21–31). Cambridge, UK: Cambridge University Press.

Tractinsky, N. (2018). The usability construct: A dead end? *Human-Computer Interaction*, *33*(2), 131–177. 10.1080/07370024.2017.1298038

Tractinsky, N. (2020). The usability construct: A concern for both theory and practice. *Human-Computer Interaction*, *35*(4), 338–353.

Wharton, C., Rieman, J., Lewis, C., and Poison, P. (1994). The cognitive walkthrough method: A practitioner's guide. In J. Nielsen and R.L. Mack (Eds.), *Usability Inspection Methods* (pp. 105–140). New York: Wiley and Sons.

White, G., Pejman, M, McAllister, G., and Good, J. (2011). Weak inter-rater reliability in heuristic evaluation of video games. In CHI '11 Extended Abstracts on Human Factors in Computing Systems (CHI EA '11). Association for Computing Machinery, New York, NY, USA, 1441–1446. 10.1145/1979742.1979788

10 Acceptability as a Design Value

So You Can Use It, but will You?

That stove top in my kitchen that I mentioned earlier clearly is a sub-optimal design. I've learned to accept the cognitive load involved in mapping the controls to the burners, so you might say that in usability terms, it is effective but not efficient or satisfying to use. But there it sits, years after installation, as my primary means of cooking food. If I were choosing a new stove I might well attend more closely to this mapping, but as most of us find out, the real experience of use occurs long after committing to ownership and once made, we subsequently learn to adjust to the foibles and irritants of poor usability.

You only need look around your home to find examples of choices you have made to use and live with over time. Is every product in your kitchen or home office an exemplar of user-centered design? Did you purchase all your furniture purely for how it served its purpose? Do you persist in using financial or commercial websites that sometimes annoy you? Take a look at your car. How many of the features and controls on the dashboard and information system can you honestly say you use with ease? My Mercedes C300 comes with a center console that allows me to input handwritten data using my finger as a stylus. Yes, really! I have no idea what usage scenario the designers of that feature imagined but I never have, and suspect I will never have, a need for it. How I wish they had spent just a little more time making the interface to the audio system a little simpler as I am unable to adjust treble and bass on that radio without consulting an online manual, which as you might imagine is not advisable when driving. Odds are, there are many products you own and services you use where the design is not optimized for usability and yet you continue to engage with them voluntarily. Examining the range of designed artefacts and services in our

DOI: 10.4324/9781003026112-10

daily lives helps one appreciate the distinction between usability and acceptability that permeates our information world.

The Innovation Diffusion model, so popular among researchers and practitioners suggests adoption of any technology is partly determined by its relative ease of use, among other factors, and characteristics of the adopting individuals. The elegance and attraction of the innovation diffusion model is its seemingly fulsome coverage of the characteristics of both the technology and the people adopting it. But this inclusive framing raises some problems for our consideration of user-centered design. Attributes of the adopted technology are not always qualities that have been designed into the product or can be easily tested during an evaluation, rather they are attributes of the adoption process (e.g., trialability or outcome observability). UX professionals cannot easily shape such considerations (when was the last time you were able to trial a dishwasher or even a can opener before purchasing?), and as Lyytinen and Damsgard (2001) showed, the process of adoption for new information technology products in particular, is usually far more complex and dynamic than suggested by diffusion theory. Obviously, we understand from socio-technical theory that implementation is crucial to success, but when releasing a design for others to use, UX professionals often act as if the results of usability tests alone will determine acceptance and adoption, which clearly is not so. So how can we determine if users will chose to use our carefully designed and usability tested products or services?

Predicting Likely Acceptance or Adoption

If we understand how to assess usability, and we acknowledge this will give us some sense of the potential for a design to succeed, what more can we determine about a design before it is set loose on the world that will increase our confidence in the design being a success? To answer this, the UX community has embraced a set of tools derived social psychological theories of choice and intent to understand not only if people *can* use a design, but given the choice, *will* they? The term employed by user-centered designers for this user response is "acceptance," and it speaks to the view of acceptability as another construct, like usability, that we should pay attention to and ideally, attempt to evaluate or measure in our design process.

In contrast to the literature on usability, with its operational standard of definition, the construct of acceptance or acceptability is rather more loosely defined by UX professionals. Typically, it is taken to refer to people's willingness to employ a tool or device for in contexts where they have discretion or choice. This focus taps into *intent* rather than *performance*, which makes acceptability a meaningful extension of usability. Interestingly, given the substantial literature that exists on user acceptance, the desire for an operational definition seems not to have been a major concern, the focus has more often been on identifying determinants of user intent that can be captured or measured. In part, this lag in definition might be explained by the traditional power of commercial or professional organizations, the major customers for information technology, to require employees use certain technologies. In other words, once usability was acknowledged and addressed, discretion in use was somewhat moot, acceptance was less a matter of choice than of compliance.

Discussion of acceptance within UX however is complicated by the application of "user acceptance tests" in some communities to demonstrate that a design has reached its contracted design goals. This software development view of "acceptance" is closer to what some UX folks would call a summative usability test completed on a final version to show completion of contract. The need to clarify the use of terms reflects an ongoing challenge of label and term ambiguity we still find in the user-centered design literature. For our present purposes, I use "acceptance" and "acceptability" to refer only to the actual or stated choice discretionary users make to use one product or service over another.

Acceptance measures originate from a very simple premise, the belief that people think and decide before they act. This rational view of our actions suggests we are privy to their own thoughts and decisions on such matters and can articulate them to others on request. In psychological terms, this suggests we are dealing with conscious processes but, as we know by now, when it comes to real, living people, it's rarely that simple. The intention to act in a particular way is itself a function of experiences, beliefs, and attitudes or even moods, and for many of us, our intentions are not entirely rational, or immediately and clearly formed before we act. We are immersed in the world, engage with it in exploration a la Neisser's cycle, use feedback to adjust course or, in this case, cement or change attitudes. Unpacking this process has been a challenge that social psychologists studying attitude formation, and the role attitudes play in our actions, have attempted for decades.

Almost all contemporary theories of IT acceptance that invoke attitudes toward use can be traced at some point back to an early theory of reasoned action (commonly referred to as TRA) proposed by Fishbein and Azjen (1975). This theory proposed three main drivers of an individual's decision to act: their attitude towards the behavior in question, the social norms for

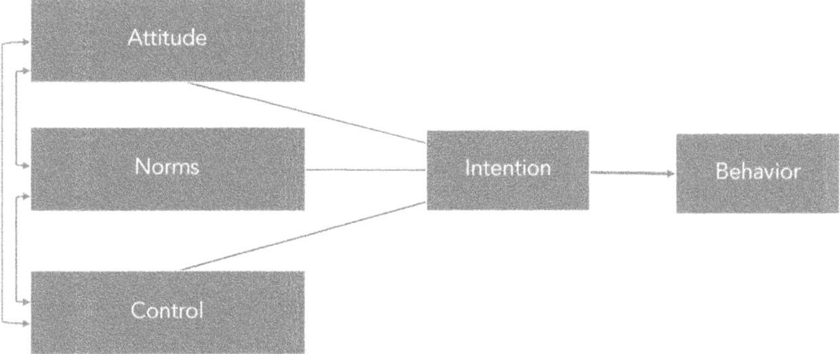

Figure 10.1 Simple representation of Ajzen's (1991) Theory of Planned Behavior (TPB) in which the intention to act precedes most conscious behaviors

such action in this context, and the individual's intentions at that moment. Assuming any individual has privileged access to their own attitude and forms an intention prior to acting, the theory suggests prompts or questions to employ, usually in the form of a survey, to gauge a person's likelihood to enact a given behavior.

On paper, this is a common-sense model that seems to explain relatively well, at least at a high level, people's actions in a given situation, but, as with so much of social science, questions were soon raised about how well such reasoned action fits with reality, and, as is the norm in theory development, it was not long before variations and additional constructs were generated. Azjen (1991) refined the original model and renamed it the theory of planned behavior (often shortened to TPB) and emphasized the importance of the control that a person believes or perceives they have in a given context (which of course is not necessarily equivalent to the actual level of control they possess, a distinction found clearly in socio-technical systems theory) (Figure 10.1). Since the behavior that UX professionals are mostly concerned with is the decision to use or not use a design, the relevance of perceived control on this decision seems obvious.

How well attitude and intent can be measured and subsequently used to predict behavior reliably when it comes to technology acceptance has become a thorny issue in the intervening years. TPB has been subjected to much criticism, particularly that it lacks consistent empirical support and is too limited to explain the complexities of human decision making in many contexts. Sniehotta et al. (2014), while acknowledging TPB's historical importance in driving research on the relationship between attitudes and behavior, went so far as to argue that the time had come to retire the theory due to its inherent limitations. Regardless TPB has not been easily displaced as a primary driver even as desire for improved models of acceptance within the information systems world has grown.

Because of its singular focus on the choice to use or not use a particular device or service, acceptance research in the UX world has sidestepped most of the theoretical wrangling over attitude formation and behavioral choice. Instead, the goal has been to identify the key drivers shaping the user's choice to use or not use any product or service. The dominant model within information systems research has for many years been the imaginatively named Technology Acceptance Model (known by all as "TAM") developed originally by Fred Davis (1989). Drawing extensively on the social psychological theories of Fishbein and Azjen, Davis also invoked the self-efficacy theory of Bandura (1982) which examines how one's beliefs in agency or control to plan action in any situation influence performance and habitual activities in life. Incorporating earlier information systems work on cost-benefit analyses to guide decision making, Davis proposed, tested, and revised scales to measure the key attitudinal drivers of choice within a planned behavior framework.

The results of this work led Davis to identify two key drivers of a user's intentions: perceived usefulness (the degree to which a person feels using a product will enhance their own performance) and perceived ease of use (the degree to which a person feels using a product will be free of effort). At first glance, this should not surprise us. The major claim here is simply that we make a decision to use a product because we believe it will help us complete a task and it will not be difficult to use. The corollary being we likely elect not to use devices that we perceive to be less helpful in meeting our needs or more difficult for us to use. Sensibly, Davis acknowledged that the simplicity of these two factors hid many more complicated forces at work, and his model allows for a range of "external variables" that might mitigate or influence our evaluation (user's motivations or prior experience, for example) but the core claim, that usefulness and ease of use are what matter, has defined this acceptance model and been the source of most discussion about how well it explains user behavior.

Of particular interest in Davis' model is the relative importance of each driver, especially since UX has long posited that ease of use is crucial. In his research and in subsequent developments of the model, usefulness is found to be the more important of the two variables. If a design offers low usefulness there is little incentive to use it and therefore acceptance will be low. People do not usually choose to adopt any product that does not serve its

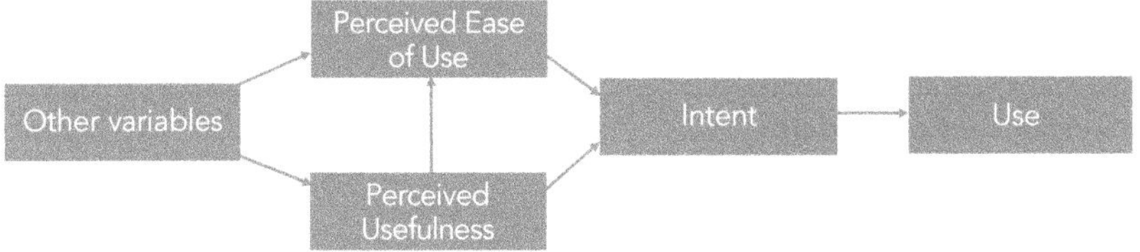

Figure 10.2 Basic constructs underlying acceptance according to Davis' (1989)

purpose for them, and no amount of usability or ease of use can overcome this. The logical extension of this is that a highly useful device might be accepted, even if difficult to use, when the user is motivated enough to do so (perhaps due to the necessity of completing a task or the lack of alternative options). The history of computing is full of such designs. As Davis put it, "users are driven to adopt an application primarily because of the functions it performs for them and secondarily for how easy or hard it is to get the system to perform those functions" (Davis, 1989, p. 333).

The model proposed by Davis suggested perceived usefulness and perceived ease of use were really the drivers of a person's attitude toward the technology, which itself shapedtheir behavioral intention to use (Figure 10.2). This framing contextualizes a user's likelihood of accepting the technology by acknowledging that the decision is not determined by usefulness and ease of use alone but from a more complex set of interactions related to the context in which the user resides (e.g., an employer might require or make the final choice on technologies in an organization and that external variable likely influences the user's attitude, and certainly their behavioral intention, significantly). In subsequent use, the model has been stripped down by some to just treat perceived usefulness and perceived ease of use as direct drivers of intention to use, again indicating the tendency of many in UX practice to seek simplified measures wherever possible, regardless of theoretical correctness.

The success of TAM probably lies in its own ease of use. The survey tool Davis generated to capture user data consists of a short 9 item survey, 4 each on usefulness and ease of use, and one on behavioral intention (a clear statement of the respondents' intention to use the product). Table 10.1 presents the TAM survey (in all items, the device or service being evaluated would replace "*this*", and responses are captured on a Likert-like scale on a Likert-like scale).

As you might imagine, this is a rather quick exercise for the user, given some exposure to a design, and people often express surprise that something as seemingly complex as a decision to adopt and use a technology can be so easily assessed. Given the model's theoretical roots, in the research on

Table 10.1 Items Underlying the Constructs in Davis (1989) TAM Survey Tool

Perceived Usefulness items
Using *this* would improve my performance in doing my job
Using *this* at work would improve my productivity
Using *this* would enhance my effectiveness in my job
I would find *this* useful in my job
Perceived Ease of Use items
Learning to operate *this* would be easy for me
I would find it easy to get *this* to do what I want it to do
It would be easy for me to become skillful in the use of *this*
I would find *this* easy to use
Behavioral Intention to use item
I intend to *use this* regularly at work

planned behaviour which is built on the simple premise that people decide to act before doing so, TAM is merely channeling a similar claim which requires little complexity for elicitation. In the intervening years, there have been various additions (the even more imaginatively named TAM2 and TAM3 were subsequent variations that unpacked the external variables and produced a seemingly unending set of other possible influences, ranging from system image to user anxiety that complicate the simplicity of the original tool). These, in my view, have little to recommend them in practical terms, though they do offer up interesting theoretical possibilities to consider when trying to understand the range of influences on humans' decisions to adopt and use a technology in their lives. The current favorite in the literature is the so-called Unified Theory of Acceptance and Use of Technology (UTAUT, Venkatesh et al., 2003) which takes this rebadging and variable unpacking even further and basically rewrites TAM with slightly different labels, an additional recognition of context, and adds multiple moderators for gender, age, experience and voluntariness of use. While a full reading of this literature might be of interest to some, for most UX professionals, Davis' TAM, with its dual constructs of usefulness and ease of use, remains popular.

But popularity aside, what is problematic for any acceptance model is the somewhat mixed evidence on how well it predicts actual usage once participants are no longer completing the survey and a technology choice has been made. In simple terms, what we really want to know is the correlation between respondents' stated intentions toward the technology and their subsequent real-world actions. If we determine that this correlation is significant (and hopefully positive, though a negative correlation would not be without value either) then we have a useful way of estimating how well our design is likely to fare upon release. The trouble is, as shown by Turner et al. (2010) in their review of more than 70 empirical studies of TAM, many did not actually measure subsequent usage, they simply reported the ratings for the two key variables (usefulness and ease of use) and the actual behavioral intention scores. Further, where actual usage data was collected, it sometimes came from more than one time sample, complicating the determination of any relationship (e.g., usage after a week might not be the same as usage after a year).

The problems don't stop there. Turner and colleagues also reported another shortcoming of these studies. Determining actual usage might be based on objectively logged usage statistics or from self-reports, and in their meta-analysis of studies, these authors revealed that self-reports correlated much more highly with TAM than objective usage statistics suggest. To what might we attribute this? There could be many reasons but it is likely this is another example of people inflating their usage, probably to maintain consistency with their stated behavioral intentions. In other words, if I report on TAM that I am going to use something, and later am asked if I did use it, there is a bias to answer in the affirmative even if I only used it for a very brief period. Where objective data on usage was collected, the correlations between TAM ratings for usefulness and ease of use, as well as behavioral intention to use, all dropped noticeably. Unfortunately, that objective data on usage was collected in less than 10 of the studies reviewed by Turner et al, which certainly reflects the challenges associated with this type of work but also leads us to ask if those pushing this model are treating stated intention to use, not real usage, as the dependent variable.

There are also documented cases where TAM got it badly wrong Keung et al. (2004) for example, reported that respondents in one organization all showed positive behavioral intentions to use, suggesting the technology would be successfully adopted within their organization. One year later, the authors reported actual use was non-existent. Further, a data set from a subsequent TAM test showed different results than the first round, perhaps not surprisingly since a year of non-adoption had passed, which then raises the question of why the original prediction was so awry. What we can probably conclude is that intention to use is a dynamic variable, what seems likely at one point in time might not be later, which forces us to consider just how reliable is any statement of intent made by a user at the earliest stage of adoption.

While the original model was developed largely for corporate decision making, including contexts where the organization might mandate use, it has now been widely used to study a variety of contexts where users have tremendous discretion over their technology usage such as open-source or free software gaming, and entertainment environments. We might recognize in such highly discretionary contexts that ease of use or usefulness are either operationalized differently in the minds of users or have less value over other attributes of a design. In the case of gaming, for example, ease of use might matter less than appropriate challenge, or the idea of "usefulness" might have no obvious value in choosing to buy or play a particular game. One might now appreciate the rather elastic nature of TAM's "external variables" category in allowing researchers to imagine and incorporate further predictors as needed (see e.g., Lue et al., 2019).

Limitations notwithstanding, the basic use of TAM or its derivatives to estimate a user group's intentions in advance of release can still be insightful. As the number of external variables and moderators continues to challenge our understanding of acceptance, we should not underestimate the practical value of quickly and easily gaining even a partially reliable estimate of user intent. Turner et al. (2010) caution us to be particularly mindful of pre-release usefulness and ease of use scores as they are uninformed by real world factors that will ultimately shape if and how the device or service is used. A recent meta-analysis of the unified model (Dwivedi et al., 2019) reminds us that a person's attitude to using any technology is not fully determined by performance or effort expectancy, indicating again how complex is the interplay between people's attitudes and their real-world behaviors. It's not that people deliberately mislead on surveys such as TAM, it is more the case that any choice behavior is, in the end, a response to multiple forces, some objective, some situational, some dispositional, and some that are harder to articulate and express in the mind of the individual.

Linking Acceptability and Usability to Use

You might wonder at this point, if acceptability research seems to have determined that ease of use is perhaps not as important as the user-centered design world has suggested? The answer seems to be that ease of use remains vital, and moreover, usefulness itself cannot be very easily distinguished from usability. While the format and basic simplicity of TAM has led to its general adoption and deployment in the research community, there is a similar survey tool more commonly employed by UX practitioners for

Table 10.2 The System Usability Scale (Brooke, 1996)

1	I think that I would like to use this system frequently.
2	I found the system unnecessarily complex.
3	I thought the system was easy to use.
4	I think that I would need the support of a technical person to be able to use this system.
5	I found the various functions in this system were well integrated.
6	I thought there was too much inconsistency in this system.
7	I would imagine that most people would learn to use this system very quickly.
8	I found the system very cumbersome to use.
9	I felt very confident using the system.
10	I needed to learn a lot of things before I could get going with this system.

gathering people's perceptions a new system, the SUS, or System Usability Scale (Table 10.2). Also originating in the 1980s, SUS was developed by John Brooke who presented the 10 items as good indicators of how users are likely to respond to a new design.

Similar to TAM, SUS reduces the evaluation of a somewhat complicated construct to a simple set of questions that users can complete quickly. Unlike TAM, Brooke did not suggest determinants or factors underlying usability, but sugggested a single ease of use measure as key. Subsequent statistical analysis of the tool by Sauro and Lewis (2009) suggests SUS really contains two dimensions: usability (8 items) and learnability (2 items), adding a further wrinkle in interpretation but SUS has shown good reliability and validity for measuring people's perceptions, and because of its widespread uptake by HCI and UX practitioners, there is now a significant body of shared SUS data which enables designers or researchers to employ SUS scores for benchmarking competing designs.

Notwithstanding the peculiarities of scoring SUS (scores on even numbered items must be subtracted from 5, scores on odd items should be reduced by 1, before adding them up and multiplying the total by 2.5 to get a number between 1 and 100), meta-analysis of multiple studies has shown that an average score is 68, thereby offering evaluators some reference for understanding how well any design compares to other products or services (of course, this assumes the comparison of any two designs is appropriate). This is valuable for UX, offering a target user experience score based on competitor products that we would like our designs to meet or exceed. What is important to understand, however, is that the correlation between SUS scores and subsequent user behavior is also modest. A product that scores well might still not be accepted or used. This is particularly true when scores represent global impressions over a range of tasks, but if we compare SUS scores at the individual task rather than full test level (e.g., by requiring people to complete a survey for each task employed in an evaluation, rather than just at the end), this correlation can be improved.

Like TAM, the basic premise of SUS is that if people find the design easy to learn and use, they are more likely to use it, and while this is not the same as acceptability in the manner conceived by Davis, the relationship between perceived ease of use (TAM) and usability (SUS) is obviously close. That relationship has been recognized and incorporated into a newer assessment tool, the Usability Metric for User Experience (UMUX) proposed by Kraig Finstad (2010). Building directly off the ISO 9241 standard definition for usability, UMIX initially aimed to capture user responses to items addressing perceived effectiveness, efficiency, and satisfaction. Reducing the item set down to four (one for each key variable plus an overall "ease of use" item), Finstad showed that UMUX correlated very positively with SUS and suggested that its own ease of scoring made is extremely attractive as an evaluation tool by UX professionals. That said, further analysis of even the 4-item tool seemed to show that it was measuring more than just usability. Lewis et al. (2015) proposed an even more simplified version, the UMUX-Lite which consisted of only two items, scored on a 5-pt scale:

> [This system's] capabilities meet my requirements.
>
> [This system] is easy to use.

As the authors note, these two items are remarkably similar to TAM's usefulness and ease of use structure, the key drivers of a user's stated intention to use. And herein lies the interesting merger of diverse efforts at determining if people will really use a new product or service. We seem to converge on the idea that a person is likely to adopt or accept a new design if it seems useful and sufficiently effortless to learn and use. The corollary also makes intuitive sense: a person is likely to reject or resist a new product or service if it is not apparently useful and usable. We might feel, and the research data would seem to support the idea, that usefulness is ultimately crucial and there is plenty of evidence in the real world that people tolerate poor user experience in products that they learn to rely on for important functions. But usefulness and effectiveness are obviously closely linked, and while the former does not appear in the ISO definition of usability, the latter clearly does, suggesting the distinction between usability and acceptability is less clear-cut than the competing models and theories might suggest.

So Where Does This Leave Us in Determining Acceptance?

Unfortunately, we must acknowledge the limitations of our ability to predict when discretionary users will and will not adopt a new information technology. Plausibly, usability is important but we now know that on its own, it is insufficient. Certainly, usefulness is essential, and key to user-centered design is ensuring we understand what people find useful and design products that provide for this and enable them to exploit this functionality. These are criteria we can operationalize and empirically determine. While this design challenge is tractable in work or formal task environments, the world has moved on somewhat from the traditional application areas that drove the original research into usability and acceptability. We are no longer delivering products or services that are only intended to meet basic requirements. As we find repeatedly, the uses to which people put designs often surprise us. If you consider a typical tablet computer, it can serve as an information access point, a writing tool, a game console, a music player, a document scanner, a banking portal, a teacher, a film screen, or a compass. In fact, the range of apps that might exploit the basic hardware and software is impossible to predict as new ones emerge continually. While this largely puts the onus on the app development team to figure out, the tablet designers have to provide an input, display and control platform that serves as a blank screen to developers and as a familiar interface for users.

A further complication comes from the dynamics of uptake in the real world. A design might test well, and users may express a strong intention to use, but between the test and the later adoption within any context there are myriad variables that can influence the outcome. People's lived experience is dynamic, subject to swings in mood, influence of others, financial developments, shifting needs, interests, and usage patterns, and the emergence of competitor products. While there is greater control in the corporate sector where usage may be mandatory, in our personal lives, what looks attractive one day might be rendered superfluous, inferior or outdated the next. Who among us has not anticipated a purchase of an item that seemed essential in one moment only to postpone the decision as life got in the way before subsequently revisiting the purchase decision? In the grey space between initial evaluation and real-world use, there is a lot of room for change.

Yet the problems of accurately predicting acceptance should not deter us from trying to understand the role of design in delivering better experiences for users. There are few precise theories in the sciences of human behavior and choice. We cannot be certain that price changes will always induce more buyers for a product or service, despite what economic rules of supply and demand predict. We cannot guarantee greater success as a result of raising awareness through costly advertising campaigns. In fact, we are living through a crisis, as I write, when we cannot even be sure the best medical evidence will sway people into accepting a vaccine to treat a deadly virus. Why then should we demand that the best theories and models in UX be capable of accurately predicting what users, given free choice, will do over time? This would be to expect more than we realistically demand of many other theories.

Instead, what we can practically claim is that we have established a basic understanding of the dynamics of acceptance and are able to identify problems, in advance, that likely will negatively impact the success of any design. If the SUS or TAM scores are all strong, acceptance may not inevitably follow but we will have cleared at least some of the obstacles we know result in design failure. Further, if these same scores indicate that the user response is not as we hoped, if usefulness is perceived to be low, for example, or if people feel that the design is not easy to use, then we can be sure there will be challenges gaining wide acceptance or adoption of the new design. In fact, the answers obtained might point us in the direction of where the design is coming up short. These can be valuable insights. The goal of UX design and indeed UX research is not always the same as pure social science, we are not determining insights and knowledge that will explain phenomena better or provide guidance for years. It is often enough just to clear the hurdles, to remove pitfalls, and to help shape the direction of an improved design in a timely fashion.

Beyond prediction, tools such as TAM and SUS can also help us identify shortcomings in our design approach. For example, if we identify low scores on usefulness then perhaps we should recognize shortcomings in the earlier user and task analyses conducted to generate requirements, possibly we missed some important needs that must be revisited. In the spirit of iteration, this might not only encourage further exploration of users, it might help us identify where our current approaches to requirements analysis or use-case generation are lacking. This is important knowledge, if we are minded to learn from it. Again, rather than treating each evaluation as a one-off event, we can pool the findings over time to learn not only what is working but what about our user-centered design process is not working as well as we imagined.

We know there are many other steps that happen in the real world and multiple variables that influence the final outcome which no user test method can fully determine. Individual users making choices for themselves are not the same as those working in an organization. In the marketplace of ideas and designs, we certainly expect some of factors Rogers listed as important to play a role: a choice must be visible to be considered, and if people have a chance to try something before buying, it's likely this will impact adoption. In short, the space between creating a good user experience and a design being broadly accepted in the real world is wide and subject to many forces. User-centered design can promise little more than helping to narrow that gap in some important ways, and in so doing, our theories and methods offer the design world some reasonable estimates. This is not everything we might hope for but to use a popular expression, "it's not nothing!"

The challenge for UX professionals then is to establish the confidence intervals, so to speak, around our evaluations and decisions. I do not mean this in a pure statistical sense, where we use the standard deviation of our sample to estimate a margin of error, rather I mean we acknowledge that we only ever have an estimate of likely acceptance, given everything we know about the target users and the results of our evaluations. In so doing, we can exploit user trials and SUS or TAM data to help us eliminate some of the design mistakes we may have made or identfy problems we have overlooked. And we can certainly employ the diffusion model or socio-technical theory to help us recognize that the process of uptake is dynamic, shaped by qualities of the design, the manner of its introduction and the nature of the people it is intended to serve. Once we have designed with these understandings and checked that we are meeting the usability and usefulness criteria we have set, then we are taking steps to improve our designs' chances of being successful.

Does this mean we will never be able to know in advance if a design will be accepted by users? It would be foolish to say "never" about the progress of our knowledge but for the foreseeable future, I do not anticipate such a radically better model emerging. This is not defeatist but a realistic interpretation of what science, and particularly social or behavioral science, offers us. The contingencies and diversities of human choice and action are wonderfully large. Patterns emerge, lawful bounds for some types of activities can be established across a large sample of people, and that is what we can exploit. We do understand some of the vectors at work in any design being accepted but we must accept that we are unlikely to know enough about every person's lived experience to identify what will determine their decisions. I am not sure I would want it any other way.

In his excellent history of numeracy, *Reckonings* author Stephen Chrisomalis (2020) traces the way humans have developed and designed numerical systems to express quantities through the ages. While most people accept the idea that our Western decimal format evolved from earlier systems such as the Roman, which dominated for more than a millennium, because of the inherent advantage it conveyed in calculation, it would be a mistake to assume that this is yet another example of usefulness and ease of use driving acceptance. Even now, when we appear to have settled on the system we know today, it continues to evolve as new problems and situations arise. Further, the apparently discarded older Roman numerals find continued use in specialized and symbolic contexts (such as the foreword pages of published books, representations of years in formal invitations, naming of royal personages, or the year of production in many film credits). Indeed,for centuries, Chrisomalis reminds us, people used both Roman and Western systems, depending on need or usage context, and the acceptance of Western numerals seems at least partially dependent on political and social changes, increasing literacy rates, control of territories, and new technologies, a set of external variables not mentioned in any version of TAM.

The printing press, for example, was hugely influential in standardizing and spreading numbering conventions. But even now, we live with a mix of bases e.g., hexadecimal (base-16) for computing, but sexagesimal (base-60) for time without much thought, once learned. And if like me, you were born before the decimalization of currency in Britain and Ireland in 1971, you might remember a monetary system that had 12 pennies to a shilling and 20 shillings to a pound (never mind the 21 shillings to a guinea, a value that was loaded with social meaning in use). All to say, the ways we communicate and view the world are not fixed, we adapt and design the means and representations we employ as a function of multiple needs forces. To be able to predict in advance how likely it is that a significant number of people will behave is no simple matter. And what Chrisomalis highlights so well with numerical systems applies even more so to contemporary information technologies which are developing at such a rapid pace.

The attempt to theorize acceptance then is ongoing, and while we might not have any great optimism for a predictive model that delivers exact results, what current research does confirm is that we must view people as multi-leveled agents in a dynamic space. Conci et al. (2009) for example examined the process of adoption among elderly mobile phone users and found that while usefuleness and ease of use mattered, these particular users recognized the value of phones for maintaining social relationships with important people in their lives so they often made a commitment to adoption regardless of ease or utility. In this, we see very literally the importance of social and cultural forces in the acceptance process, just as the socio-technical theorists suggested but, in this case, not in any organizational setting but in a family and kinship context. While the authors, like most social scientists, sought to develop their own variant of an acceptance model that added new boxes and arrows to the process, the real lesson here is that we can only really understand and predict users if we broaden our analysis across all time slices and acknowledge that people's behavior is typically the product of more than one or two variables.

So How Can We Best Evaluate the User Experience?

In teaching User Experience and observing how usability or acceptability test results are often interpreted by design teams, I am convinced that as set-up and run, most evaluations fail to capture key insights. There's nothing wrong with deriving measures of of usability according to ISO-9241-11, or trying to estimate people's intentions to use a new design through TAM, but if the goal is help shape better products and services, we may have taken these two approaches about as far as they can go in their present form, and the recent push to reduce these complex questions to ever shorter survey tools leaves so much potential data unexplored.

At a fundamental level, user experience can be viewed through three important lenses: process, outcome, and affect (see Table 10.3).

Any interaction involves an observable process, a set of actions and responses between user and interface. Typically, we capture such data points as screen-by-screen transactions, time per step or per task, errors, navigation choices, and so forth. We can extend these basic data points to compare how such interactions map with ideal paths performed by an expert, moments of deviations from the ideal, explorations of how users recover from problems and so forth but we are obviously interested here in understanding action, what a user does with our design when operating it in a typical usage context. Process measures help us see if our imagined usage paths are the journeys taken by real users.

Outcome refers to the range of variables that measure or capture what the user attains from the interaction, usually in the short-term. In typical usability evaluations we measure task completion (an effectiveness score) but we might also consider learning, purchases made, data submitted, target information located, or anything that brings closure to the user's interaction and signals an end-point for an interaction. Increasingly, different outcomes

Table 10.3 The Broad Categories of User Experience

	PROCESS: WHAT USER DOES	OUTCOME: WHAT USER ATTAINS	AFFECT: WHAT USER FEELS
Aim	Understanding user's moves and attention through the information space	Observe what it means for user to feel accomplishment or closure	Identify what the interaction means for the user in their world
Data	Navigation paths taken Use of features Focus of attention Input choices	Purchase made? Details submitted? Conversation completed? Information located? Comprehension attained?	Empowered? Annoyed, frustrated? Enriched? Unsure or wary? Confident? Willing to use again?

will be enabled by interactive technologies and our evaluations need to reflect these. Outcome measures for entertainment technologies, for example, are not always the same as those we consider important for health information or financial transactions.

Affect covers the host of attitudinal, emotional, and mood-related elements of experience. These exist in all human endeavor yet have been seriously overlooked in studies of usability. Certainly, the recognition within usability circles that satisfaction remains a key component of the experience underscores the importance of looking beyond task speed or accuracy, but satisfaction itself is a vague concept. There is now far greater recognition that the drivers of user preference, perception of aesthetics, frustration, or sense of enhancement and accomplishment with an interaction might all underlie a satisfaction rating and might even provide partially independent indices of important user experiences. And however else we might consider TAM and SUS, they ultimately are capturing affect, a user's estimate of their likelihood of using the design successfully at some future point.

I believe we must cast the data net much further than we have traditionally done in understanding how people experience information technologies if we are to design the type of experiences that enhance and augment our lives. Once we move from thinking about usability or acceptability as predefined constructs and allow for a broader evaluation of processes, outcomes and affects, we can start to consider user experience as a combination of actions, results and emotions, a series of human variables that reflect life as lived in reality, not just as the completion of tasks or estimate of acceptability. We can acknowledge that non-rational aspects of interaction affect our thinking and decisions with information tools, that we may adopt or reject for reasons not entirely related to price or performance, and that how we feel about our place in the group, the organization, and the world colors our judgment of use, and it does so in the short and the long-term. Can we really expect a user trial or a survey tool to capture all this for us?

Alternative Measures of UX

The list of potential variables to study is long and it is pleasing to note that over the last few years there has been increased interest in extending our evaluations beyond time and performance scores to address this richer set of concerns all humans have of their information experiences. Aesthetics, long ignored by social scientists, are finally acknowledged as important to users, even if the correlations we find between ratings of appeal and ease of use are not always clean. Hassenzahl and Tractinsky (2006) spoke for many when they argued that the incorporation of non-instrumentalist views of user experience was long overdue, and these authors argued that the experiential turn in HCI allows for and encourages a greater attendance on both hedonic qualities such as aesthetics and on emotional and affective aspects of interaction. A more recent model of technology adoption, Parasumaran and Colby's (2014) Technology Readiness Index tries to capture enablers and inhibitors of adoption that are reflected in people's optimism, innovativeness, discomfort and insecurity, tying outcomes to individual characteristics that are shaped by context, personality and experience. This is not a radical shift in acceptance theory but it does offer a potential bridge between utilitarian and hedonic framings of the process, as seen, for example in Aboelmaged et al. (2021).

But Why Do We Continue to Ignore Time?

While it is encouraging that UX is opening up to new measures, there remains a significant shortcoming in all human studies of interaction that dwarfs the choice of what measures or data we capture. To me, this is the failure of UX to address the impact of time. By this I mean that user evaluations continue to treat user experience as if it is a relatively fixed or stable property of an interaction, captured at the moment of a test, rather than as a dynamic, temporally extended quality of our engagement with information technologies in the world.

Most UX tests are based on quick samples of interaction, frequently captured as the user is learning to interact with the application for the first time. At best, such data provides an estimate of learnability, not even usability. Even where users may be trained to a criterion before conducting the formal evaluation, overcoming the learning phase, there is still the sense that such interactions are occurring at a earliest stage of use that may not provide the best predictors of extended interaction. Yet most users are fairly stable in their choice of applications, investing the time to learn only rarely, and for the most part sticking with applications for months or even years before changing or updating.

It is almost certain that a user's initial reaction to an interface is determined by multiple factors, chief among them being the perception of aesthetics, experience with equivalent designs, and immediate feedback. Vital as it is to understand these responses, a predictable shift occurs as users spend more time with any device or interface. What was initially seen as unusable sometimes comes to be liked over repeated use (I observed this phenomenon in detail in Dillon, 1987). What starts out appearing attractive and acceptable may later be disliked and rejected. But the corollary is also true: what is initially disliked or considered hard to use can later be adopted or rated more highly once training or repeated use has occurred. This is the reality of human behavior with information technologies. We adapt. Basing an evaluation of a design solely on the early or first reactions of users can be extremely misleading, and evaluators need to acknowledge and incorporate the role of time when planning and conducting tests.

To some extent this distinction is already acknowledged in UX with the recognition of learnability as a usability factor. In this case, we are particularly interested in how quickly users overcome problems with a design, either through practice, instruction or persistence. However, even learnability estimates are based on short term exposure, often single or two-trial user tests where we observe changes over minutes rather than hours, certainly not days and weeks. This is obviously important, but it is infrequently measured. Moreover, even if learnability was routinely evaluated distinctly from usability in testing, it would still leave us very short of the type of insights we might gain by studying users over more extended periods. With students I have conducted several usage evaluations that captured data over months (see e.g., Vaughan and Dillon, 2006) and such studies always show that changes in user experience continue to occur long after the first or second use of a design. In fact, it might be difficult to map the point at which changes in user experience cease happening during long-term exposure to and adoption of technologies.

If one examined the literature on human-computer interaction from the late 1970s on, now approaching half a century of scholarly work and documented practice, you will find that longitudinal studies of interaction are a rarity. We might admit there are many challenges, that experimental controls over long periods are difficult to implement, that people are slow to commit their time to being studied repeatedly, and of course, the pay-off to researchers for all this effort is low when one's peers are all producing results at a faster rate. This is the reality of research but in my view it remains a damning criticism of UX and HCI design scholarship. And it's not only a consideration for scholars, there are practical issues here too. Kjelsdov et al. (2010) performed an extended study of the usability of a patient records system, reporting effectiveness, efficiency and cognitive load results from users who were assessed at the start and end of one year of usage, during which they moved from novice to expert (or at least very experienced) users of the system. While the authors report that effectiveness improved over the year, as we might hope, efficiency did not shift. In terms of cognitive load, frustration levels diminished across the year, but general ratings of mental effort remained high. In examining the usability problems reported across tests, the authors found that experience changed the users' ratings of severity, and while even a year later, some usability problems were still reported by experienced users, there was no principled way of determining from the first test which problems were going to persist and which would cease to bother users after a year. As the authors note, "time does not heal usability problems" (p. 142), after a year of use, people are not using technologies in the same way.

What this should tell us is that the classic evaluation approach to user experience, the study of usability and the estimation of acceptability, will not provide us with all the answers we require in being truly user-centered. We exist as creatures over time, influenced by the past, the present, and our interpretation or estimates of the future. We think, behave and act in a physical, social, and cultural world, subject to forces that are not easily reduced to or understood by short-term observations and survey tools. User-centered design has made real progress, but it remains engaged in catch-up mode, too concerned with limited, time-sliced aspects of human action and reactions to possible designs that tell us too little about people's real behavior over extended periods. For progress to occur, we need to get in front of the question: how can technology make our lives better? Answering this will require a major shift in our views of users and use.

References

Aboelmaged, M., Hashem, G., and Mouakket, S. (2021). Predicting subjective well-being among mHealth users: a readiness – value model. *International Journal of Information Management, 56*(1), 1–16. 10.1016/j.ijinfomgt.2020.102247

Azjen, I. (1991). The theory of planned behavior. *Organizational Behavior and Human Decision Processes, 50*(20), 179–211.

Bandura, A. (1982). Self-efficacy mechanism in human agency. *American Psychologist, 37*(2), 122–147.

Brooke, J. (1996). SUS: A quick and dirty usability scale. In P.W. Jordan, B. Thomas, B.A. Weerdmeester, and I. McClelland (eds.), *Usability Evaluation in Industry* (pp. 189–194). London: Taylor and Francis.

Chrisomalis, S. (2020). *Reckonings: Numerals, Cognition and History*. Cambridge MA: MIT Press.

Conci, M., Pianesi, F., and Zancanaro, M. (2009). Useful, social and enjoyable: Mobile phone adoption by older people. In T. Gross et al. (ed.), *Human-Computer Interaction – INTERACT 2009*. Lecture Notes in Computer Science, vol 5726. Berlin, Heidelberg: Springer. 10.1007/978-3-642-03655-2_7

Davis, F. (1989). Perceived usefulness, perceived ease of use, and user acceptance of information technology. *MIS Quarterly, 13*(3), 319–340.

Dillon, A. (1987). Knowledge acquisition and conceptual models: A cognitive analysis of the interface. In D. Diaper and R. Winder (eds.), *People and Computers III* (pp. 371–379). Cambridge: Cambridge University Press.

Dwivedi, Y.K., Rana, N.P., Jeyaraj, A. *et al.* (2019). Re-examining the unified theory of acceptance and use of technology (UTAUT): Towards a revised theoretical model. *Information Systems Frontiers, 21*, 719–734. 10.1007/s10796-017-9774-y

Finstad, K. (2010). The usability metric for user experience. *Interacting with Computers, 22*(5), 323–327. 10.1016/j.intcom.2010.04.004

Fishbein, M., & Ajzen, I. (1975). *Belief, Attitude, Intention, and Behavior: An Introduction to Theory and Research*. Reading, MA: Addison-Wesley.

Hassenzahl, M., and Tractinsky, N. (2006). User experience—A research agenda. *Behaviour and Information Technology, 25*(1), 91–97. 10.1080/01449290500330331

Keung, J., Jeffery, R., and Kitchenham, B. (2004). The challenge of introducing a new software cost estimation technology into a small software organisation, in: Proceedings of the 2004 Australian Software Engineering Conference 11. (ASWEC'04), IEEE Computer Society Press, pp. 52–59.

Kjeldskov, J., Skov, M.B., and Stage, J. (2010). A longitudinal study of usability in health care: Does time heal? *International Journal of Medical Informatics, 79*(6), 135–143. 10.1016/j.ijmedinf.2008.07.008

Lewis, J., Utesch, B., and Maher, D. (2015). Investigating the correspondence between UMUX-LITE and SUS scores. In A. Marcus (ed.), *Design, User Experience, and Usability: Design Discourse*. Lecture Notes in Computer Science, vol 9186. Cham: Springer. 10.1007/978-3-319-20886-2_20

Lue, Y., Papagiannidis, S., and Alamanos, E. (2019). Exploring the emotional antecedents and outcoms of technology acceptance. *Computers in Human Behavior, 90*, 153–169. 10.1016/j.chb.2018.08.056

Lyytinen, K. and Damsgaard, J. (2001). What's wrong with the diffusion of innovation theory? In M. Ardis and B. Marcolin (eds.), *Diffusing Software Product and Process Innovations* (pp. 173–190). TDIT 2001. IFIP — The International Federation for Information Processing, vol 59. Boston, MA: Springer. 10.1007/978-0-387-35404-0_11

Parasumaran, A. and Colby, C.L. (2014). An updated and streamlined technology readiness index: TRI 2.0. *Journal of Service Research*, *18*(1), 59–74. 10.1177/1094670514539730

Rahimi, B., Nadri, H., Lotfnezhad Afshar, H., and Timpka, T. (2018). A systematic review of the technology acceptance model in health informatics. *Applied Clinical Informatics*, *9*(3), 604–634. 10.1055/s-0038-1668091

Sauro, J., and Lewis, J. (2009). Correlations among prototypical usability metrics: Evidence for the construct of usability. In CHI '09: Proceedings of the SIGCHI Conference on Human Factors in Computing Systems, April 2009, pp. 1609–1618. 10.1145/1518701.1518947

Sniehotta, F., Presseau, J., and Araújo-Soares, V. (2014). Time to retire the theory of planned behaviour. *Health Psychology Review*, *8*(1), 1–7. 10.1080/17437199.2013.869710

Turner, M., Kitchenham, B., Brereton, P., Charters, S., and Budgen, D. (2010). Does the technology acceptance model predict actual use? A systematic literature review. *Information and Software Technology*, *52*, (5), 463–479. ISSN 0950 5849, 10.1016/j.infsof.2009.11.005

Vaughan, M., and Dillon, A. (2006). Why structure and genre matter for users of digital information: A longitudinal experiment with readers of a web-based newspaper. *International Journal of Human-Computer Studies*, *64*(6), 502–526.

Venkatesh, V., Morris, M., Davis, G., and Davis, F. (2003). User acceptance of information technology: Toward a unified view. *MIS Quarterly*, *27*(3), 425–478.

Augmentation as the REAL Value 11

The Path to Truly Humane Design

By now, the idea that we live in an information-based age that distinguishes our current existence from our ancestors' pasts might seem questionable to you. Since earliest times, humans have created and exchanged information, not always with the intent of leaving permanent or even long-lasting records but at least of allowing for the sharing of ideas, data, and symbols beyond the immediate moment. In so doing our fellow humans have continually leveraged the materials and objects of our world as signals to others of ownership, identity, and location. Across the course of history, the information technologies we have produced and exploited have certainly evolved significantly, sometimes rapidly, other times slowly, but as the producers and the consumers of information, we humans have remained relatively unchanged in core ways. In other words, humans have always lived in an information age, perhaps not always one as rich or complex as today's, but each era has its unique or identifiable information tools and technologies that reflect our seemingly innate drive to mark, organize, and externally represent our inner worlds.

Clearly, some of our current information technologies would be unrecognizable and even unimaginable to people living centuries ago, just as today most of us have little sense of what will come into routine use over the next two centuries. Try this little thought experiment for yourself and imagine right now what the primary form of input will be in 2223. Are you still envisaging keyboards and screens? What alternatives are you considering? Are we using gestures and speech, or maybe thoughts? It is not simple, is it? Some technologies have survived long enough to outlast generations without radical alteration. The format and cost of books might have changed with the

DOI: 10.4324/9781003026112-11

mass production of paperbacks, but a 17th-century scholar would not find the format or use of a modern book to pose any great usability challenge or require any great leap of imagination to appreciate. Other than capacity and durability, early writing implements such as styli and ink are not radically different from contemporary ballpoint pens. Yes, we have improved ink storage on the device side and in so doing reduced the repetition of dipping nibs in ink every few traces but in user experience terms this is mainly an efficiency and satisfaction gain. Using one's hand to control a slim device that can shape a line of ink on paper has a consistency of action the permeates most writing tools across time. Let's go further, what stone-age artist, seeing for the first time a modern paintbrush and palette, would struggle for very long to exploit their capabilities?

Of course, we have also created new technologies that would be difficult for people of another era to fathom. Harnessing electricity, circuit boards, and microchips to deliver computational power at a level that exceeds the lifetime abilities of great mathematicians from even decades ago would surely seem incredible. And to package that power in a device as small as an iPhone still seems impressive given living memory of early computers. So too, the ability to talk to (and see), in real time, anyone on the planet who owns a smart phone, regardless of distance, would probably be viewed by most in the past as a special kind of magic. That the pace of development in the last 100 years has been rapid is undeniable, from first airplane flight to a manned lunar landing in a matter of decades, compared, for example, to the centuries of time between early writing tools and the mechanical printing press, or the leap from horse-drawn transportation to motor vehicles, but we should avoid the trap, pushed endlessly in the media and business world, of thinking that only in our age has our relationship to information technologies changed.

On the contrary, the minds of our ancestors were not remarkably different than those of our great grandparents, or of today's born digital generation. We still make meaning out of sensory stimuli, we still have a limited range of vision, restricted working memory capacity and a tendency to rely on context, habit, and mood to influence our decisions. As a species, we use our hands in much the same way we always did (though we might be a little more thumb-active now than we were even 20 years ago). As humans, we tend to form connections with those around us to create a sense of community and inevitably, to develop a certain wariness of outsiders. For our species long history we have been attracted by beauty, found our attention captured by movement, and struggled to distinguish signals from noise. We've always needed sleep, manipulated our surroundings for our comfort and safety, and communicated through symbols, sounds, and actions. These attributes of our minds when engaging with the world around us are the closest we have to constants or invariants in lived experience, and our efforts at understanding ourselves for the purposes of creating new information technologies should always acknowledge them. Better yet, we should design intentionally around these invariants.

The difficulties of true user-centered design are non-trivial. There is a continual tension in our information design world between profit and need. The commercial impact of a successful artifact encourages many designers to seek our attention and offer solutions that seem to have immediate pay-off for us. As consumers, we typically are attracted to products or services that are faster, smaller, glitzier, and cheaper, or some combination of these. The profit-need relationship might be considered user-centric by some since customers, consumers and users are treated as one and the same and competition generates better products. In an idealized free-market view of the world, consumer choice is equated to user preference, and surely that is user-centeredness in action? This is true in only the most superficial understanding of user-centeredness. Yes, economically-advantaged people often have a choice of designs but as we know, our ability to make an informed choice, to select a design that is best for us in anything other than the near-term, is limited. And once we have committed to a choice, spent our funds, or expressed our views, few people are able to correct a mistake or revisit their choice without incurring considerable costs. More often, it is the user who adjusts or adapts to the design, and this is yet another invariant quality of our minds and bodies, we demonstrate such flexibility even if the resulting interactions are sub-optimal.

We now have enough research evidence to recognize that, given the chance to try designs for ourselves, we tend to put value on utility and on usability. However, for most of our purchases, that window to try things out, to determine the goodness of fit between an information product and ourselves, is short. Take a car for a test drive and you might get some idea of how it handles on the road but only for a relatively short journey. If you decide to purchase, it is likely you will spend more time arranging the finances or signing the paperwork at the dealers than you will having the dashboard control functions explained to you. Yet it is that same interface you will be engaging every time you drive the car for the next six years (the average length of ownership for a new car in the US according to *Autotrader*), and that same set of controls you will find yourself cursing when you can't adjust the radio or the air conditioning in a hurry.

What we know about utility and usability is limited, reminding us there is much more to understand about why some designs are better than others in meeting our long-term needs. As we saw in the research on user acceptance, many of our theoretical frameworks and their resulting empirical tests derive from studies where users were not even the ultimate arbiters of purchase. The foundational work on the Technology Acceptance Model, for example, comes from organizational contexts where a company or group leaders can ultimately mandate specific technology choices and use cases. This is likely to remain true, even in distributed work contexts where many organizations will continue making the decisions, especially in any context involving sensitive information (video-conferencing tool Zoom has taken over the world during the pandemic and few of us have been able to avoid it, but how many of us had any real influence on its selection?). Predicting acceptance in such environments is often tied to norms on compliance and organizational citizenship. But the world of consumer technology has grown significantly in the last 20 years, and people are increasingly making choices of information tools that are used exclusively by themselves and their loved ones. Does the nature of acceptance change in domestic or personal rather than formal work or organizational contexts? I would think so. Our personal selections result in a technological environment of interconnected devices that exist across home and non-work spaces tying entertainment, financial, communication and health tools together. Smart homes, smart vehicles, smart devices, and sometimes smart people make for a heady mix of design options. Attempting to be user-centered in that space demands more than a quick survey on behavioral intention, or a few checks against imprecise heuristics. In such a technological world, how might we best proceed?

One approach I believe we cannot rely on is the naïve, some might say mindless, empiricism of design thinking that advocates for the generation of ideas coupled with quick tests to weed out the problems. The approach certainly has its uses, and in the absence of an alternative might be the best we can do in some situations, but it comes with a very high risk of groupthink driving design and no assurances of successful adoption. Even if there was no science base for guiding key design decisions, it would be difficult for humans to design in a completely empirical manner without biases, personal preferences, and assumptions influencing our suggestions because this is how we are wired. If nothing else, the scientific study of ourselves has revealed how deeply our own belief systems shape our interpretation of data and reality. We simply cannot step outside ourselves to see the world as it really is, in some raw form for which we can design, unfiltered by our own mental models and constructs. Once we accept this, we allow ourselves to recognize the limitations of our immediate sense impression or of our own framing of the problem to be solved. What we can do though, is use the knowledge we have created of ourselves and our mental processes to serve as a check and balance on our data streams, opinions, first reactions, and impressions of how we or others will behave, therefore encouraging and enabling ourselves to discern probabilities and likely outcomes of our design choices on a stronger basis than imagination or opinion.

This book has presented an outline of the layers of knowledge we can employ to help us understand the ways humans respond to information contexts. Obviously, there are problems with the science base we have. First, it is not intended or articulated in a manner that makes it easily digestible by non-specialists, and most of what we know from studying ourselves was not generated for the purpose of guiding design. So, there is a need for translation or mediation between laboratory and field social sciences and the practical application of this knowledge. We are witnessing the emergence of this bridging language, not least in the work and the deep literature on HCI which did not exist at the dawn of the computer age, but there is still a long way to go. While I invest much hope on the education of new professionals to help us shape user-centered design, I worry that current curricula in many programs shortchanges science and research findings in favor of methods and practice. This results in our equipping graduates with skills in data elicitation or prototyping, which supports an empirical, design thinking type of approach to problems but fails to ground new professionals fully in the theories of human thinking and behavior that could help them exploit and gain real insights from their data. As Wittgenstein famously said of psychology and which we might now apply justifiably to UX education, the main problem continues to be that, "theory and method pass one another by" (Wittgernstein, 1958, p. 232).

Second, there remains a significant problem in the framing of our scientific knowledge which we have inherited from the Cartesian division of social science into largely independent layers of study. This apportioning of distinct framings on the basis of temporality makes for convenient boundaries within and between disciplines, but does not serve us particularly well in gaining a holistic understanding of people as users of information technology. As we continually see when we examine the dynamics of human response to designs, issues interact. A design challenge at the physical interface can cause problems at the social level of adoption. A poor choice of language or terminology may reflect mistaken or incomplete cognitive analyses of interaction that induces errors impacting stakeholders many miles away. A decision to adopt one product based on test results might entail requirements in the supporting infrastructure that were never considered part of the design and evaluation process. Each of these problems can be related to the way we think of humans as "users," bound to a view of use as one human at one interface, or, if we are so inclined, as a group that exists at the social level without perceptual or physical vectors of note. Social science carves our world up this way but in reality, we all exist at multiple-layers, concurrently living, working, and playing as physical, cognitive, social, and cultural beings, engaged with and within a network of interconnected devices.

Throughout history, inspired individuals have certainly generated wonderful designs, and we likely will continue to see such individualism lauded and rewarded in the marketplace. However, we cannot pin our hopes on the Steve Jobs and Elon Musks of the world, if only because there's always too few of them to go round. We might argue that these people are not so much great designers as great business minds, but that's less my concern. We can substitute Henry Dreyfuss, Charles Eames, or Jon Ive for Musk, or Jobs and the point remains. The "great person," or "genius designer" model of innovation will not deliver us the reliable, robust and humane technological infrastructure we need to ensure ethical and equitable access to information (just look what they have given us so far) To get there, we need a discipline of design that can better incorporate knowledge of people, and people's values, systematically into our problem solving and solution generation. We need to be less reliant on great individuals than on truly user-centered design processes that yield usable and augmenting technologies. The goal will not be achieved without a richer and deeper form of design education, informed by science, engineering, art and practice, widely available to all so that we have thousands of great designers, not a few genius ones.

What's Ahead Then for UX?

If we examine the media coverage of technological advances, it is easy to get caught up in the fashionable discussions of new devices exploiting the power of artificial intelligence, big data and machine learning to create world-altering environments which will unleash either utopian or dystopian conditions for ordinary people. Take a casual look at the regular predictions of what's looming and you'll get the laundry list of usual suspects: AI will take over decision making, self-driving cars will alter lifestyles, robots will displace workers, and the Internet of Things (IoT) will permeate our environments. To some extent, these developments are inevitable, but it still leaves us asking if these are really outcomes or, more likely given our history as a species, mere stepping-stones on the way to even greater developments in the decades ahead.

Our ability to predict the technological future is poor. I used to advise people to apply "a rule of 10," to any futuristic claim i.e., reduce every outcome or multiply the timeline by a factor of ten if you wish to be remotely accurate in predicting the future. By this I mean that we have predicted complete social reorganization of work through networked computing since the early 1980s, and it was due to happen before the end of that century. We're still making that prediction today, yet the biggest driver of employment practices has not really been the computer than the Covid-19 pandemic which forced us to rapidly exploit communication technologies to keep work organizations going. Yes, without the emergence of Zoom and an information infrastructure to enable us to make that transition we might have struggled in the last few years, but it is hard to attribute the disruption of work in the 2019–2022 window to technology alone. I believe what was predicted to occur within 10 or so years back in 1980 is more likely to work itself out slowly over the coming decades as the world learns to adjust and exploit new work opportunities. We're now 40 years into widespread adoption of computers in the workplace and we're still not sure how to structure our working lives optimally. Will it take until 2080 for the imagined revolution to fully occur? Probably. And even then, the results will likely be more evolutionary.

It's not just our own working lives we are unable to predict, there have been innumerable claims made about the future which simply proved wrong. Digital books never did replace paper; people do stream movies but they still flock to cinemas; school children (mainly) learn in face-to-face classrooms; customers shop in stores and while credit cards are ubiquitous, many people worldwide still carry cash. Each of these older products or services was predicted to die a relatively quick death as networks and data reduced our reliance on material objects and physical locations but even as Spotify and Tidal offered almost limitless access to comparatively high-resolution music, vinyl records made a resurgence as people recognized the inherent pleasure in analog existence. This should remind us is that humans are complicated, capable of multiple-levels of engagement with the world, able to transcend and exploit the digital and the material realms, and are wired to shape their lives through patterns of activities that can be resistant to sudden change.

But the technologies of information are evolving, and we might reasonably envisage a time when information devices are ivirtual, embedded in our world, our clothes, our possessions, and living spaces, called upon as needed and instantiated in a form that is not limited by current hardware interfaces. While users will likely continue to "feel" they are physically engaging, and be aware of the presence of such tools about them, new "hardware" might be a constellation of sensory signals interfaced to users directly, enacted via sensors, skin pads, glasses, ambient signals, and ultimately, brain activity. The division between material and digital will likely become seamless as our technology is distributed through our built environments. If we can call on data and figure out how to generate a user interface virtually, anywhere, how would such interactions appear, how would we share, how would we manage them? How might we tailor our level of immersion in such a space, turn it off, or restrict it to certain tasks, actions, and periods in our lives. How might people respond to such interactions and how could their responses, across all parameters, be used to shape the user experience? Such questions take us far beyond typical considerations of usability or user experience, raising questions about affective engagement, sense of self and of space, connectivity, community, identity, and more. We need to envisage the future of user experience occurring in dynamically constructed information spaces that exploit real-time configurability, immersion, automation, and connectivity wherever we are.

While I question our ability to predict the future, the user experience of information and its associated technologies is evolving at a pace that exceeds traditional human-computer interaction (HCI) knowledge. The dominant paradigm of interaction continues to be a human engaging a physical device, with full or partial keyboard for mostly text-based input. More recently, limited touchscreen capability and even more limited voice controls have pushed the interaction envelope but this traditional framing has given us a series of design principles or guidelines, fixed methods of evaluation, and a view of interaction as tool or device dependent. UX, as currently conceived, is tied to a method and skill set that treats design as a soft science or hybrid of art and engineering, frequently reactive and evaluative rather than prescriptive, with a limited view of how we to imagine, never mind instantiate alternative information acts.

Rather than privileging technical innovations as the driver of advances, how might we exploit the multi-leveled information processing architectures of humans to illuminate new directions for technologies? In a time when not only is there greater access to information than ever, but where almost all human endeavors are or can be mediated by digital tools, it is necessary for us to think about the type of desirable and ethical information experiences humans are themselves designed for, courtesy of our material and psycho-social architectures, so as to create the technical infrastructure that reflects a world we desire to engage more than one to which we simply adapt. If we are to retain the term "user" to describe the human component of this system then we should at a minimum adjust our understanding of users to reflect our full human sensory, cognitive and affective capabilities, enacted within material, social, and cultural environments. We need to treat users as the multi-level beings we are, not as the time-sliced operators modeled from social science, forever pressing keys or touching screens in a Skinnerian reinforcement loop.

Why Is This Necessary?

The complexity of design and the need for a richer, multi-level sense of the user are both apparent in the recent tragic accidents involving the Boeing 737 Max airplane. After fatal crashes involving significant loss of lives, investigations revealed just how decisions taken across a distributed development process came to a head at the point where pilots met the controls, with tragic consequences. An anti-stall system, designed to deal with a very specific set of flying conditions, was adjusted late in the process after test flights revealed occasional issues related to the attack angle of the plane in flight. Airplanes usually fly within a small range of angles but the new, more powerful engines on the 737 Max tended to increase the angle at certain speeds. Using a single sensor to monitor this and send corrective instructions to the engine, a system called MCAS was introduced but, it seems, not included in the necessary training for pilots due to pressures to meet deadlines.

Since pilots could turn the system off, and it was envisaged that MCAS would only kick-in during rare, unlikely to occur conditions, routine regulatory checks for safety somehow did not happen. But more than this, mention of the new system was absent in training manuals, and pilots were not prepared appropriately in its use. What we know of one crash indicates the system kicked in shortly after take-off, incorrectly based on readings of a single sensor, forcing the nose of the plane down. The pilots, unaware of what was happening kept adjusting the angle of attack, ending up in tug-of-war with the airplane's computer for control of this angle. Worried pilots on this flight seemingly tried to read the manuals to determine the best course of action while adjusting the controls in real time, with fatal consequences.

Now in one sense, this represents a failure of project management and design. Indeed, a spokesman for the American Airlines pilots' union, Dennis Tajer, was quoted in the *New York Times* as saying of Boeing:

> "They completely discounted the human factor component, the startle effect, the tsunami of alerts in a system that we had no knowledge of that was powerful, relentless and terrifying in the end."
>
> (Boeing 737 Max: What's Happened After the 2 Deadly Crashes, *New York Times*, October 21, 2019)

But continuing review of these accidents throws up an even more complicated set of dynamics at work. Safety regulations were not checked and met, training opportunities were missed, information in manuals was not fully provided (seemingly for fear of triggering new regulatory requirements and thus delaying delivery) and the diffusion of the new design across the international aviation industry took little account of the realities of pilot knowledge and experience in the field. Startling as it may be, pilots in some parts of the world lack first-hand flight experience in a real airplane before taking a professional position, developing their skills, and gaining their license on the basis only of simulator practice. The trouble with MCAS was that its behavior in simulation seemingly failed to reflect the plane's handling in real flights. Most pilots flying Boeing planes did not even know of its existence until the crashes highlighted the problem. Further, investigation revealed that regulators in the US had outsourced some regulatory requirements to Boeing, in effect allowing the company to serve as its own regulator even though it seems many of those involved in the design of the new 737 had no awareness that MCAS even existed.

The loss of life was tragic. This disaster highlights the interconnected nature of important design decisions, and the need to consider more than the moment where the user touches the controls when trying to understand the full implications of any interaction. This is obviously a highly specialized form of technology, with trained users, operating in a regulated space but even if more than one sensor had been designed into MCAS and the manuals had been updated, there would still be a need to ensure flight teams knew that the system existed and how they should react when the system was deployed. For that to happen, simulators would need to be designed appropriately and company- and even industry-wide awareness of the plane's new system needed to be raised. What might at first glance appear to be a poor user interface reveals upon fuller consideration to reflect a series of limited understandings of the human-technology interactions, from the direct users to the broader stakeholders involved and impacted. Pilots operate airplanes in a team context, with co-pilots and crew responsible for passenger safety. They do so on the basis of specialized knowledge acquired through training and experience, and are subject to licensing requirements that are supposed to reflect the skills and knowledge needed to perform their work. There are almost 10,000 airplanes flying in our skies at any time and every interface in this environment is a component in a globally distributed socio-technical system involving a contingent set of relationships that are impacted by the choices and actions of individual users. User centeredness here demands a fuller appreciation of what use entails (learning, practice, ability to adjust to dynamic conditions while communicating with others) while acknowledging that multiple stakeholders, most of whom never directly touch a particular interface, are key parts of the system's usability and acceptance.

Like most major product manufacturer's Boeing has human factors or user experience professionals on staff but, how much influence can they have on the complete product design and implementation? Since the earliest human factors professionals identified the need for greater involvement, the discipline has struggled to place members where strategic decisions are taken. This has certainly been a long-standing concern in HCI (see earlier coverage of this issue in studies of the European software industry (Dillon et al., 1993) or in the US IT management sector (Morris and Dillon, 1996). While recruitment indicators suggest UX research and design roles are in higher demand than ever, the roles rarely involve positions of strategic influence. In the case of MCAS, it is not clear that a thorough usability test of the type conducted in UX would have been sufficient as the lack of training and communication across the network of stakeholders proved so crucial to the crashes. While it is easy to be wise after the event, we will never be sufficiently informed in advance of a product's release if we continue to view UX as a single layer concern of usability or error-reduction. To enable user-centred design to be a driver not a palliative we have to rethink the role and education of user-centered designers so as to address the multi-layered engagement and connection of people with technologies.

Real Design: Respect Experience, Augment Life

I ofte refer to the need for a new way of thinking as an attempt to engage in "REAL" design, where real is an acronym for "Respecting Experience, Augmenting Life." For me, this more directly captures the essential aims of a truly user-centered design philosophy while avoiding the "user" term. While I understand that people do not mean to employ "user" in any derogatory manner, the word is inherently limiting and strips away from ourselves some of the most fundamental qualities of our humanity that I

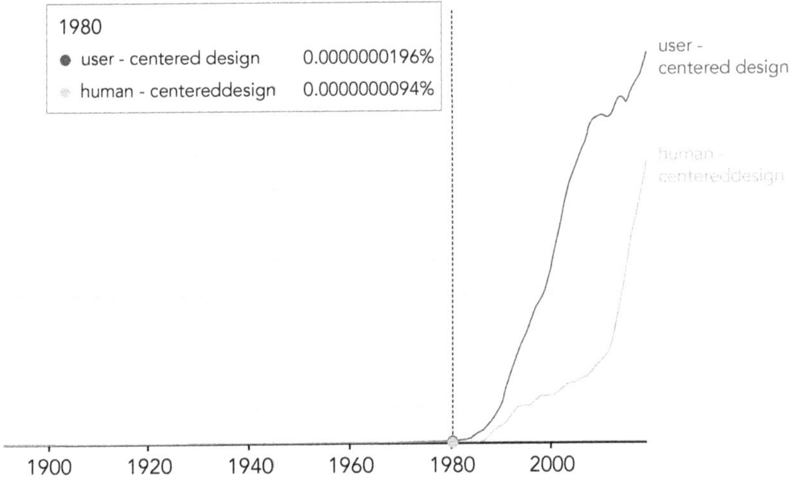

Figure 11.1 N gram representation showing frequency of terms "human-centered design" and "user-centered design" since 1980

believe we should leverage and reflect in our information technologies. While it is certainly an improvement to refer to the process as human-centered design, this term has never really managed to displace user-centered in the professional literature (though interestingly, a Google nGram analysis (see Figure 11.1) shows "human-centered" as a more frequently employed term in general usage, but once we append "design" to the phrase, "user-centered design" dominates).

By unpacking the acronym "REAL," my intent is to reframe the discussion about what we are trying to achieve when we engage in the study and development of new information spaces and tools.

First, we must question "user-centeredness" as a concept. Despite its origins, I fear that the term has become sufficiently diluted by business interests that make no distinction between users and customers, shifting the focus from quality of experience to commercial value. In this world view, 'use' is a series of transactions to be analyzed and supported for their most effective and efficient completion. For sure, satisfaction has been retained in mainstream HCI as a key measure, coupled often with net promoter scores that aim to estimate how likely a user might be to speak well to others of a product. While this is not in itself the death-knell, the user-customer conflation places humans at the center only in as far as they are transactionally beneficial. It is this type of design thinking that has yielded captive design, sticky websites and user nudges that leverage core principles from human psychology but in a manner that we might not think of as human-centric. It would not be an unfair question to ask if the ethics of such interaction designs are all they might be? If we don't take back control of the term, user-centeredness will mean little more than customer-friendly.

Second, I believe we can better design information spaces with an enriched understanding of natural dispositions and behavioral emergence. We have the sciences of human physiology and psychology to draw upon, but we now also have decades of experiencing how our information designs are leading us to forms of communication, misinformation, and exploitative practices that are too easily enabled with digital platforms. It's not simply a matter of letting the science catch up, it is unlikely ever to do so, or of adding an ethics course to a design curriculum (necessary but hardly sufficient), people are built to act and engage, consequently there are dynamics in our human responses that are never entirely predictable. Further, the timeline for these dynamic responses is greater than typically captured in our user studies, even in the field. When we study usability, for example, are we open to the possibility that increasing speed on task, highly desirable as we imagine it to be on an occasional routine task, might actually have a negative impact for some people engaged in repetitive tasks over extended periods? Can we acknowledge the design of group discussion tools that have diminished rather than enhanced our sense of open discourse or community sharing despite the apparent ease of use they provide? In short, as we live through the changes, are we measuring the slow processes which emerge in human activities and interactions, and are we feeding such knowledge or observations back into our design imagination?

Primarily though, my use of "real" design is to remind ourselves of the challenge set by Doug Engelbart some 60 years ago, that we seek to create new tools that augment human capabilities. This must surely be the ultimate goal of a truly human-centered approach to design. It requires us to move beyond usability and acceptance, important as these qualities are, and beyond the hedonic (another consumer-oriented takeover seems inevitable here too) to imagining a world where our information infrastructure truly supports all people across their lifespan. Can we build environments that allow fellow global citizens to speak comprehensibly across linguistic barriers? Knowing that aging humans will nearly all suffer predictable declines in their perceptual systems, can we design technologies that gracefully adjust and address or compensate for these changes? Better yet, can we create an information environment where we supplement our memories, soothe our anxieties, increase our skill acquisition, monitor and improve our health or enhance our educational practices on a scale that raises everybody up, no matter where they connect?

To even think of doing so, we must truly respect people's lived experience, short and long-term, and recognize that common patterns of engagement with the world offer insights into ways in which we can improve the human condition. That is the key to augmentation, enabling people to engage, perform, and live better than they otherwise might do without our interventions. That is a form of design that would truly be human-centered.

Broadening the Lens on Use

Let us consider two topical areas of interaction concern that would benefit from a rethinking of how we conceive of user-centeredness: cybersecurity and accessibility.

In a world that increasingly understands the threats to security and privacy of a global information infrastructure, much effort is, justifiably placed on protecting government and industrial processes from outside interference. If the frontline of future criminal or military operations is our networks, it is vital that we develop and maintain technical strengths in artificial intelligence, cryptography, and threat management. Important as these concerns are, the weak spot in many cybersecurity scenarios is often not the technology but the human. People are not naturally wired to follow stringent protocols, are poor password generators, and of course, suffer from a variety of attentional and memory limitations that are easily manipulated and preyed upon.

A typical weakpoint for online security is the personal email address. It is estimated that more than 30,000 addresses are hacked daily (https://techjury.net/blog/how-many-cyber-attacks-per-day/#gref) and many users are blissfully unaware of this happening. A study by Mayer et al. (2021) revealed that as many as 73% of people had their email stolen. Despite the repeated warnings and even requirements for stronger passwords on many sites, identity theft remains a huge problem. If people are not generating poor passwords, even systems that commonly generate hard to hack passwords and automatically remember these for users are subject to predictable human frailty.

A tension exists in analyses of security between improving the interface between user and security protocols or diminishing it by designing it out. In other words, either find better ways of helping users to be secure, such as password helpers and managers, mandatory schedules and rules, etc., or of by-passing the user's unreliable memory entirely by employing potentially unique attributes they carry around with them at all times and cannot forget, such as their face or fingerprint. Both of these can work but as we know, neither is infallible. In the face of mandatory rules for regular password changes, people often recycle the same few they can remember easily, or write them down in less secure spaces. Password management software can be a boon here, automating both the generation and the storage of hard-to-hack passwords for regularly visited sites. But such a system still requires a user-generated master-password for the user to unlock the management tool, a modern example of the old insight that a chain is only as strong as its weakest link. Even facial recognition, which one would think of as carrying no cognitive load in use can be simply defeated. The American Civil Liberties CLU trains its observers to switch off their iPhone's facial recognition option when participating in civil events lest their rightful and legal refusal to unlock their phones without a warrant is easily by-passed by someone holding the phone up to the owner's face.

What these examples reveal is that even as apparently simple a task as password protection is nuanced and complicated in real-world usage. It is certainly important to consider memory and broader cognitive concerns in designing password protocols and to seek out exploitable qualities of the user's unique identity we can leverage for solutions, but neither completely solves the problem. The best knowledge we have of human cognition tells us that memory and attention frailties will inevitably impact security at some point. Contextual analysis of use reveals even biometric features, which might be uniquely possessed are not uniquely exploitable. As we engage even more across interconnected information networks, security becomes distributed, passwords go out of date, are stolen, are forgotten, and the load on users only increases across time to stay on top of their own identity practices. Most people are frustrated at some point by an inability to gain lawful access to their own information (Lloyds Bank in the UK recently made it almost impossible for me to even access a personal account online, at one point requiring me to register a new password by using a code delivered via postal mail that invariably took so long to deliver that my registration window was closed by the time it arrived!).

Nordpass Security estimated recently that typical users employ over 100 passwords across their various usage contexts, surely a sign that something is not working well here (Rowe, 2021). Everything we know about human psychology tells there is inevitable weaknesses in this type of "security" system. The standard "user-as-customer" response has been to sell or push password managers but as we can see, this approach only addresses one layer of the vertical slice, treating the problem as a purely memory and effort issue. The only way we can fully understand this and design appropriately for it is to observe real people across time grappling with the multiple security procedures they must inevitably follow in using a host of information technologies in their lives. Such consideration would surely address not only memory but attitudes to security and privacy which vary significantly across individuals, and even within individuals depending on context. It may not be entirely rational, but one suspects that people might be more worried, for example, about bank or email security online than newspaper or Netflix accounts, even though each opens an access path to valuable personal information. In a world where our data and interaction histories are captured and sold, the complete study of security must embrace social and cultural facets of norms, expectations, and values as much as physical biometrics or cognitive effort.

A second area of design challenge where we can perhaps appreciate the need for a more holistic view of the user deals with accessibility and in particular, the design of assistive technology, the devices, software, and systems designed to increase, maintain, or improve the functional capabilities of people with disabilities (Assistive Technology Industry Association, 2020). Too often, the UX challenge has focused on developing software under a single user model where a learner's disability is tackled through interface modifications to input and output devices, or mode of information presentation. As noted in Ayon and Dillon (2021) much of the design work has not kept up with current views of accessibility which have shifted from a medical view of disability as the problem to be overcome through technology to a view of accessibility being a condition of the world in which certain features (or their absence) disable participation or use by certain people.

This inversion of the problem from a medical to an environmental or contextual condition is particularly apparent in education. Ayon and Dillon's (2021) review of findings in that area reveal that design interventions frequently fail to address the many ways in which a learner with a disability must employ the technology. Too often, set-up can be complicated and require more than one person. In-classroom use can separate the learner from other students in a manner that many users find uncomfortable or unduly attention-gaining, not in a positive way. Learners using such designs often feel they are being treated differently or that the added effort of learning to use the technology on top of learning the material they are studying is an extra burden. Taken even at face value, this research shows that the user experience involves obvious physical and cognitive concerns but it also comes with strong emotional and environmental dimensions that are not typically considered in a usability test.

But the accessible technology concerns don't stop at the individual. Most studies of implementation reveal how social are these practices. Obviously, classroom technology relies on teachers being able to exploit the capabilities as much as the direct student user. It's also clear that in domestic (non-classroom) settings, family members might be actively engaged in the successful use and management of the design. Pihlainen et al. (2017) showed that successful accessible technologies might rely heavily on family members acting as co-designers, which is commonly recognized but rarely implemented in design processes. As they note, "providing an active role for parental co-development of technological activities fosters technology acceptance and family integration in long-term technology co-design, co-evaluation and co-intervention. This has strong implications towards social inclusiveness, technology demystification and innovative co-creation" (p. 19).

Sharma et al. (2020) studied families in Finland attempting to use assistive technologies and while confirming the general finding that parents wish such technologies were more engaging to use for their children, also highlighted the significant cultural dynamics at work in the adoption and application of such technologies in society. These authors emphasize what they term the "socio-technical aspirations" prevalent within a context, at the family unit, school, and social levels, as crucial in understanding how best to leverage technology for greater accessibility.

As with the issue of cybersecurity, designing for accessibility asks questions of our understanding of people that pushes us beyond easy layering of human experience into one or two layers derived from social science theory. To truly address the challenges of accessible design we need to move beyond a view of disabilities as a condition to be overcome and learn to see them as part of a broader shaping of a complete environment of interactions where perhaps previously unnoticed properties become obstacles for some. In this way, we can recognize certain people are therefore disabled from access and use because of the world as presented, not from some deficit or condition in themselves. In conceiving design solutions there must be recognition of the social groups in which the interventions may operate, incorporating more stakeholders into the design process and helping shape a broader cultural awareness of how design choices reflect values and civic engagement. Traditional human or user-centered design has too often had little to say on such issues, I believe, because it has borrowed its view of users unquestioningly from academic and social science theories of human behavior and experience. This is less a criticism than an observation, it made sense for those concerned with UX to begin there but it is now time to recognize that our understanding of users and user-centered design cannot end there.

Getting to Augmentation: A Multi-Layered Education

To advance our efforts at being truly user-centered we need to address both the framing of users across all levels of experience, and the education of new user experience professionals.

It is not a difficult step to broaden one's conception of users because, ultimately, we all recognize in ourselves the multi-level nature of our being in the world. When we engage with a new device or space for the first time, we all go through a process of orienting ourselves and "getting a feel" for it that invariably involves the full range of human psychosocial responses. We look, touch, sense, move, and adjust to the new. The very term "get a feel" implies physicality but it also brings perceptual and cognitive dimensions to the fore. In new environments we "get our bearings," suggesting a need to orient ourselves to an environment, positioning oneself in respect to the space, the situation and to others, literally and figuratively. This orientation is as much social and cultural as it is physical. When we comment that the terminology or labeling on a new interface is or is not to our liking, we highlight a range of experiential and linguistic preferences that carry cultural and cognitive baggage. In sum, we are, at all times, operating as multi-level beings.

Of course, our limited attention might encourage us to see a situation or interaction as mainly occurring at one level, e.g., if we struggle with a virtual key press we might imagine the only issue here is physical use, or if we can't remember a password it might seem like the only issue is memory, but these are instances, sub-units of meaningful interaction with technologies. Each is important but not sufficient in understanding use, and every sub-unit carries with it a set of understandings that reflect far wider experiential demands. To press a key correctly is indeed a physical act but to perform it requires an awareness of that small object on the screen being "pressable", which we call an affordance, and that by doing so one is issuing a form of command that will induce a response in a device, the use of which is part of a much larger knowledge frame that carries cognitive, social and cultural meaning. Forgetting a password is certainly a memory issue but the experience of this will likely invoke an emotional reaction, an awareness of the implications of being unable to perform some routine activity that likely involves other people, and forms part of your understanding how and why security procedures are applied in organizational and social settings. There simply is no interaction we might have with technologies that does not tie in, however loosely, all the layers of human experience.

Considered this way, the solution might seem obvious: let's make sure that all user analyses we conduct capture the multiple levels of experience that are in play. That's certainly true but it is about as useful as telling a student who is struggling to reach some learning goal that they should "try harder," it does not really offer much educational value. What we need is to explicitly state the relevant issues by walking step by step through the layers and noting the experiential components that seem important. This means unpacking the full range of issues that might help us understand what user we are designing for might bring to the interaction and not limiting ourselves to one level, no matter how particular the immediate design challenge might be.

A simple exercise I conduct with my students early in the semester is to ask them to consider an everyday device such as a mobile phone or kitchen appliance and to outline the user issues that might exist at each level, from the physical ergonomics to the cultural aspects of use. This is really a brainstorming exercise to force them out of a narrow consideration of the user interface and immediate ease of use. At first, this can be a struggle but as the groups discuss the challenge, they tentatively begin to fill in the details on a whiteboard to share with other groups. In the first few classes, the user issues are predominantly physical or cognitive. By the end of the semester, by which time they will have covered much of the material in this book, the distribution flows more uniformly across all levels the students now informed by terms, theories, and findings from each level of the social science base they have explored.

I make no great claims that this type of exercise on its own produces radical change in the design professionals we produce but it does offer the students a framework for thinking about human-computer interaction that I believe is richer than being tied to one theory, one school of thought or one method of design. It encourages an integration of theoretical and methodological frameworks since no one theory or method can cover the levels appropriately. It also offers a way of ensuring that important differences between users might be identified (we all might have the same physical properties, or we might not; and if we imagine our users all share the same cultural background, what questions might this raise about the assumptions underlying our design?), and it does so in a way that is more natural or emergent than reading books of guidelines or generating a set of personas.

The broader front to advance is incorporating this type of multi-level thinking across the curriculum of education for UX professionals. The "divide and conquer" approach has not only driven social science, but it has formed the basis for much of the coursework we offer students in their programs. Consequently, I find there are generally two types of UX education available to new professionals, one that ties theory in by employing the divided layers approach, with separate courses in perception, in cognition, in ergonomics, and so forth, with little real effort at combining these together. This produces robust professionals who tend to focus or specialize in one or other layer, usually the cognitive, with some acknowledgement of the secondary importance of physical or social aspects. The second type emphasizes method over theory, pushing a form of design practice that encourages the development of skills related to the quick identification of requirements, prototyping, and the basics of running rapid tests on design ideas. Here, theory not only takes a back seat, it might be considered superfluous to the agile gathering of data and the production of quick solutions.

What I believe we need is a new form of user-centered design education that recognizes the limitations of either approach and emphasizes greater integration of a theoretical layers, which tied to methods for user analysis and scenario generation, would push a richer, multi-layered view of users as human beings, immersed in the real world. To get beyond classic measures of usability and acceptability, recognizing they are useful but insufficient as a basis for creating the types of information technologies that augment our existence, we must embrace a complete view of our experiences. This is why a vertical slice through the rich theoretical work on human nature is required as a foundation for those who wish to practice user or human-centered design.

Of course, some will argue that *less* rather than *more* theory is what we need, that we should design primarily by creating and testing. I have some sympathy for this approach. We simply cannot rely on theory alone so we must create and test, I doubt it will ever be different. Most of our theories are not suggestive or directive for design, they are explanatory and somewhat predictive of human response but they are not articulated in a manner where they can be easily employed for generating new products or services. However, in the context of user-centered design, I offer two reasons why the "create and test" method alone is flawed.

First, we cannot avoid theory. There is no blank slate creation that occurs in absence of some theory or mix of theories in the mind of a designer. Paraphrasing philosopher Karl Popper there really is no such thing as theory-free observation. When a designer imagines an interface, or conceives of an interaction to be supported, they are drawing on their understanding and mental models of the world. Even if they are using data from usability tests as a guide, they must interpret and generate solutions from a range of options. The mental processes underlying these choices rely on concepts, ideas, knowledge, intuition all reflecting and manifesting the designer's theoretical understanding. Until such time as a design solution is logically determined by a specification or finding, and there is no space for alternatives, a designer must apply the theoretical knowledge they possess to generate a solution. The designer might not refer to their thinking as theoretical but that hardly matters, it is unavoidable, our mental processes are theory driven. All the better then that we enhance the relevant knowledge that is being applied to increase the chances of achieving a user-centered solution.

Second, theory informs method. We have learned much over recent decades on what makes for a reliable and valid user test, how the underlying constructs of usability and acceptability are related, how to gather user requirements appropriately, and what statistical tests are most applicable to UX data. Simply asking people questions, or generating a survey without understanding response biases is a quick way of gaining flawed data. Alternatively, simply adopting a standard evaluation protocol for every test is likely to miss some important data that can improve a particular design. A richer theoretical understanding of user experience makes us ask questions of our methods and helps us interpret the data they provide. If I test only for ease of learning or efficiency on task, what am I not understanding about the role of culture, or the user's emotional response? Perhaps those layers are less important in some instances, but we must determine this appropriately not overlook them through ignorance or accident.

In sum, we need to build a broader theoretical understanding of user experience that recognizes the richness of human life. We have moved on from the largely instrumental view of information technologies as tools, framed in terms of work and tasks for which they offer some utility and, as their complexity grew, raised concerns with usability. Our ecology of information is shifting toward new forms of user interface, greater sensory engagement, and dynamic design, which in combination could deliver some of the promises made for this technology for decades. Each of these is briefly discussed below but while these are interesting, it is the consequences of such developments in human and social terms that are most compelling. How we address these will challenge what we know about UX design and determine how human-centered we really can be.

Shifting Interface Boundaries

One obvious development where we have made rapid progress is the portability of information technologies. Mainframe to mobile has happened in less than a lifetime but a quick examination of people's routine use indicates that laptops, tablets, and large screen mobile phones tie us firmly to rather familiar devices. Beyond the challenges of reliable power and connectivity for our hardware, we have seemingly accepted the physical keyboard as a constraint. Mobile devices demonstrate how keyboards can be presented virtually but even here they demand significant screen space to employ and are often non-optimal for human physiology. As technologies require less physical size, a breakthrough in design that lessens the need to carry a keyboard or even learn to type could exploit more natural human communicative acts based on voice, gesture, facial expression, and touch. Fully articulated 3-D handtracking systems offer the potential for true direct manipulation of simulated physical objects, which opens up the potential to create interactive experiences that transcend the typical physical-digital divide by allowing for naturalistic control processes and rich haptic feedback that simulates the material world.

While brain-computer interfacing might be decades from deployment, the short-term impact of direct manipulation could significantly lessen our reliance on hardware input devices, allowing for the generation of on-the-fly control interfaces through the use of tablets, depth cameras and modeling software that exploit routine surfaces. Moving, controlling, writing, sizing and maneuvering of objects in a virtual space could be leveraged by the physiological skills humans refine routinely through their interactions with the physical world (see e.g., Li et al., 2020). But such practical applications are only the start since we can envisage augmentations to the human hand that allow for extended reach, precision aiming, or rapid responses that exploit the automatic neuro-physiological processing of humans, not only enhancing our physical capabilities but enabling full participation in digital spaces for all, especially offering enhancements for those with reduced or limited abilities.

Further, by closing the loop in terms of tactile feedback, we approach the potential to touch and engage with digital representations in a manner that incorporates sensory signals for size, texture, weight, and so forth. Applying sensors to clothing and surfaces can allow us to reside in the physical and digital realms simultaneously. This cueing might also signal the presence of digital spaces that can be exploited by users as they move through the world, affording them on-demand, any place interactions via gesture-controlled and sensor-enabled virtual interfaces. In this way, we not only design with our bodies in mind, we aim to augment our physical movements and skills. Ergonomic analysis might then shift from concerns with comfort and efficiency to considering power and precision.

Multi-Sensory Engagement

In combination with shifting hardware boundaries, let us recognize how information is more than text, words, or screens. The opportunity to incorporate greater sensory involvement in interaction is long overdue. While sound has been partially exploited for attention capture, properties of auditory processing that give rise to cues on location, trajectory, relative mood, and more can potentially deliver richer information experiences that are rarely considered currently. One can imagine the computational activities of search and retrieval exploiting sonic cues to suggest time and effort, potentially offering private signals to a user via earphones during multitasking, or being designed to correlate with ongoing real-time data streaming for monitoring of background or secondary activities.

Similarly, we can treat other sensory channels such as taste and smell (see e.g., Neves and Camara, 2020), which to date have largely been explored only in gaming or entertainment scenarios but which again offer an opportunity to engage with the user to complement their activities and experiences. The aim here is less an olfactory interface, for example, but the additive value of combinatory sensory stimuli to enrich the information experience or extend the user's sources of information over time. Imagine, for example, wearables that signal the presence or location of others, or that capture and convey important contextual information to an otherwise distracted person. How much do we actually know about how humans synthesize different sensory information and how little have we exploited our minds' processing capabilities when designing information applications?

Advances in epidermal VR interfaces suggest we explore further the potential to exploit the human's largest sense organ, the skin, in ways that have rarely been utilized in experience design. What might our skin offer as means to capture and communicate relevant health data, where the user is both passive provider and active user of information? Subtle cues of physiological processes (stress, posture, position, blood pressure, etc.) could be obtained in a relatively unobtrusive manner and we could design ways of feeding this back to people to enable them to monitor their own well-being. Environmental state could be conveyed in a manner that might extend the capabilities of humans to understand their world around them without overloading the visual channel. Skin-sourced data could be used to improve speech recognition through the exploitation of muscle signals and vocal vibration, demonstrating the convergence of sensory data to improve all aspects of the human-computer interface. Skin based interfaces might also enable control and input by using parts of our limbs such as the back of the forearm as emergent input devices (see e.g., Bergstrom and Hornbaek, 2019). In short, we can and are envisaging a form of material-digital connection that can better exploit our physical and behavioral nature as users.

Dynamic Design

Leveraging the benefits of emergent interfaces addresses one core aspect of user experience but the focus of much interaction design still resides on a fixed view of tasks, decomposed discretely, and used to derive design solutions. Again, this places experience design behind the curve, designing for recognized actions that may or may not be what users want or will do. Yet users do not exploit technology in its given form, they adapt it and adapt to it. The challenge then is how to apply sensor technologies, machine learning and natural language processing to move beyond direct user input (the commands or terms employed) to exploit multiple data signals from humans to tailor interactions in real time. In so doing, we will likely discover new opportunities for human-information interactions that are not tied to immediate tasks or needs.

Adoption of voice-controlled info-appliances has been limited by the range of tasks supported through unambiguous and vocabulary-constrained input. Language is a supremely subtle information resource that is under-exploited due to the limitations of current computational linguistics but we can anticipate progress in machine learning and natural language processing (NLP) to allow more sophisticated language processing that will support conversational interactions between users and devices. The potential then is for data exploration by humans that is cognitively richer than the submission of search terms, incorporating sentiment analysis, and even quality indices that will deliver digital assistants with capabilities to problem solve with users, not just deliver discrete answers.

Through such interactions the choices, utterances and actions of users might serve as a guide to many important qualifiers of their needs and preferences such as depth or complexity of information sought, reading and language ability differences, and even temporal preferences for types of information or experience. The challenge of contextualizing language processing is not simply computational, it involves increased understanding of how human speech patterns reflect intention and meaning. Much of the practical application of NLP resides in creating more sophisticated bots or automated responders but the insights gained from computational linguistics can be applied to the tailoring of more aspects of user experience than question and answer pairings, it would enable more contextual communicative exchanges that enable the exploitation of massive data repositories for multiple query types in commercial and private spaces. Further, the experience of using such resources can serve to augment human learning through interrogation, exchange, and requests for tailored instruction. Applying eye-tracking to gain an index of domain knowledge and attention, for example, we can envisage the process of interaction being more than a sequence of task steps or discrete acts but as an unfolding, dynamic process where the cues provided by users over time offer further characterizations of their intent, gathered over longer sequences than single tasks, to more fully understand how the user is engaged (Gwizdka and Dillon, 2020). Design then is an extended and adaptive process occurring through actual use rather than staged tests, requiring us to reconsider the meaning of user-centered design.

Implications

By shifting the focus of UX from qualities such as usability and acceptance of devices toward a view of interaction as the multi-leveled, temporally extended information processing tendencies and preferences of humans, we can begin to envisage new opportunities to exploit and direct technical developments. Specifically, moving beyond traditional hardware boundaries, leveraging multi-sensory processing, and designing for dynamic, adaptive performance that exploits the data intensity of machine learning and AI, we can envisage new forms of user experience design that better support the diversity and complexity of human endeavors. But as I have repeatedly tried to argue in this book, new designs are rarely adopted wholesale, used only as the designers intended, and divorced from the real-world concerns beyond an isolated task.

A shift in interaction from devices to environments represents a significant change in the sense of ownership, storage, location, and possession of information. Virtual and dynamic interfaces evoke intangibility and require consensual acceptance by users of forms of monitoring and data capture that pose serious questions of user willingness to engage across hybrid applications.

Ability to control depth and range of immersion will likely be a key factor in early acceptance of such environments and raise the question of immersion levels that might reflect human comfort in specific contexts.

Dynamic design based on continual machine learning of user behavior requires a commitment by users to significantly more of their behavior being captured. Despite popular claims otherwise, there is compelling evidence that privacy still matters for most adult users in the US (Pew Research, 2019) even if they feel relatively powerless to ensure it. Post-pandemic acceptance of shared workspaces raises the challenge of heightened privacy needs in communal environments. For discretionary system adoption, where personal monitoring of all aspects of our lives is more advanced, it is likely users will raise more rather than fewer concerns.

The rapid adoption of mobile and increasingly integrated information technologies indicates growing expectations for user experiences tied less to distinctive, standalone hardware than interoperable environments and common platforms. An aging and growing population will increasingly include technology-savvy users who will anticipate digital environments for ambient assisted living that augment their physical, perceptual, and cognitive capabilities at a time of predictable declines in acuity. Tailorability will become an assumed quality of future information technologies even while users raise more concerns about data rights.

Despite my reservations about predictions, the next decade or so is likely to see a growth in wearables, gaze directed interaction, and commercial data mining-sourced adaptive systems as stepping stones to more immersive and integrated, cross platform user experiences. The future will likely be shaped by hybrid digital-physical interfaces which combine advances in material engineering, computer science and social science to guide design choices. Genuine citizen concerns with privacy and trust will likely drive more discourse on UX in the coming decade particularly as we enact adaptive data-driven design. Long -term, informed tailorability will be an important design frontier for user experience and to design well for this environment, we need a richer and more integrated understanding of humans. If we wish to augment our lives, not just make tasks easier to do, user-centered design needs to become a real discipline.

References

Assistive Technology Industry Association. (2020). What is AT? *Assistive Technology Industry Association*. https://www.atia.org/home/at-resources/what-is-at/

Autotrader (2019). Buying a car: How long can you expect a car to last? https://www.autotrader.com/car-shopping/buying-car-how-long-can-you-expect-car-last-240725

Ayon, V. and Dillon, A. (2021). Assistive technology in education: Conceptions of a socio technical design challenge. *International Journal of Information, Diversity and Inclusion, 5*(2), 174–184.

Bergstrom, J. and Hornbaek, K. (2019). HCI on the skin. *ACM Computing Surveys, 52*(4), 1–14.

Dillon, A., Sweeney, M., and Maguire, M. (1993). A survey of usability evaluation practices and requirements in the European IT industry. In *People and Computers IX*, Proceedings of the British Computer Society's Annual Conference, HCI'93, Cambridge: Cambridge University Press, pp. 81–94.

Gwizdka, J. and Dillon, A. (2020). Eye-tracking as a method for enhancing research on information search. In W.T. Fu, and H. van Oostendorp (Eds.), *Understanding and Improving Information Search: A Cognitive Approach* (pp. 161–181). Cham: Springer International Publishing. 10.1007/978-3-030-38825-6_9

Li, Z., Lei, Z., Yan, A., Solovey, E., and Pahlavan, K. (2020). ThuMouse: A micro-gesture cursor input through mmWave radar-based interaction. In *2020 IEEE International Conference on Consumer Electronics (ICCE)*, pp. 1–9. 10.1109/ICCE46568.2020.9043082

Mayer, P., Zou, Y., Schaub, F., and Aviv, A. (2021). 'Now I'm a bit angry': Individuals' awareness, perception, and responses to data breaches that affected them. In Proceedings of the 30th USENIX Security Symposium (USENIX 21), pp. 393–410.

Morris, M. and Dillon, A. (1996). The importance of usability in the establishment of organizational software standards for end user computing. *International Journal of Human-Computer Studies, 45*(2), 243–258. 10.1006/ijhc.1996.0050

Neves, P. and Câmara, A. (2020). Multisensory HCI design with smell and taste for environmental health communication. In C. Stephanidis, et al., (eds.), *HCI International 2020 - Late Breaking Papers: User Experience Design and Case Studies. HCII 2020.* Lecture Notes in Computer Science, vol 12423. Cham: Springer. 10.1007/978-3-030-60114-0_31

Pew Research Center (2019). *"Americans and Privacy: Concerned, Confused and Feeling Lack of Control Over Their Personal Information."* https://www.pewresearch.org/internet/2019/11/15/americans-and-privacy-concerned-confused-and-feeling-lack-of-control-over-their-personal-information/

Pihlainen, K., Montero, C., and Karna, E. (2017). Fostering parental co-development of technology for children with special needs informal learning activities. *International Journal of Child-Computer Interaction, 11*, C (January), 19–27. 10.1016/j.ijcci.2016.10.010

Rowe, A. (2021). Study Reveals Average Person Has 100 Passwords. TechCo News, Nov 9, 2021. https://tech.co/password-managers/how-many-passwords-average-person

Sharma, S., Avellan, T., Linna, J., Achary, K., Turunen, M., Hakulinen, J., and Varkey, B. (2020). Socio-technical aspirations for children with special needs: A study in two locations – India and Finland. *ACM Transactions on Accessible Computing, 13*(3), 1–27. 10.1145/3396076

Tajer, D. (2019). Quoted in "Boeing 737 Max: What's Happened After the 2 Deadly Crashes", *New York Times*, October 21, 2019.

Wittgernstein, L. (1958). *Philosophical Investigations*. Oxford: Blackwell.

Index

Note: **Bold** page numbers refer to tables and *italic* page numbers refer to figures.

Aboelmaged, M. 215
acceptance or acceptability 233; aesthetics and 215; choices, and impact on adoption 211–212; Davis' model, and user's intentions drivers 202, *203*; defined 199; determining, and real world dynamics 209–211; elderly mobile phone users, case 212; as extension of usability 198–200, 206, 208–209; numerical systems, case 212; self-efficacy theory 202; social and cultural forces in 212–213; SUS or TAM scores 210; System Usability Scale (SUS) **207**, 208; Technology Acceptance Model (TAM) 202, 203–205, 223; theory of planned behavior (TPB), Ajzen's 200, *201*; within UX 200, 202, 206. *See also* usability
adopter types (Rogers theory): distribution of, bell curve *152*, 153; early adopters 152; early or late majority categories 152; innovators 151–152; laggards 152–153; proportion of *152*; traits or dispositions 151
advertisements 25
aesthetics 215, 216
Africa, colored art in 3
Ajzen, I. 200, 201, 202
Al-Beruni 77
Alexander, C. 31, 55
Altamira cave, Spain 1, *2*; de Sautola, claims 1–3; image of bison 1, *2*
Amazon.com 23
America 168
American Civil Liberties CLU 234
American Publishers Association 6
Apple 100
Applying Cognitive Psychology to User Interface Design (Gardiner and Christie) 131
archaeologists 79
Aristotle 53
art, and paintings: Egyptian tomb 12; expressions and representation through 12, 13; as means of co-habitation 13; shift in representational form 12
assistive technology 235–236
augmentation, term 5
Ayon, V. 235

Bandura, A. 202
Barnes, L. 135
Baxter, G. 143, 144
Bazos, J. 24
behavioral sciences 79
Benbasat, I 151
Berry, D.M. 67
Boehm, B. 35

Boeing 737 Max airplane 228; fatal crashes, and design decisions 228, 229; human factor component 229–230; trouble with MCAS 228, 229
Book of Judges 31
books, digital 6, 220–221, 227
Brewer, W.F. 117
Brooke, J. 207
Byazit, N. 30, 31

camera switch 108
7+/-2 capacity rule 122
Card, S. 86, 87, 88, 89, 90, 111, 118, 190
Cartailhac, E. 2
Cartesian divide and conquer approach 83, 239
cave art, and paintings 1, 8; analysis, and technique of 2, 3, 10; animals, representations of 10, 11; and computers 8; human form, depiction 11; images, common 10; memorable events as 11; origin and meaning 1–3; technological progress 3, 4; utilitarian nature of, images 10
Center for Advanced Research on Language Acquisition 159
Chiagouris, L. 154
Chrisomalis, S. 212
Christie, B. 131
classroom technology 236
clay potters 48
client-centered financial advice 25
coal mining industry: idea of people and technologies 139–140; mechanization in 139; Trist observations 139
Cognitive Psychology (Eysenck and Keane) 114
Cognitive Walkthrough (CW) method 186, 188; goal and questions, addressed 189; HE comparison to 189–190
Colby, C. L. 215
collectivism, culture 165–166
common-sense model 201
computer revolution 23, 140
Computer Science 5, 67, 70
Conci, M. 212
"conjecture" or hypotheses 62–63
Conjectures and Refutations (Popper) 63
consumer goods 49
context of use, designed artifact 40
control issues, and enhancement desires 145–147
Cooper, M. 24
cottage industries 57
COVID-19 pandemic: communication technologies use 226; Deloitte survey 141; surge in device ownership 141
craft-based knowledge: design activity, form of 52–53; drawbacks 53–54; limitations of, cartwheel case 54–55; rationalizing improvements 54; rise of mechanization, threat to practitioners 55; skill transfer issue 53–54; slow response time problem 55; trial and error approach 54
craft-based practices 49
Cross, N. 62
culture: challenges, community response to 164; collectivism/individualism 165–166; comparison of four countries, on six dimensions *169*, 170; concept, and world 158–159; criticism of Hofstede model 171; defined, key aspects 159–160; differences, and user preferences 161; dimensions of, Hofstede's 164–168, *169*; femininity/masculinity 166; globalization and 161; Hofstede et al.'s onion model of 162–163, 170; indulgence *vs.* restraint 167–168; information "haves" and "have-nots 160; key figures, and rituals 162, 163; layer of values 162–163; manifestations of 162; "modesty-assertive" labels 166; and nation, distinction 170–171; orientation, long-term *vs.* short-term 167; power distance 165; tales and symbols 161–162, 163; uncertainty avoidance 166–167
customer-centered retail 25
CW *see* Cognitive Walkthrough method

Darke, J. 63
data science 80
dating techniques 2, 3
Davis, F. 202, 208
degree programs, design as focus 51–52, 69
Deloitte, U.S. 141
de Quincey, T. 176

de Sautola, M. 1, 4, 8; Altamira cave art finding 1, *2*; discovery, lessons of 3–4
Descartes, R. 77, 78, 89
design: act of, Simon's claims 58–60, 65–66; assistive technology 235–236; challenges, and solution 50, 72–73; characteristics of successful 149–151; as cognitive and physical act 51; degree programs 51–52, 69; digital realm, challenges 28; dynamic, and machine learning 245; educational programs 67, 68–72; as form of thinking 64; as human act, routine 48, 51, 52, 57–59, 66; image of traditional craft and 49; industrial production rise 56 (*see also* mechanization, of manufacture); Lawson/Dorst views, distinct framings 66; making sense of, problematic 65–67; physical ergonomics of 105; practices, craft- and science-based 49; problem-solving approaches 63–65; "REAL" 230–233; reasoning, Lawson's study 51; Schon's, description of 60–61; Schon *vs.* Simon description of 61–62; shift from craft to machine-aided 56; shift in meaning of 57–58; tactile and tangible interfaces 106, 242, 243; term, definitions and interpretations 48–49; understanding of 58–65, 72–73; universal curriculum, need for 64, 94–95; user-centered, education challenge 69–73, 94–95; wearable and portable devices 105. *See also* processes, of design; user-centeredness design
designers: job openings, and education 51, 67, 69–72, 224; label, types 50–51; problem-solving approaches 63–65; qualifications for 65; Simon's views 65; skilled performance 64; user-centered, challenge with educating 69–72, 224, 239; UX professionals, challenges faced 72, 235; working practices, conjecture or hypotheses 62–63
Design Research Society, UK 30
design thinking: "*Design Thinking is Bullshit*" (Jen) 42–43; method for innovation 42; theoretical basis, lack of 43
digital books 6, 220–221, 227
digital documents 90–91
Digital Equipment Corporation 24
digital technologies: accounts of design challenges 29; development of 27, 28; focus on users 29
digit span test 122
Dillon, A. 43, 235
disabilities, and assistive technology 235–236
Discourse on Method (Descartes) 78
dished cartwheel 29
divide-and-conquer style 84, 85, 90, 91
Donald, M. 13; stages of cognitive evolution 14; summary of (1998) layers of culture **15**
Dorst, K. 60, 66
Dourish, P. 40
Dreyfuss, H. 225
Drulhe, L. 161
Dudek, C. 181, 194

Eames, C. 225
Eason, K. 141, 155, 156; propositions 141, **142**, 143; new information adoption and 155; organizational setting, emphasis 142; relevant parties, involvement 143; view of users in, propositions 142
economists 79
educational programs, for design 68–70, 94–95, 224
electric vehicle (EV): Barnes' journey, experience 135–136, 140; challenges of 135, 137; supporting infrastructure, need for 135–136; work system 140
emotions, and information-processing 132–133
Engelbart, D. 5
enhancement desires, and control issues 145–147
epidermal VR interfaces 242
Ergonomics 32, 89; and "human factors" 100, 111; idea of physical 101; physical analysis, of users 101, **102**, 103–104; term use in UX 100
experience, of users 227; acceptability, estimate of 213–215; aesthetics, perception of 215, 216; broad categories of **214**; designers, digital documents and 90–91; dynamic design, and machine learning 245; evaluations, as fixed property 213, 215–217; interest,

and understanding of 44–45, 240; as multi-layered/level interaction 92, *93*, 227, 237–238, 244; satisfaction, estimates of 179, 180–181, 195, 214; sensory involvement, in interaction 242–243; tactile feedback 241; TAM and SUS use 214; with technologies 135–137, 227; term "group dynamics" 137
expert-based evaluation 185–190; Cognitive Walkthrough 186, 188; heuristic evaluation 186–188
eye-tracking methods 184
Eysenck, M. 114

Facebook 18, 19, 20
fake video, and AI 23
feminine-leaning societies 166
Fields, A. 114
Finstad, K. 207
Fishbein, M. 200, 202
Fitts, P. 109
Fitts' Law 94, 104, 109, 111, 112
frame design 29
Frascara, J. 95
Fuller, B. 6

Gardiner, M. 131
Gartner technical report in 2010 106
Gates, B. 24
genius designer, model of innovation 225
Gestalt principles of visual form 94
Girardi, P. 154
Google 5, 160
Google Glasses 27
Gould, J.D. 185
Grandjean, E. 102
Greenwich Observatory 158
Guardian newspaper 135
Gutenberg, J. 24
Gutenberg printing 9, 24

Haddad, S. 171, 172
handheld devices, physical interactions 103–104
handwriting, index finger-based 103
Hargreaves, J. 55
Harrison, S. 33
Hassenzahl, M. 215
HCI professionals, and degree programs 39, 69
HE *see* heuristic evaluation method
Hertzum, M. 190
heuristic evaluation (HE) method 186; CW comparison to 189–190; Nielsen's heuristics for evaluating usability *187*, 188; shortcomings 188
Hobbes, T. 98
Hofestede-Insights.com 168–169
Hofstede, G. 158, 162, 163–168, 164, 167, 172
Home computers 24
Hoober, S. 104
How Designers Think (Lawson) 51
human behavior: activities range, time estimates (Newell and Card) 86, **87**; adaptation 216; bodies and mind work 107; cognition over time, responses automation and 126–131; cognitive theories of mind and 114; Descartes views 77; mistakes 130–131; movement time, precision 108–109; psychophysiological level of 105–106; science, study of 75, 77, 86; social relations, analysis 138; with technologies, individual factors and 136–137, 139–140 (*see also* experience, of users)
human-computer interaction (HCI) 33, 36–38, 217, 227, 238; design values 145; formal model of, time estimates 118, *119*; "hard science" 88; multi-sensory engagement 242–243; Newell and Card, paper 86–89, 111; process, within perceptual cycle framework 118; psychological level, theories and insights 87; time-sliced distinctions **87**, 89, 111
The Human Factor (Vicente) 70
human-machine interface 33, 39, 242, 243
human mind, study of 114
human psychology: active 116; attention, ability 124–125; automated tasks/routine performance 118, 119; automatic to controlled processing 128–129; "available information" 117; characteristics of 116; cognition over time, automation of responses 126–128; cognitive architecture of users *119*; cognitive view of 115, *116*; control, desire of 145; emotional aspects 132–133; enhancement, desire

of 145–147; learning, musical instrument 128–129; "long-term" memory role 123–126; mistakes 130–131; Neisser's representation 115, *116*, 117, 118, 120; sensory inputs, filtering signals 120, 124; short-term sensory store 120–121; sound awareness, and perception 120; Wickens' model 119; working memory role 121–123; world's signals interpretation 117

humans: attention allocation and consciousness 124–125; attributes of mind 221–222; automatic to controlled processing 128–129; cognition 20; cognition over time, and responses automation 126–128; cognitive architecture of users *119*; as cognitive beings 115; cognitive evolution of 14, 16; concerns with IT 19; conversation 126; cycle of interaction, with world 115, *116*, 118; Donald's, development stages 14, **15**; emotional side, and responses 132–133; experience, research and education on 76; form depiction, in art 11–12; history of 13–14; information processing 124, 224; as information users 5, 6, 16, 19, 221 (*see also* information); language learning 125; linguistic capabilities, emergence 14; "long-term" memory role 123–126; material level of existence 99; mimetic, and theoretic 14, **15**; mind's inner workings model 118, *119*; movement time, precision 108–109; multi-layered interaction, with designed interface 92–94, 108, 227; perception and cognition in 114–115, *116*; as physical beings, "users" 84, 89, 98–99, 106–107; reading, complex act 128; representation act, as cognitive extension 17; sensory involvement, in interaction 242–243; short-term sensory store 120–121; social and technical infrastructures, evolution 18; social scientists, enquiry space on 82–86; sound awareness, and perception 120; tendencies, and design methods 31–32; user-centered design 19, 21, 31, 33–34, 89; "vertical slice," multi-layered analysis of 77, 88, 90, 91, 92, 93; working memory in 121–123

IBM 164, 171

Iivari, J. 43

Iivari, N. 43

imagining of ideas 17

Indian parable, of blind men and the elephant 75

individualistic work culture 165

indulgence *vs.* restraint, in culture 167–168

industrial revolution 56, 57

information: ability to imagine 17; availability, and use of 5–6; -based age 221; CDs, and LPs 6; and collectivism 13; history, process 8–9, 221; human engagement with, pattern of 7, 8; imagination ability 17; infrastructure, global 5, 17–19, 20, 23, 81; internet use 6; knowledge doubling curve 6; lived experiences theme and 16–17; mobile computing tools and 6; practices/ record analyses 7–8; representation, as cognitive extension 17; space, designed/ networked 22; technologies, progress of 4–6, 18, 22; user-centeredness, as core value of 25–26

information technology 3, 6, 19, 81, 220; emergence of user-centeredness design 25, 33; genius designer, innovation model 225; human communication, development in 81, 227; hybrid physical-digital environments 105–106; impact on world, changing 81–82, 105; interactions with, in group/collective 137, 140; interface boundaries, shifting 241–242, 244; lived experience, reshaped areas of 80–83; nuanced history of, evolution 25, 227; people as users of 136; portability of, progress 241; process of adoption for 199, 200; user-friendly, all sectors 26

information tools, downsides 23–24

Inkeles, A. 164

Innovation Diffusion model 199

Innovation Diffusion Theory (Rogers') 148, 156, 171; communication channels, and diffusion process 154; five stages, adoption process 148, 199; impulsivity in 154; innovation characteristics 149–151; limitations to 154, 155; personality role 156; strength of 153–154; types of adopters/users 151–155

innovations characteristics (Rogers theory): compatibility 149; degree of discretion 151; outcomes, observability 150–151; relative advantage 149; trials or test runs 150; usability, ease of 150, 156, 198–199
Interaction Design Foundation 39
interactive technologies, in digital realm 28–29
International Standards Organization (ISO) standards 179; *Guidance on Usability Specification and Measures* (1998) 179
internet 161
Internet of Things (IoT) 225
iPhone X 100
Islamic Golden Age 77
Ive, J. 225

Jacobsen, N. 190
James, W. 128
Jen, N. 42
Jobs, S. 24, 225

Keane, M. 114
Keung, J. 205
Khajouei, R. 188
Kjeldskov, J. 217
knowledge doubling curve 6
Kroemer, K. 102
Kyriakoullis, L. 173

Lamar, H. 25
Land, F. 143
language processing 125, 243–244
laptop 99
Lawson, B. 51, 54, 63–64, 66
learning, musical instrument 128–129
Levinson, D. 164
Lewin, K. 138
Lewis, C. 185
Lewis, J. 185, 195, 208
Lewis, J.R. 181, 194, 207
Licklider, J. 30
Lindgaard, G. 181, 194
long-term memories: attention allocation and consciousness 124–125; conversation making 126; language learning 125–126; several forms 123; "what" and "how" distinction 124
Loranger, H. 71
Lovelace, A. 25
Ludd, N. (General) 56

machine-learning 80
man-computer symbiosis 31
maps, and world 158–159
masculine culture 166
mass production age 49
Mayer, P. 233
McEleney, J. 27
Mead, M. 163
mechanization, of manufacture: Crompton's "Spinning Mule" 56; Hargreave's "Spinning Jenny" 55, 56; human labor employment, shift in 56; industrialization 56, 57; Luddites against 56; Wright's views, on social progress 57
medicines, label instructions on 26
mental experiences, aspects of 76–77
menu design choices 109, *110*, 111
misinformation campaigns 23
mobile technologies 24, 100, 105–106, 241
model-based approach 190–192; basic task elements for **191**; GOMS method 190; If-THEN rule 192; limitations 192
Moore, G.C. 151
mouse-style input device 5
Musk, E. 225

national character 164
national culture 170
nationalities, and culture 170, 171
natural language processing (NLP) 243, 244
Neisser, U. 115, 116, 117, 118, 120
Neolithic era 13
Newell, A. 86, 87, 88, 89, 90, 111, 190
new technologies 221; adoption, Rogers' model 148–149; supporting infrastructure need 135–136
see also information technology
Nielsen, J. 186, *187*
Nielsen-Norman Group 71
Noel, G. 95
noise 120
Non-Zero, The Logic of Human Destiny (Wright) 57
Nordpass Security 234
Norman, D. 43, 175
numerical systems 212

olfactory interface 242
Olsen, K. 24
online global retail market 23
online security: designing for accessibility 236; and identity theft 233; password protection 234–235
orientation dimension, of culture 167

Parasumaran, A. 215
Parsons, T. 163
password management software 234
peak shift principle 11, 12
physical analysis, users: age and nationality 101, 104; anthropometric data 101, **102**; data, for products physical aspects 101, 102; ergonomics study for 101–103, 108, 111–112; gaming contexts, and age 104; handheld devices, physical interactions with 103, 104; humans "physical beings" 106–107; hybrid environments emergence 105–106; movement time, precision 108–109; physical acts and control, connection 108–109
physical device interactions 103–104
physical ergonomics, idea of 101
pictographic theory 7
Pihlainen, K. 236
Plato 77
Popper, K. 63, 239
portable information environment 105–106, 241
power distances, in culture 165
Poyner, B. 31
principle of desirability 12
privacy, and cybersecurity 45, 233–234, 236, 245
processes, of design: control, and enhancement issue 146–147; "goodness of fit" 32, 39, 222; human involvement in 30, 31–32, 33; human-machine interfaces, and systems 32, 33, 241, 242; management of 30; modeling of users, approach 32; Primary Generator model (Darke') 63; problem-solving approach, varied 63–64; Scientific Management approach to 31; systematic design methodologies 29–30; Taylor's work 31; user-centeredness key to 31–32, 33–34, 48. *See also* (user-centeredness design); user experience, qualitative aspects of 33, 43; Vardouli views, in disciplinary-wide terms 30
psychologists 79
The Psychology of Everyday Things (Norman) 175
Psychology science 114–115
psychophysiology 107

QWERTY keyboard 100

Rachmandran, V. S. 11
reading, complex act 128
"REAL" design 230
"real" design use 230–233
Reckonings (Chrisomalis) 212
The Reflective Practitioner (Schon) 62
representation act 17; purposes, tools for 20–21
Ritter, F. 37
Rogers, E. 6, 148, 171, 211. *See also* Innovation Diffusion Theory (Rogers')
Roman numerals 212
Roozenburg, N. 60
routine technologies 140
Royce, W. 34
rural living, people in 22

Sauro, J. 181, 194, 207
Schmand-Besserat, D. 7
Schon, D. 60–62
science base, and problems with 76; units of analysis 76; "vertical slice," idea 77, 90, 91
sciences: "social" prefix use 78–79; term, plural 78
Sciences of the Artificial (Simon) 58–59
Scientific Management approach 31
Second World War (1939–1945) 30
self-efficacy theory 202
Shackel, B. 176, 177, 178
Sharma, S. 236
Shils, E. A. 163
Ship of Theseus challenge 98, 112
Simon, H. 58–62, 64, 65, 66, 70, 71
Sinclair, C. 24
skilled craftspeople 49
skin based interfaces 242–243
smart glasses, idea 27

smartphones 100, 105; addiction 23; elderly users 212; gaming contexts, and age role 104; physical interactions with handheld 103–104
smart spectacle design 28
Sniehotta, F. 201
social adaptation process 57
social media: mass adoption of 18, 20; spread of 23, 24; usage, during COVID-19 pandemic 141
social practices, evolution 25
social sciences: behavioral sciences, term use 79; Cartesian approach to 83, 86, 224; disciplines evolved, from enquiries 80; divide-and-conquer mentality 84, 85, 90, 91, 239; enquiries, diverse 79–80; enquiry space on humans 82–86; facets of human experience, specialize in 76; four-level distinction 87; interdisciplinarity and 80; Newell and Card's framing of 86, **87**, 88; origins, history of 77; prefix "social" in 78; specialized practices and 79; theoretical models of humans in 82; theories breakdown, based on temporal concerns 86, **87**, 88, 90; time-sliced division 76; user-centered design, focus 82–86, 88
social scientists, challenges 75–76
sociologists 79
socio-technical systems 141; Eason's ten propositions 141, **142**
socio-technical theory 144–145
socio-technical thinking 138; control issues, and enhancement desires 145–147, 156; Eason's propositions 141, **142**, 143; idea of people and technologies 139–140; impact on, quality of life and work 143–144; participatory, design movement 142–143; technological imperative 139; technology adoption, understanding 147; Trist research 138–139, 144; view of users 144; work system, and unit level analysis 139. *See also* user-centeredness design
Socrates 77
software development: spiral model of Boehm 35; waterfall model of 34–35, *35*
Software Engineering 67
Sommerville, I. 143, 144
specialized knowledge, and training 229–230
Spinning Jenny 55, 56
spiral model of Boehm 35
Spivey, N. 12
Spotify 227
Steering Law 109, *110*, 111
stepped or "walking" menu design 109, *110*
Sturt, G. 54
SUS *see* System Usability Scale
Sweeney, M. 43
System Usability Scale (SUS) **207**, 208. *See also* Technology Acceptance Model (TAM)

Tajer, D. 228
TAM *see* Technology Acceptance Model
Tavistock Institute in London 138
Taylor, F. 31
technological progress: Barnes' EV journey 135–136; emergence of, history 23–24, 25; fake video, and AI 23, 225; great-thinkers view of 25; impact in, other domains 38; and innovation 3, 4, 18, 25; media coverage of 225; misinformation campaigns 23; negative impacts 23; new technology, adoption 148–149, 221; pace of development 221; rule of 10, futuristic claim 226; self-driving cars/robots 225; smartphone addiction 23
Technology Acceptance Model (TAM) 202, 203, 204, 223; additions in, and popularity 204; Davis' survey tool, constructs in 203, **204**; intuitive sense 208; organizational contexts 223; review of, challenges 205; SUS similarity to 207–208; use for, intentions estimation 206; UTAUT and 204
technology-oriented studies 71
Technology Readiness Index 215
theory-free observation 240
theory of innovation adoptions 148
theory of planned behavior (TPB): Ajzen's 200, *201*; limitations, criticism 201–202
Thomas, D. 138
Thomas, W. 138
3-D handtracking systems 241

Tidal 227
Tjendra, J. 42
TPB *see* theory of planned behavior
Tractinsky, N. 194, 215
Treyens, J.C. 117
Trist, E. 138–139, 144
Turner, M. 205, 206
Twitter 4

uncertainty avoidance, cultures 166–167, 168
Understanding the Human Mind (Fields) 114
Unified Theory of Acceptance and Use of Technology (UTAUT) 204
Uranium-thorium mass spectrometry 3
urban environment 22
usability: and acceptability 198–199, 206, 208–209; approaches, comparison 192, **193**; defined 176, 177; effectiveness and efficiency 179, 180–182, 195; evaluation methods for 182–192; ISO defined 179; key indices 179; learnability estimate of 216; limitations of, as design value 193–195; Nielsen's heuristics for evaluating 186, *187*; operational emphasis 177; satisfaction, estimates of 179, 180–181, 195; software industry in, 1980s/1990s 184; source of data 183; System Usability Scale **207**; test, process involves 182; as testable quality, operational interpretation 195
usability evaluation: comparing approaches 192, **193**; criticisms of 194, 195; expert-based 185–190; inconsistency of 193; model-based 190–192; practices, method classes 182–185; rates of heuristic evaluation 193–194; user-based 183–185
Usability Metric for User Experience (UMUX) 208; SUS correlated with 208; UMUX-Lite 208
user as, physical being 98–101
user-based evaluation 183–185; retrospective verbal protocol 183; sample size, issue 185; think-aloud protocols 183; user provides, data points 183
user-centeredness design 20, 25–26, 217, 222, *231*; "acceptance," term 199–200; activities/steps included in 41–42; advertisements for 25–26; approach, challenge before 37; artifact, within multiple contexts 39–40; challenge of delivering, services 27, 37, 41, 45; cognition over time, automation of responses 126–131; common sense 28, 41, 108, 110–111; "create and test" method 239–240; cultural awareness, and dimension for 171–173; cybersecurity, and accessibility 233–236; design historians, views 28; development, and aspects of 36, 37; difficulties of 222; digital document interactions 90–91; digital realm, design challenge of 28; digital technology and 29; ease of use, importance 28; empiricism, emphasis on 36, 223; essence of, approach 39; "human-centered" approaches 38, *231*; international standards and 178–179; key focus, of modern methods 31–32, 34; learning or training, need for 26, 37, 229–230; look-and-feel aspects of 45; mapping challenge 175; meaning 34–38; multi-layered interaction 92, *93*, 94, 237; participatory goal 142–143; as phased process, defining 40–41, 45; principal claim of 26; privacy issue 45; process, generic model 39, *40*; product's "usability"/usefulness 176–177, 209 (*see also* (usability); professionals views 39; profit-need relationship 222; "REAL" design 230–233; role in, four steps 39; social scientific framing of users 144; socio-technical approach to 141–145; socio-technical thinking influence on 143–144; as system personalization 44; testing design with people 36, 37; thematic analysis of 43–44; underscores professional education 37; as user focus 44; "user-friendliness" and concept of 26, 41; as user participation 44; users as, multilayered beings 89–91; users' reactions/response to 36, 40, 45, 89, 224–225; value on utility, and usability 222; Vicente's perspective 83–84
user-centered term, meanings 34
user-centric approaches 31, 32
user-experience *see* experience, of users

'user,' term 178, 227–228, 230
UX design, and professionals 37, 39; alternative measures 215; challenges 72, 235; design values 145; education 89, 224, 239; impact of time 215–218; process 37, 42; researchers *vs.* designers 48, 49, 106; research in, Newell and Card 87–88; role 185–186; term "ergonomics" 100, 106; understanding 49; view of interaction 244–245

Vardouli, T. 30
"vertical slice" approach 77, 86, **87**, 88, 90, 91, 93
Vicente, K. 70, 83
virtual digital environments 28
voice-controlled info-appliances 243

Wall St model of innovation 18, 23
waterfall model, of software development 34–35, *35*
wearable and portable devices 105
web browsers 23
Western decimal format 212
The Wheelwright's Shop (Sturt's) 54
Wickens, C. 119
Williams, B. 98
Wired magazine 103
Wittgernstein, L. 101, 224
working memory 121–123
workstations 107–108
Wright, R. 57
writing, and literacy 86; counting systems and 7; pictographic theory of 7; quill and ink use 10, 221

YouTube 160

Zaphiris, P. 173
Zoom 227
Zuckerberg, M. 24

For Product Safety Concerns and Information please contact our EU representative GPSR@taylorandfrancis.com
Taylor & Francis Verlag GmbH, Kaufingerstraße 24, 80331 München, Germany

www.ingramcontent.com/pod-product-compliance
Ingram Content Group UK Ltd.
Pitfield, Milton Keynes, MK11 3LW, UK
UKHW021449080625
459435UK00012B/430